Ninja Foodi Grill Cookbook for Beginners 2022

1000 Easy, Delicious and Affordable Recipes for Indoor Grilling and Air Frying

Rebecca J. McKinney

CONTENTS

Sides, Snacks & Appetizers..31

Meats..44

Meatless...78

Poultry...96

Seafood

Sauces, Dips, And Dressings

Desserts

Introduction

There's nothing like the smell of freshly grilled steak. The enticing and inviting aroma in the air around you, the sizzling when the meat touches the hot plate, the blackened seared lines you enjoy so much. But when the weather turns against you, it is hard to plan a grilling day in the backyard. But how about your home?

With the Ninja Foodi Grill, you can have it all -freshly grilled specialties in the comfort of your own home. Away from the rain, wind, or hot sun, with the indoor grill, there is no guesswork involved. Just follow the grill instructions, and delights are guaranteed. And this cookbook is created to give you just that. 1000 mouthwatering recipes you can make on your indoor grill. Whether looking for a meal for breakfast, snack, side dish, dinner, or even dessert (pretty cool, right?), we've got you covered.

And with the ultimate tips on how to use the Ninja Foodi Grill included, it is safe to say that this cookbook is the only indoor grilling guide you will ever need. Read on and see for yourself!

Starting with Your Ninja Foodi Grill

The Features of Ninja Foodi Grill

1. The unique Ninja Foodi Grill is Integrated Smart Probe. The grill sears, sizzles, and air fry crisps as well as mainly indoor grill and air fryer.

2. You can cook food with precision and quality and without generating smoke indoor.

3. The air circulates inside the Ninja Foodi grill of about 500°F on all sides of the grill.

4. The 500°F air circulates all around the food for amazing crispiness and searing while the high-density grill creates amazing char-grilled marks and lovely flavors to food.

5. The Ninja Foodi Grill allows awesome control of setting: Low, Medium, High, and Max.

6. The wide temperature range of 105°F-500°F and variable fan speed enable 5 fast, and versatile cooking functions: Grill, Air Crisp, Dehydrate, Roast, and Bake.

7. Air fry crisp with up to 75% less fat than deep-frying, using the included 4-qt crisper basket

8. No need to cut into foods or constantly probe them like when using an instant-read thermometer. Thus, you can eliminate guesswork and never worry about under or overcooking with the Integrated Smart Probe. Multi-task with peace of mind as food cooks to perfection

9. Instinctive digital display lets you easily choose a cooking function and see your food's internal temperature as the Integrated Smart Probe monitors it. The grill will conveniently help you when your food is perfectly cooked

10. Virtually smoke-free with unique Smoke Control Technology. The combination of a temperature-controlled grill grate, splatter shield, and cool-air zone reduces smoke, keeping it out of the kitchen.

How to Use Your Ninja Foodi Grill

When you are cooking for the first time with your Foodi grill, you must first wash the detachable cooking parts with warm soapy water to remove any oil and debris. Let air dry and place them back inside once you are ready to cook. An easy-to-follow instruction guide comes with each unit, so make sure to go over it before cooking.

Position your grill on a level and secure surface. Leaving at least 6 inches of space around it, especially at the back where the air intake vent and air socket are located. And you should ensure that the splatter guard is installed whenever the grill is in use. It is a wire mesh that covers the heating element on the inside of the lid.

1. Grilling. Plug your unit into an outlet and power on the grill. Use the grill grate over the cooking pot and choose the grill function. There are four default temperature settings of low at 400°F, medium at 450°F, high at 500°F, and max at 510°F. Set the time needed to cook. You may check the grilling cheat sheet that comes with your unit to guide you with the time and temperature settings. It is best to check the food regularly depending on the doneness you prefer and to avoid overcooking. Once the required settings are selected, press starts and waits for the digital display to show 'add food'. The unit will start to preheat similar to an oven and will show the progress through the display. This step takes about 8 minutes. If you need to check the food or flip it, the timer will pause and resume once the lid is closed. The screen will show 'Done' once the timer and cooking have been completed. Power off the unit and unplug the device. Leave the hood open to let the unit cool faster.

2. Bake. Remove the grates and use the cooking pot. Choose the bake setting and set your preferred temperature and time. Preheating will take about 3 minutes. Once done with preheating, you may put the ingredients: directly on the cooking pot, or you may use your regular baking tray. An 8-inch baking tray can fit inside as well as similar-sized oven-safe containers.

3. Roasting. Remove the grill grates and use the cooking pot that comes with the unit. You may also purchase their roasting rack for this purpose. Press the roast option and set the timer between 1 to 4 hours according to the recipe requirements. The food will preheat for 3 minutes regardless of the time you have set. Once ready, place the meat directly on the roasting pot or rack. If you check the food occasionally for doneness. A meat thermometer is another useful tool to get your meats perfectly cooked.

4. Air crisping. Put the crisper basket in and close the lid. You should press the air crisp option and the start button. The default temperature is set at 390° F and will preheat at about 3 minutes. You can adjust the temperature and time by pressing the buttons beside these options. If you do not need to preheat, just press the air crisp button a second time and the display will show you the 'add food' message. You should put the food inside and shake or turn it every 10 minutes. And you should use oven mitts or tongs with silicone when doing this.

5. Dehydrating. Place the first layer of food directly on the cooking pot. Add the crisper basket and add one more layer. Choose the dehydrate setting and set the timer between 7 to 10 hours. You can check the progress from time to time.

6. Cooking frozen foods. Choose the medium heat, which is 450° F using the grill option. You can also use the air crisp option if you are cooking fries, vegetables, and other frozen foods. Set the time needed for your recipe. Add a few minutes to compensate for the thawing.

Caring for Your Ninja Foodi Grill

Despite looking a bit complicated, cleaning the Ninja Foodi Grill actually pretty easy. Especially if it takes a methodical and well-defined approach.

It is recommended that you clean up your appliance after every use to keep the appliance crisp and daisy fresh.

The process of safely and effectively cleaning up your appliance is as follows:

1. The first step is to allow the appliance to cool down after a cooking session.

2. Once the appliance is cool, carefully unplug the device from the power outlet.

3. A good tip will be to keep the hood of your appliance open if you want to let it cool quickly.

4. The grill gate, splatter shield, crisper basket, cooking pot, cleaning brush, and other accessories are completely dishwasher safe, so you can directly put them in your dishwasher/ or clean them by hand.

5. The thermometer, though, is not dishwasher safe, and hence you are to clean it manually using a damp cloth.

6. You may rinse the accessories with additional water and clean them using the provided cleaning brush for an additional polish.

7. If your cooking basket has baked-on cheese/sauce stuck onto the surface, then you may use the other end of the provided cleaning brush and use it as a scraper to clean them off.

8. Once done, use a towel or a dryer to dry all of the accessories.

9. You should keep in mind, though, that the main unit is not dishwasher safe. Therefore, you are to take a simple damp cloth and rub the exterior gently. Make sure that you don't use any sort of rasping cleaner as they might damage the surface of the appliance.

10. The thermometer is also a very sensitive part, and you should never use any sort of cleaning solution while cleaning it.

11. A cotton swab or can of compressed air is suggested to clean the thermometer.

12. Once you are done with the initial cleaning, you may still find some food residue stuck on the surface of the accessories; if that is the case, do the following:

●   If you have any residue stuck on the splatter shield, soak it in warm soapy water solution and clean it up as needed.

●   If you have more stubborn dirt, boil the splatter shield for about 10 minutes for a deep cleaning.

If you need to deep clean the thermometer, soak the silicone grip and stainless-steel tip in a container full of warm water.Keep in mind that neither the cord nor the jack should be immersed, so make sure they are not soaked.

The thermometer holder is very sensitive and is to be washed using a damp cloth.

If you follow these instructions properly and to the letter, your appliance will stay in tip-top shape for years to come.

Useful Tips for Your Ninja Foodi Grill

Here are some useful tips you can use when cooking with the Ninja Foodi and some commonly asked questions to guide you if you are planning to purchase one for yourself.

1. Brush or spray the grates with some canola, corn, or avocado oil to avoid smoke.

2. A light coating of oil will make your air-fried French fries taste better.

3. Use the time charts as a guide but make sure you check the food regularly since the grill gets hot and can cook quickly. You may also use a meat thermometer for your food to cook exactly the way you want.

4. Use silicone or wooden utensils. Never stick metal tongs or cutleries on your grill to avoid electric shock and damaging the ceramic coating.

5. If you are planning to do a lot of dehydrating and baking, it will be helpful to purchase their food rack and baking pan.

6. If the timer was up but you need to cook the food longer, simply adjust the timer and press the start button to continue cooking.

7. Although preheating is recommended to get the finest results, you can skip this step by pressing the option a second time.

8. To get juicier meat, let it rest at least 5 minutes before slicing.

Frequently Asked Questions

1. Is it worth the price?

If you are getting the Foodi grill as a secondary appliance, it may seem pricey. But given the various functions, you are getting with one piece of equipment, the value for money will be apparent with continuous use.

2. Can it heat the kitchen as most ovens do?

No. One great thing about portable cookers like the Ninja Foodi grill is that it does not make the kitchen uncomfortably hot making it ideal for use even during summer.

3. What button should I press to pause the timer?

Opening the lid will automatically pause the timer.

4. Why is my food not evenly cooked when air-fried?

It is best not to overcrowd food inside the crisper basket and create an even layer to get better results. You need to flip or shake the food every few minutes to have even browning.

5. How do I convert cooking temperatures from recipes meant for regular ovens?

You can simply reduce the temperature required by 25 degrees Fahrenheit when using the Ninja Foodi Grill. You will have to check the food regularly to make sure it will not get overcooked.

Breakfast

Honey-lime Glazed Grilled Fruit Salad

Servings: 4
Cooking Time: 4 Minutes
Ingredients:
- ½ pound strawberries, washed, hulled and halved
- 1 can pineapple chunks, drained, juice reserved
- 2 peaches, pitted and sliced
- 6 tablespoons honey, divided
- 1 tablespoon freshly squeezed lime juice

Directions:
1. Insert the Grill Grate and close the hood. Select GRILL, set the temperature to MAX, and set the time to 4 minutes. Select START/STOP to begin preheating.
2. While the unit is preheating, combine the strawberries, pineapple, and peaches in a large bowl with 3 tablespoons of honey. Toss to coat evenly.
3. When the unit beeps to signify it has preheated, place the fruit on the Grill Grate. Gently press the fruit down to maximize grill marks. Close the hood and GRILL for 4 minutes without flipping.
4. Meanwhile, in a small bowl, combine the remaining 3 tablespoons of honey, lime juice, and 1 tablespoon of reserved pineapple juice.
5. When cooking is complete, place the fruit in a large bowl and toss with the honey mixture. Serve immediately.

Bread Pudding

Servings: 6 To 8
Cooking Time: 30 Minutes
Ingredients:
- 1 loaf (about 1 pound) day-old French bread, cut into 1-inch cubes
- 3 large eggs
- 4 tablespoons (½ stick) unsalted butter, melted
- 1 cup milk
- ¾ cup heavy (whipping) cream, divided
- 2 cups granulated sugar, divided
- 1 tablespoon cinnamon
- 1 teaspoon vanilla extract
- 8 ounces cream cheese, at room temperature

Directions:
1. Line the inside bottom and sides of the Cooking Pot with aluminum foil. This will wrap the bread pudding, so make sure it fits the sides of the Cooking Pot.
2. Place the bread cubes in the Cooking Pot.
3. In a large bowl, whisk together the eggs, melted butter, milk, ½ cup of heavy cream, 1 cup of sugar, cinnamon, and vanilla. Evenly pour the mixture over the bread cubes. Place another foil layer on top of the bread cubes, then fold over all the foil ends to seal all around. Place the Cooking Pot in the refrigerator for at least 30 minutes, or overnight, for the bread to absorb the liquid.
4. Insert the Grill Grate and close the hood. Select GRILL, set the temperature to HI, and set the time to 30 minutes. Select START/STOP to begin preheating.
5. While the unit is preheating, prepare your frosting. In a large bowl, whisk together the cream cheese, remaining 1 cup of sugar, and remaining ¼ cup of heavy cream until smooth. Set aside.
6. When the unit beeps to signify it has preheated, place the Cooking Pot with the foil-wrapped bread pudding on top of the Grill Grate. Close the hood and cook for 30 minutes.
7. When cooking is complete, remove the pot from the grill. Use grill mitts to carefully open up the top foil lining. Drizzle the frosting over the bread pudding. Allow the bread pudding to cool before serving.

Buttermilk Biscuits

Servings:12
Cooking Time: 5 Minutes
Ingredients:
- 2 cups all-purpose flour, plus more for dusting the work surface
- 1 tablespoon baking powder
- ¼ teaspoon baking soda
- 2 teaspoons sugar
- 1 teaspoon salt
- 6 tablespoons cold unsalted butter, cut into 1-tablespoon slices
- ¾ cup buttermilk

Directions:
1. Spray the Crisper Basket with olive oil.
2. Insert the Crisper Basket and close the hood. Select BAKE, set the temperature to 360ºF, and set the time to 5 minutes. Select START/STOP to begin preheating.
3. In a large mixing bowl, combine the flour, baking powder, baking soda, sugar, and salt and mix well.
4. Using a fork, cut in the butter until the mixture resembles coarse meal.
5. Add the buttermilk and mix until smooth.
6. Dust more flour on a clean work surface. Turn the dough out onto the work surface and roll it out until it is about ½ inch thick.
7. Using a 2-inch biscuit cutter, cut out the biscuits. Put the uncooked biscuits in the greased Crisper Basket in a single layer.
8. Close the hood and BAKE for 5 minutes. Transfer the cooked biscuits from the grill to a platter.
9. Cut the remaining biscuits. Bake the remaining biscuits.
10. Serve warm.

Banana Bread

Servings:3
Cooking Time: 22 Minutes
Ingredients:
- 3 ripe bananas, mashed
- 1 cup sugar
- 1 large egg
- 4 tablespoons (½ stick) unsalted butter, melted
- 1½ cups all-purpose flour
- 1 teaspoon baking soda
- 1 teaspoon salt

Directions:
1. Coat the insides of 3 mini loaf pans with cooking spray.
2. In a large mixing bowl, mix the bananas and sugar.

3. In a separate large mixing bowl, combine the egg, butter, flour, baking soda, and salt and mix well.
4. Add the banana mixture to the egg and flour mixture. Mix well.
5. Divide the batter evenly among the prepared pans.
6. Select BAKE, set the temperature to 310ºF, and set the time to 22 minutes. Select START/STOP to begin preheating.
7. Set the mini loaf pans into the pot.
8. Close the hood and BAKE for 22 minutes. Insert a toothpick into the center of each loaf; if it comes out clean, they are done.
9. When the loaves are cooked through, remove the pans from the Crisper Basket. Turn out the loaves onto a wire rack to cool.
10. Serve warm.

Grilled Sausage Mix

Servings: 4
Cooking Time: 22 Minutes
Ingredients:
- 8 mini bell peppers
- 2 heads radicchio, each cut into 6 wedges
- Canola oil, for brushing
- Sea salt, to taste
- Freshly ground black pepper, to taste
- 6 breakfast sausage links
- 6 hot or sweet Italian sausage links

Directions:
1. Insert the Grill Grate and close the hood. Select GRILL, set the temperature to MAX, and set the time to 22 minutes. Select START/STOP to begin preheating.
2. While the unit is preheating, brush the bell peppers and radicchio with the oil. Season with salt and black pepper.
3. When the unit beeps to signify it has preheated, place the bell peppers and radicchio on the Grill Grate; close the hood and GRILL for 10 minutes, without flipping.
4. Meanwhile, poke the sausages with a fork or knife and brush them with some of the oil.
5. After 10 minutes, remove the vegetables and set aside. Decrease the temperature to LOW. Place the sausages on the Grill Grate; close the hood and GRILL for 6 minutes.
6. Flip the sausages. Close the hood and GRILL for 6 minutes more. Remove the sausages from the Grill Grate.
7. Serve the sausages and vegetables on a large cutting board or serving tray.

Egg And Avocado Burrito

Servings: 4
Cooking Time: 3 To 5 Minutes
Ingredients:
- 4 low-sodium whole-wheat flour tortillas
- Filling:
- 1 hard-boiled egg, chopped
- 2 hard-boiled egg whites, chopped
- 1 ripe avocado, peeled, pitted, and chopped
- 1 red bell pepper, chopped
- 1 slice low-sodium, low-fat American cheese, torn into pieces
- 3 tablespoons low-sodium salsa, plus additional for serving (optional)
Directions:

1. Insert the Crisper Basket and close the hood. Select AIR CRISP, set the temperature to 390ºF, and set the time to 5 minutes. Select START/STOP to begin preheating.
2. Make the filling: Combine the egg, egg whites, avocado, red bell pepper, cheese, and salsa in a medium bowl and stir until blended.
3. Assemble the burritos: Arrange the tortillas on a clean work surface and place ¼ of the prepared filling in the middle of each tortilla, leaving about 1½-inch on each end unfilled. Fold in the opposite sides of each tortilla and roll up. Secure with toothpicks through the center, if needed.
4. Transfer the burritos to the Crisper Basket. Close the hood and AIR CRISP for 3 to 5 minutes, or until the burritos are crisp and golden brown.
5. Allow to cool for 5 minutes and serve with salsa, if desired.

Banana And Oat Bread Pudding

Servings: 4
Cooking Time: 16 To 20 Minutes
Ingredients:
- 2 medium ripe bananas, mashed
- ½ cup low-fat milk
- 2 tablespoons maple syrup
- 2 tablespoons peanut butter
- 1 teaspoon vanilla extract
- 1 teaspoon ground cinnamon
- 2 slices whole-grain bread, cut into bite-sized cubes
- ¼ cup quick oats
- Cooking spray

Directions:
1. Select AIR CRISP, set the temperature to 350ºF, and set the time to 20 minutes. Select START/STOP to begin preheating.
2. Spritz a baking pan lightly with cooking spray.
3. Mix the bananas, milk, maple syrup, peanut butter, vanilla, and cinnamon in a large mixing bowl and stir until well incorporated.
4. Add the bread cubes to the banana mixture and stir until thoroughly coated. Fold in the oats and stir to combine.
5. Transfer the mixture to the baking pan. Wrap the baking pan in aluminum foil.
6. Place the pan directly in the pot. Close the hood and AIR CRISP for 10 to 12 minutes until heated through.
7. Remove the foil and cook for an additional 6 to 8 minutes, or until the pudding has set.
8. Let the pudding cool for 5 minutes before serving.

Pesto Egg Croissantwiches

Servings: 4
Cooking Time: 8 Minutes
Ingredients:
- 4 large eggs
- 4 croissants
- 8 tablespoons pesto
Directions:
1. Insert the Cooking Pot and close the hood. Select GRILL, set the temperature to HI, and set the time to 8 minutes. Select START/STOP to begin preheating.
2. While the unit is preheating, in a small bowl, whisk together the eggs.

3. When the unit beeps to signify it has preheated, pour the beaten eggs into the Cooking Pot. Close the hood and cook for 4 minutes.

4. While the eggs are cooking, split the croissants. Place the croissant halves on top of the Grill Grate.

5. After 4 minutes, open the hood and scramble the eggs with a spatula. Spoon the scrambled eggs onto the bottom halves of the croissants. Remove the Cooking Pot from the unit.

6. Insert the Grill Grate into the unit. Spoon 2 tablespoons of pesto on top of each egg-topped croissant, then top each sandwich with the croissant top. Close the hood and cook for 4 minutes.

7. When cooking is complete, the croissant crust should be toasted. Serve.

Maple Walnut Pancake

Servings: 4
Cooking Time: 20 Minutes
Ingredients:
- 3 tablespoons melted butter, divided
- 1 cup flour
- 2 tablespoons sugar
- 1½ teaspoons baking powder
- ¼ teaspoon salt
- 1 egg, beaten
- ¾ cup milk
- 1 teaspoon pure vanilla extract
- ½ cup roughly chopped walnuts
- Maple syrup or fresh sliced fruit, for serving

Directions:
1. Select BAKE, set the temperature to 330ºF, and set the time to 20 minutes. Select START/STOP to begin preheating.

2. Grease a baking pan with 1 tablespoon of melted butter.

3. Mix together the flour, sugar, baking powder, and salt in a medium bowl. Add the beaten egg, milk, the remaining 2 tablespoons of melted butter, and vanilla and stir until the batter is sticky but slightly lumpy.

4. Slowly pour the batter into the greased baking pan and scatter with the walnuts.

5. Place the pan directly in the pot. Close the hood and BAKE for 20 minutes until golden brown and cooked through.

6. Let the pancake rest for 5 minutes and serve topped with the maple syrup or fresh fruit, if desired.

Tomato-corn Frittata With Avocado Dressing

Servings: 2 Or 3
Cooking Time: 20 Minutes
Ingredients:
- ½ cup cherry tomatoes, halved
- Kosher salt and freshly ground black pepper, to taste
- 6 large eggs, lightly beaten
- ½ cup corn kernels, thawed if frozen
- ¼ cup milk
- 1 tablespoon finely chopped fresh dill
- ½ cup shredded Monterey Jack cheese
- Avocado Dressing:
- 1 ripe avocado, pitted and peeled

- 2 tablespoons fresh lime juice
- ¼ cup olive oil
- 1 scallion, finely chopped
- 8 fresh basil leaves, finely chopped

Directions:
1. Put the tomato halves in a colander and lightly season with salt. Set aside for 10 minutes to drain well. Pour the tomatoes into a large bowl and fold in the eggs, corn, milk, and dill. Sprinkle with salt and pepper and stir until mixed.

2. Select BAKE, set the temperature to 300ºF, and set the time to 20 minutes. Select START/STOP to begin preheating.

3. Pour the egg mixture into a baking pan. Place the pan directly in the pot. Close the hood and BAKE for 15 minutes.

4. Scatter the cheese on top. Increase the grill temperature to 315ºF and continue to cook for another 5 minutes, or until the frittata is puffy and set.

5. Meanwhile, make the avocado dressing: Mash the avocado with the lime juice in a medium bowl until smooth. Mix in the olive oil, scallion, and basil and stir until well incorporated.

6. Let the frittata cool for 5 minutes and serve alongside the avocado dressing.

Grilled Kielbasa And Pineapple Kebabs

Servings: 4
Cooking Time: 12 Minutes
Ingredients:
- ½ cup soy sauce
- ¼ cup light brown sugar, packed
- 2 (8-ounce) cans pineapple chunks, drained
- 2 (12-ounce) packages kielbasa sausages, cut into ½-inch slices

Directions:
1. In a large bowl, mix together the soy sauce, brown sugar, and pineapple chunks until the sugar is dissolved. Add the sausage slices and set aside for 10 minutes.

2. Thread the kielbasa and pineapple onto 10 to 12 skewers, alternating meat and fruit. Set aside any glaze that remains in the bowl.

3. Insert the Grill Grate and close the hood. Select GRILL, set the temperature to HI, and set the time to 12 minutes. Select START/STOP to begin preheating.

4. When the unit beeps to signify it has preheated, place half of the skewers on the Grill Grate. Brush them with extra glaze. Close the hood and grill for 3 minutes.

5. After 3 minutes, open the hood and flip the skewers. Close the hood and cook for 3 minutes more. After a total of 6 minutes, remove the skewers. Repeat with the remaining skewers.

6. When cooking is complete, remove the skewers from the grill and serve.

Spinach With Scrambled Eggs

Servings: 2
Cooking Time: 10 Minutes
Ingredients:
- 2 tablespoons olive oil
- 4 eggs, whisked
- 5 ounces fresh spinach, chopped
- 1 medium tomato, chopped
- 1 teaspoon fresh lemon juice

- ½ teaspoon coarse salt
- ½ teaspoon ground black pepper
- ½ cup of fresh basil, roughly chopped

Directions:
1. Grease a baking pan with the oil, tilting it to spread the oil around.
2. Select BAKE, set the temperature to 280ºF, and set the time to 10 minutes. Select START/STOP to begin preheating.
3. In the pan, mix the remaining ingredients, apart from the basil leaves, whisking well until everything is completely combined.
4. Place the pan directly in the pot. Close the hood and BAKE for 10 minutes.
5. Top with fresh basil leaves before serving.

Spinach Omelet

Servings: 1
Cooking Time: 10 Minutes
Ingredients:
- 1 teaspoon olive oil
- 3 eggs
- Salt and ground black pepper, to taste
- 1 tablespoon ricotta cheese
- ¼ cup chopped spinach
- 1 tablespoon chopped parsley

Directions:
1. Grease a baking pan with olive oil.
2. Select BAKE, set the temperature to 330ºF, and set the time to 10 minutes. Select START/STOP to begin preheating.
3. In a bowl, beat the eggs with a fork and sprinkle salt and pepper.
4. Add the ricotta, spinach, and parsley and then transfer to the baking pan. Place the pan directly in the pot.
5. Close the hood and BAKE for 10 minutes or until the egg is set.
6. Serve warm.

English Pumpkin Egg Bake

Servings: 2
Cooking Time: 10 Minutes
Ingredients:
- 2 eggs
- ½ cup milk
- 2 cups flour
- 2 tablespoons cider vinegar
- 2 teaspoons baking powder
- 1 tablespoon sugar
- 1 cup pumpkin purée
- 1 teaspoon cinnamon powder
- 1 teaspoon baking soda
- 1 tablespoon olive oil

Directions:
1. Select BAKE, set the temperature to 300ºF, and set the time to 10 minutes. Select START/STOP to begin preheating.
2. Crack the eggs into a bowl and beat with a whisk. Combine with the milk, flour, cider vinegar, baking powder, sugar, pumpkin purée, cinnamon powder, and baking soda, mixing well.

3. Grease a baking pan with oil. Add the mixture to the pan. Place the pan directly in the pot. Close the hood and BAKE for 10 minutes.
4. Serve warm.

Banana Churros With Oatmeal

Servings: 2
Cooking Time: 15 Minutes
Ingredients:
- For the Churros:
- 1 large yellow banana, peeled, cut in half lengthwise, then cut in half widthwise
- 2 tablespoons whole-wheat pastry flour
- ⅛ teaspoon sea salt
- 2 teaspoons oil (sunflower or melted coconut)
- 1 teaspoon water
- Cooking spray
- 1 tablespoon coconut sugar
- ½ teaspoon cinnamon
- For the Oatmeal:
- ¾ cup rolled oats
- 1½ cups water

Directions:
1. To make the churros
2. Put the 4 banana pieces in a medium-size bowl and add the flour and salt. Stir gently. Add the oil and water. Stir gently until evenly mixed. You may need to press some coating onto the banana pieces.
3. Spray the Crisper Basket with the oil spray. Put the banana pieces in the Crisper Basket and AIR CRISP for 5 minutes. Remove, gently turn over, and AIR CRISP for another 5 minutes or until browned.
4. In a medium bowl, add the coconut sugar and cinnamon and stir to combine. When the banana pieces are nicely browned, spray with the oil and place in the cinnamon-sugar bowl. Toss gently with a spatula to coat the banana pieces with the mixture.
5. To make the oatmeal
6. While the bananas are cooking, make the oatmeal. In a medium pot, bring the oats and water to a boil, then reduce to low heat. Simmer, stirring often, until all the water is absorbed, about 5 minutes. Put the oatmeal into two bowls.
7. Top the oatmeal with the coated banana pieces and serve immediately.

Avocado Quesadillas

Servings: 4
Cooking Time: 11 Minutes
Ingredients:
- 4 eggs
- 2 tablespoons skim milk
- Salt and ground black pepper, to taste
- Cooking spray
- 4 flour tortillas
- 4 tablespoons salsa
- 2 ounces Cheddar cheese, grated
- ½ small avocado, peeled and thinly sliced

Directions:
1. Select BAKE, set the temperature to 270ºF, and set the time to 8 minutes. Select START/STOP to begin preheating.
2. Beat together the eggs, milk, salt, and pepper.

3. Spray a baking pan lightly with cooking spray and add egg mixture.
4. Place the pan directly in the pot. Close the hood and BAKE for 8 minutes, stirring every 1 to 2 minutes, until eggs are scrambled to the liking. Remove and set aside.
5. Spray one side of each tortilla with cooking spray. Flip over.
6. Divide eggs, salsa, cheese, and avocado among the tortillas, covering only half of each tortilla.
7. Fold each tortilla in half and press down lightly. Increase the temperature of the grill to 390ºF.
8. Put 2 tortillas in Crisper Basket and AIR CRISP for 3 minutes or until cheese melts and outside feels slightly crispy. Repeat with remaining two tortillas.
9. Cut each cooked tortilla into halves. Serve warm.

Potato Bread Rolls

Servings: 5
Cooking Time: 20 Minutes
Ingredients:
- 5 large potatoes, boiled and mashed
- Salt and ground black pepper, to taste
- ½ teaspoon mustard seeds
- 1 tablespoon olive oil
- 2 small onions, chopped
- 2 sprigs curry leaves
- ½ teaspoon turmeric powder
- 2 green chilis, seeded and chopped
- 1 bunch coriander, chopped
- 8 slices bread, brown sides discarded

Directions:
1. Insert the Crisper Basket and close the hood. Select AIR CRISP, set the temperature to 400ºF, and set the time to 15 minutes. Select START/STOP to begin preheating.
2. Put the mashed potatoes in a bowl and sprinkle on salt and pepper. Set to one side.
3. Fry the mustard seeds in olive oil over a medium-low heat in a skillet, stirring continuously, until they sputter.
4. Add the onions and cook until they turn translucent. Add the curry leaves and turmeric powder and stir. Cook for a further 2 minutes until fragrant.
5. Remove the skillet from the heat and combine with the potatoes. Mix in the green chilies and coriander.
6. Wet the bread slightly and drain of any excess liquid.
7. Spoon a small amount of the potato mixture into the center of the bread and enclose the bread around the filling, sealing it entirely. Continue until the rest of the bread and filling is used up. Brush each bread roll with some oil and transfer to the basket.
8. Close the hood and AIR CRISP for 15 minutes, gently shaking the Crisper Basket at the halfway point to ensure each roll is cooked evenly.
9. Serve immediately.

Cinnamon Sugar Roll-ups

Servings: 4
Cooking Time: 10 Minutes
Ingredients:
- 1 sheet frozen puff pastry, thawed
- 3 tablespoons cinnamon
- 5 tablespoons granulated sugar
- 2 tablespoons unsalted butter, melted, divided

Directions:
1. Insert the Grill Grate and close the hood. Select GRILL, set the temperature to LO, and set the time to 10 minutes. Select START/STOP to begin preheating.
2. While the unit is preheating, unroll the pastry dough on a flat surface. In a small bowl, combine the cinnamon and the sugar. Brush 1 tablespoon of butter over the surface of the pastry. Then sprinkle on the cinnamon sugar evenly.
3. Carefully roll the pastry into a log. Using a sharp knife, cut the log into 1- to 2-inch slices. Lightly brush the top and bottom of the roll-ups with the remaining 1 tablespoon of butter.
4. When the unit beeps to signify it has preheated, place the roll-ups on the Grill Grate. Close the hood and grill for 5 minutes.
5. After 5 minutes, open the hood and flip the roll-ups. Close the hood and cook for 5 minutes more.
6. When cooking is complete, the roll-ups will be a nice golden brown. Serve.

Lush Vegetable Omelet

Servings: 2
Cooking Time: 13 Minutes
Ingredients:
- 2 teaspoons canola oil
- 4 eggs, whisked
- 3 tablespoons plain milk
- 1 teaspoon melted butter
- 1 red bell pepper, seeded and chopped
- 1 green bell pepper, seeded and chopped
- 1 white onion, finely chopped
- ½ cup baby spinach leaves, roughly chopped
- ½ cup Halloumi cheese, shaved
- Kosher salt and freshly ground black pepper, to taste

Directions:
1. Select BAKE, set the temperature to 350ºF, and set the time to 13 minutes. Select START/STOP to begin preheating.
2. Grease a baking pan with canola oil.
3. Put the remaining ingredients in the baking pan and stir well.
4. Place the pan directly in the pot. Close the hood and BAKE for 13 minutes.
5. Serve warm.

Soufflé

Servings: 4
Cooking Time: 22 Minutes
Ingredients:
- ⅓ cup butter, melted
- ¼ cup flour
- 1 cup milk
- 1 ounce sugar
- 4 egg yolks
- 1 teaspoon vanilla extract
- 6 egg whites
- 1 teaspoon cream of tartar
- Cooking spray

Directions:
1. In a bowl, mix the butter and flour until a smooth consistency is achieved.

2. Pour the milk into a saucepan over medium-low heat. Add the sugar and allow to dissolve before raising the heat to boil the milk.
3. Pour in the flour and butter mixture and stir rigorously for 7 minutes to eliminate any lumps. Make sure the mixture thickens. Take off the heat and allow to cool for 15 minutes.
4. Select BAKE, set the temperature to 320ºF, and set the time to 15 minutes. Select START/STOP to begin preheating.
5. Spritz 6 soufflé dishes with cooking spray.
6. Put the egg yolks and vanilla extract in a separate bowl and beat them together with a fork. Pour in the milk and combine well to incorporate everything.
7. In a smaller bowl mix the egg whites and cream of tartar with a fork. Fold into the egg yolks-milk mixture before adding in the flour mixture. Transfer equal amounts to the 6 soufflé dishes.
8. Put the dishes in the grill. Close the hood and BAKE for 15 minutes.
9. Serve warm.

Mushroom And Onion Frittata

Servings: 4
Cooking Time: 10 Minutes
Ingredients:
- 4 large eggs
- ¼ cup whole milk
- Sea salt, to taste
- Freshly ground black pepper, to taste
- ½ bell pepper, seeded and diced
- ½ onion, chopped
- 4 cremini mushrooms, sliced
- ½ cup shredded Cheddar cheese

Directions:
1. In a medium bowl, whisk together the eggs and milk. Season with the salt and pepper. Add the bell pepper, onion, mushrooms, and cheese. Mix until well combined.
2. Select BAKE, set the temperature to 400ºF, and set the time to 10 minutes. Select START/STOP to begin preheating.
3. Meanwhile, pour the egg mixture into the baking pan, spreading evenly.
4. When the unit beeps to signify it has preheated, place the pan directly in the pot. Close the hood and BAKE for 10 minutes, or until lightly golden.

Mixed Berry Dutch Baby Pancake

Servings: 4
Cooking Time: 12 To 16 Minutes
Ingredients:
- 1 tablespoon unsalted butter, at room temperature
- 1 egg
- 2 egg whites
- ½ cup 2% milk
- ½ cup whole-wheat pastry flour
- 1 teaspoon pure vanilla extract
- 1 cup sliced fresh strawberries
- ½ cup fresh raspberries
- ½ cup fresh blueberries

Directions:

1. Select BAKE, set the temperature to 330ºF, and set the time to 16 minutes. Select START/STOP to begin preheating.
2. Grease a baking pan with the butter.
3. Using a hand mixer, beat together the egg, egg whites, milk, pastry flour, and vanilla in a medium mixing bowl until well incorporated.
4. Pour the batter into the pan. Place the pan directly in the pot. Close the hood and BAKE for 12 to 16 minutes, or until the pancake puffs up in the center and the edges are golden brown.
5. Allow the pancake to cool for 5 minutes and serve topped with the berries.

Western Omelet

Servings: 2
Cooking Time: 18 To 21 Minutes
Ingredients:
- ¼ cup chopped bell pepper, green or red
- ¼ cup chopped onion
- ¼ cup diced ham
- 1 teaspoon butter
- 4 large eggs
- 2 tablespoons milk
- ⅛ teaspoon salt
- ¾ cup shredded sharp Cheddar cheese

Directions:
1. Select AIR CRISP, set the temperature to 390ºF, and set the time to 6 minutes. Select START/STOP to begin preheating.
2. Put the bell pepper, onion, ham, and butter in a baking pan and mix well. Place the pan directly in the pot.
3. Close the hood and AIR CRISP for 1 minute. Stir and continue to cook for an additional 4 to 5 minutes until the veggies are softened.
4. Meanwhile, whisk together the eggs, milk, and salt in a bowl.
5. Pour the egg mixture over the veggie mixture.
6. Reduce the grill temperature to 360ºF and BAKE for 13 to 15 minutes more, or until the top is lightly golden browned and the eggs are set.
7. Scatter the omelet with the shredded cheese. Bake for another 1 minute until the cheese has melted.
8. Let the omelet cool for 5 minutes before serving.

Egg And Bacon Nests

Servings:12
Cooking Time: 30 Minutes
Ingredients:
- 3 tablespoons avocado oil
- 12 slices bacon
- 12 eggs
- Salt
- Freshly ground black pepper

Directions:
1. Insert the Grill Grate and close the hood. Select GRILL, set the temperature to HI, and set the time to 30 minutes. Select START/STOP to begin preheating.
2. While the unit is preheating, brush the avocado oil in the bottom and on the sides of two 6-cup muffin tins. Wrap a bacon slice around the inside of each muffin cup, then crack an egg into each cup. Season to taste with salt and pepper.

3. When the unit beeps to signify it has preheated, place one muffin tin in the center of the Grill Grate. Close the hood and grill for 15 minutes.

4. After 15 minutes, remove the muffin tin. Place the second muffin tin in the center of the Grill Grate, close the hood, and grill for 15 minutes.

5. Serve immediately or let cool and store in resealable bags in the refrigerator for up to 4 days.

Cheesy Hash Brown Casserole

Servings: 4
Cooking Time: 30 Minutes
Ingredients:
- 3½ cups frozen hash browns, thawed
- 1 teaspoon salt
- 1 teaspoon freshly ground black pepper
- 3 tablespoons butter, melted
- 1 can cream of chicken soup
- ½ cup sour cream
- 1 cup minced onion
- ½ cup shredded sharp Cheddar cheese
- Cooking spray

Directions:
1. Put the hash browns in a large bowl and season with salt and black pepper. Add the melted butter, cream of chicken soup, and sour cream and stir until well incorporated. Mix in the minced onion and cheese and stir well.

2. Select BAKE, set the temperature to 325ºF, and set the time to 30 minutes. Select START/STOP to begin preheating.

3. Spray a baking pan with cooking spray.

4. Spread the hash brown mixture evenly into the baking pan.

5. Place the pan directly in the pot. Close the hood and BAKE for 30 minutes until browned.

6. Cool for 5 minutes before serving.

Ham And Corn Muffins

Servings:8
Cooking Time: 6 Minutes
Ingredients:
- ¾ cup yellow cornmeal
- ¼ cup flour
- 1½ teaspoons baking powder
- ¼ teaspoon salt
- 1 egg, beaten
- 2 tablespoons canola oil
- ½ cup milk
- ½ cup shredded sharp Cheddar cheese
- ½ cup diced ham

Directions:
1. Select BAKE, set the temperature to 390ºF, and set the time to 6 minutes. Select START/STOP to begin preheating.

2. In a medium bowl, stir together the cornmeal, flour, baking powder, and salt.

3. Add the egg, oil, and milk to dry ingredients and mix well.

4. Stir in shredded cheese and diced ham.

5. Divide batter among 8 parchment paper-lined muffin cups.

6. Put 4 filled muffin cups in the pot. Close the hood and BAKE for 5 minutes.

7. Reduce temperature to 330ºF and bake for 1 minute or until a toothpick inserted in center of the muffin comes out clean.

8. Repeat steps 6 and 7 to bake remaining muffins.

9. Serve warm.

Avocado Eggs

Servings: 4
Cooking Time: 10 Minutes
Ingredients:
- 4 ripe avocados, divided
- 3 tablespoons extra-virgin olive oil
- 1 teaspoon salt
- ½ teaspoon freshly ground black pepper
- 8 small eggs
- Hot sauce or salsa, for garnish (optional)

Directions:
1. Insert the Grill Grate and close the hood. Select GRILL, set the temperature to HI, and set the time to 10 minutes. Select START/STOP to begin preheating.

2. While the unit is preheating, cut the avocados in half lengthwise and remove the pits, but leave the skin on. You may need to scoop out some of the green flesh so the egg fits once added. Set the extra flesh aside to use as an additional topping later.

3. In a small bowl, whisk together the olive oil, salt, and pepper. Brush the seasoned olive oil on the flesh of the avocados. Then, crack an egg into the center of each avocado half.

4. When the unit beeps to signify it has preheated, place the avocados on the grill, egg-side up. Close the hood and grill for 10 minutes.

5. Cooking is complete when the egg whites are firm. Remove the avocados from the grill. Garnish with the reserved avocado and top with your favorite hot sauce or salsa, if desired.

Bacon And Egg Bread Cups

Servings: 4
Cooking Time: 8 To 12 Minutes
Ingredients:
- 4 crusty rolls
- 4 thin slices Gouda or Swiss cheese mini wedges
- 5 eggs
- 2 tablespoons heavy cream
- 3 strips precooked bacon, chopped
- ½ teaspoon dried thyme
- Pinch salt
- Freshly ground black pepper, to taste

Directions:
1. Select BAKE, set the temperature to 330ºF, and set the time to 12 minutes. Select START/STOP to begin preheating.

2. On a clean work surface, cut the tops off the rolls. Using your fingers, remove the insides of the rolls to make bread cups, leaving a ½-inch shell. Place a slice of cheese onto each roll bottom.

3. Whisk together the eggs and heavy cream in a medium bowl until well combined. Fold in the bacon, thyme, salt, and pepper and stir well.

4. Scrape the egg mixture into the prepared bread cups.

5. Place the bread cups directly in the pot. Close the hood and BAKE for 8 to 12 minutes, or until the eggs are cooked to your preference.
6. Serve warm.

Brie And Apple Tart

Servings: 4
Cooking Time: 10 Minutes
Ingredients:
- 1 sheet ready-to-bake puff pastry (thawed, if frozen)
- 1 small apple, cored and thinly sliced
- 3 tablespoons honey
- 1 teaspoon light brown sugar, packed
- 1 (8-ounce) round Brie cheese
- 2 tablespoons unsalted butter, melted

Directions:
1. Insert the Grill Grate and close the hood. Select GRILL, set the temperature to LO, and set the time to 10 minutes. Select START/STOP to begin preheating.
2. While the unit is preheating, unroll the pastry dough on a flat surface. Place the apple slices in the center of the dough. Drizzle the honey over the apples and sprinkle the brown sugar on top. Unwrap the Brie and place it on top of the apple slices. Fold the ends of the pastry around the Brie, similar to wrapping up a package, making sure to fully enclose the Brie and apples. Using a basting brush, brush the pastry all over with the melted butter.
3. When the unit beeps to signify it has preheated, place the pastry on the grill. Close the hood and grill for 10 minutes.
4. When cooking is complete, the pastry will be a nice golden brown. The Brie may leak out while cooking, and this is okay. The filling will be hot, so be sure to let it cool for a few minutes before serving.

Olives, Kale, And Pecorino Baked Eggs

Servings: 2
Cooking Time: 10 To 12 Minutes
Ingredients:
- 1 cup roughly chopped kale leaves, stems and center ribs removed
- ¼ cup grated pecorino cheese
- ¼ cup olive oil
- 1 garlic clove, peeled
- 3 tablespoons whole almonds
- Kosher salt and freshly ground black pepper, to taste
- 4 large eggs
- 2 tablespoons heavy cream
- 3 tablespoons chopped pitted mixed olives

Directions:
1. Place the kale, pecorino, olive oil, garlic, almonds, salt, and pepper in a small blender and blitz until well incorporated.
2. Select BAKE, set the temperature to 300ºF, and set the time to 12 minutes. Select START/STOP to begin preheating.
3. One at a time, crack the eggs in a baking pan. Drizzle the kale pesto on top of the egg whites. Top the yolks with the cream and swirl together the yolks and the pesto.
4. Place the pan directly in the pot. Close the hood and BAKE for 10 to 12 minutes, or until the top begins to brown and the eggs are set.

5. Allow the eggs to cool for 5 minutes. Scatter the olives on top and serve warm.

Country-fried Steak And Eggs

Servings: 4
Cooking Time: 16 Minutes
Ingredients:
- For the country-fried steak
- 1 cup milk
- 2 large eggs
- 2 cups all-purpose flour
- 2 teaspoons salt
- 1 teaspoon freshly ground black pepper
- 1 teaspoon garlic powder
- 1 teaspoon onion powder
- ¼ teaspoon cayenne pepper
- ¾ teaspoon paprika
- 4 (8-ounce) cube or round steaks
- For the eggs and gravy
- 4 to 8 large eggs
- 4 tablespoons (½ stick) unsalted butter
- 4 tablespoons all-purpose flour
- ½ cup heavy (whipping) cream
- ¼ teaspoon salt
- ¼ teaspoon freshly ground black pepper

Directions:
1. Create an assembly line with 3 shallow dishes. In the first dish, whisk together the milk and eggs. In the second dish, combine the flour, salt, black pepper, garlic powder, onion powder, cayenne pepper, and paprika. Place a steak in the flour mixture to coat both sides, then dip it into the egg mixture to coat both sides. Dip the steak back in the flour mixture, coating both sides. Place the coated steaks in the third shallow dish.
2. Insert the Grill Grate and close the hood. Select GRILL, set the temperature to HI, and set the time to 6 minutes. Select START/STOP to begin preheating.
3. When the unit beeps to signify it has preheated, place all 4 steaks on the Grill Grate. Close the hood and cook for 3 minutes.
4. After 3 minutes, open the hood and flip the steaks. Close the hood and cook for 3 minutes more.
5. When grilling is complete, transfer the steaks to a plate. Using grill mitts, remove the Grill Grate from the unit, leaving any excess fat drippings from the Grill Grate in the Cooking Pot.
6. Select AIR CRISP, set the temperature to 400°F, and set the time to 10 minutes. Select START/STOP and then press the PREHEAT button to skip preheating. Crack the eggs in the Cooking Pot. Close the hood and cook for 5 minutes, until the egg whites are opaque and firm. Remove the eggs from the pot.
7. Place the butter and flour in the Cooking Pot with the remaining fat drippings. Stir with a wooden spoon or silicone whisk until the butter has melted. Pour in the heavy cream and add the salt and pepper. Stir until completely mixed.
8. Close the hood and cook for 3 minutes. After 3 minutes, open the hood, stir the gravy, then close the hood to cook for 2 minutes more.

9. When cooking is complete, stir the gravy again and let it sit until you're ready to serve. To serve, pour the gravy over the country-fried steaks next to the eggs.

Coconut Brown Rice Porridge With Dates

Servings: 1 Or 2
Cooking Time: 23 Minutes
Ingredients:
- ½ cup cooked brown rice
- 1 cup canned coconut milk
- ¼ cup unsweetened shredded coconut
- ¼ cup packed dark brown sugar
- 4 large Medjool dates, pitted and roughly chopped
- ½ teaspoon kosher salt
- ¼ teaspoon ground cardamom
- Heavy cream, for serving (optional)

Directions:
1. Select BAKE, set the temperature to 375ºF, and set the time to 23 minutes. Select START/STOP to begin preheating.
2. Place all the ingredients except the heavy cream in a baking pan and stir until blended.
3. Place the pan directly in the pot. Close the hood and BAKE for 23 minutes until the porridge is thick and creamy. Stir the porridge halfway through the cooking time.
4. Remove from the grill and ladle the porridge into bowls.
5. Serve hot with a drizzle of the cream, if desired.

Bacon And Broccoli Bread Pudding

Servings: 2 To 4
Cooking Time: 48 Minutes
Ingredients:
- ½ pound thick cut bacon, cut into ¼-inch pieces
- 3 cups brioche bread, cut into ½-inch cubes
- 2 tablespoons butter, melted
- 3 eggs
- 1 cup milk
- ½ teaspoon salt
- Freshly ground black pepper, to taste
- 1 cup frozen broccoli florets, thawed and chopped
- 1½ cups grated Swiss cheese

Directions:
1. Insert the Crisper Basket and close the hood. Select AIR CRISP, set the temperature to 400ºF, and set the time to 10 minutes. Select START/STOP to begin preheating.
2. Put the bacon in the basket. Close the hood and AIR CRISP for 8 minutes until crispy, shaking the basket a few times to help it cook evenly. Remove the bacon and set it aside on a paper towel.
3. AIR CRISP the brioche bread cubes for 2 minutes to dry and toast lightly.
4. Butter a cake pan. Combine all the remaining ingredients in a large bowl and toss well. Transfer the mixture to the buttered cake pan, cover with aluminum foil and refrigerate the bread pudding overnight, or for at least 8 hours.
5. Remove the cake pan from the refrigerator an hour before you plan to bake and let it sit on the countertop to come to room temperature.

6. Select BAKE, set the temperature to 330ºF, and set the time to 40 minutes. Select START/STOP to begin preheating.
7. Place the covered cake pan directly in the pot. Fold the ends of the aluminum foil over the top of the pan. Close the hood and BAKE for 20 minutes. Remove the foil and bake for an additional 20 minutes. If the top browns a little too much before the custard has set, simply return the foil to the pan. The bread pudding has cooked through when a skewer inserted into the center comes out clean.
8. Serve warm.

Breakfast Tater Tot Casserole

Servings: 4
Cooking Time: 17 To 19 Minutes
Ingredients:
- 4 eggs
- 1 cup milk
- Salt and pepper, to taste
- 12 ounces ground chicken sausage
- 1 pound frozen tater tots, thawed
- ¾ cup grated Cheddar cheese
- Cooking spray

Directions:
1. Whisk together the eggs and milk in a medium bowl. Season with salt and pepper to taste and stir until mixed. Set aside.
2. Place a skillet over medium-high heat and spritz with cooking spray. Place the ground sausage in the skillet and break it into smaller pieces with a spatula or spoon. Cook for 3 to 4 minutes until the sausage starts to brown, stirring occasionally. Remove from heat and set aside.
3. Select BAKE, set the temperature to 400ºF, and set the time to 15 minutes. Select START/STOP to begin preheating.
4. Coat a baking pan with cooking spray.
5. Arrange the tater tots in the baking pan. Place the pan directly in the pot. Close the hood and BAKE for 15 minutes. Stir in the egg mixture and cooked sausage. Bake for another 6 minutes.
6. Scatter the cheese on top of the tater tots. Continue to bake for 2 to 3 minutes more until the cheese is bubbly and melted.
7. Let the mixture cool for 5 minutes and serve warm.

Chocolate Banana Bread With White Chocolate

Servings: 4
Cooking Time: 30 Minutes
Ingredients:
- ¼ cup cocoa powder
- 6 tablespoons plus 2 teaspoons all-purpose flour, divided
- ½ teaspoon kosher salt
- ¼ teaspoon baking soda
- 1½ ripe bananas
- 1 large egg, whisked
- ¼ cup vegetable oil
- ½ cup sugar
- 3 tablespoons buttermilk or plain yogurt (not Greek)
- ½ teaspoon vanilla extract

- 6 tablespoons chopped white chocolate
- 6 tablespoons chopped walnuts

Directions:
1. Select BAKE, set the temperature to 310ºF, and set the time to 30 minutes. Select START/STOP to begin preheating.
2. Mix together the cocoa powder, 6 tablespoons of the flour, salt, and baking soda in a medium bowl.
3. Mash the bananas with a fork in another medium bowl until smooth. Fold in the egg, oil, sugar, buttermilk, and vanilla, and whisk until thoroughly combined. Add the wet mixture to the dry mixture and stir until well incorporated.
4. Combine the white chocolate, walnuts, and the remaining 2 tablespoons of flour in a third bowl and toss to coat. Add this mixture to the batter and stir until well incorporated. Pour the batter into a baking pan and smooth the top with a spatula.
5. Place the pan directly in the pot. Close the hood and BAKE for 30 minutes. Check the bread for doneness: If a toothpick inserted into the center of the bread comes out clean, it's done.
6. Remove from the grill and allow to cool on a wire rack for 10 minutes before serving.

Fried Potatoes With Peppers And Onions

Servings: 4
Cooking Time: 35 Minutes
Ingredients:
- 1 pound red potatoes, cut into ½-inch dices
- 1 large red bell pepper, cut into ½-inch dices
- 1 large green bell pepper, cut into ½-inch dices
- 1 medium onion, cut into ½-inch dices
- 1½ tablespoons extra-virgin olive oil
- 1¼ teaspoons kosher salt
- ¾ teaspoon sweet paprika
- ¾ teaspoon garlic powder
- Freshly ground black pepper, to taste

Directions:
1. Insert the Crisper Basket and close the hood. Select AIR CRISP, set the temperature to 350ºF, and set the time to 35 minutes. Select START/STOP to begin preheating.
2. Mix together the potatoes, bell peppers, onion, oil, salt, paprika, garlic powder, and black pepper in a large mixing and toss to coat.
3. Transfer the potato mixture to the Crisper Basket. Close the hood and AIR CRISP for 35 minutes, or until the potatoes are nicely browned. Shake the basket three times during cooking.
4. Remove from the basket to a plate and serve warm.

Chorizo Sausage And Eggs

Servings: 4
Cooking Time: 20 Minutes
Ingredients:
- ½ onion, diced
- 2 pounds chorizo, casings removed if using links
- 6 large eggs
- 1 large tomato, diced
- Chopped fresh cilantro, for garnish

Directions:

1. Insert the Cooking Pot and close the hood. Select GRILL, set the temperature to HI, and set the time to 20 minutes. Select START/STOP to begin preheating.
2. When the unit beeps to signify it has preheated, place the onion in the pot. Then place the chorizo on top of the onion. Use a wooden spoon or silicone spatula to break the sausage apart into bite-size pieces. Close the hood and cook for 15 minutes.
3. After 15 minutes, open the hood and stir the sausage and onion. Crack the eggs on top of the mixture and add the diced tomato. Close the hood and cook for 5 minutes more.
4. When cooking is complete, garnish with the cilantro and serve. You can also serve with your favorite flour or corn tortillas for breakfast tacos.

Mini Caprese Pizzas

Servings: 4
Cooking Time: 10 Minutes
Ingredients:
- 1 (14-ounce) package refrigerated pizza dough
- 2 tablespoons extra-virgin olive oil
- 2 large tomatoes, thinly sliced
- 8 ounces fresh mozzarella cheese, cut into thin discs
- 12 fresh basil leaves
- Balsamic vinegar, for drizzling or dipping

Directions:
1. Insert the Grill Grate and close the hood. Select GRILL, set the temperature to MED, and set the time to 10 minutes. Select START/STOP to begin preheating.
2. While the unit is preheating, lay the pizza dough on a flat surface. Cut out 12 small round pizzas 1½ to 2 inches diameter each. Brush both sides of each dough round with the olive oil.
3. When the unit beeps to signify it has preheated, place the dough rounds on the Grill Grate, 4 across, in 3 rows. Close the hood and grill for 5 minutes.
4. After 5 minutes, open the hood and flip the rounds. Top each round with the tomato and cheese slices. Close the hood and cook for 5 minutes more.
5. When cooking is complete, remove the pizzas from the Grill Grate. Top each with the basil. When ready to serve, drizzle each pizza with the balsamic vinegar, or keep the vinegar on the side in a small bowl for dipping.

Sourdough Croutons

Servings:4
Cooking Time: 6 Minutes
Ingredients:
- 4 cups cubed sourdough bread, 1-inch cubes
- 1 tablespoon olive oil
- 1 teaspoon fresh thyme leaves
- ¼ teaspoon salt
- Freshly ground black pepper, to taste

Directions:
1. Combine all ingredients in a bowl.
2. Insert the Crisper Basket and close the hood. Select AIR CRISP, set the temperature to 400ºF, and set the time to 6 minutes. Select START/STOP to begin preheating.
3. Toss the bread cubes and transfer to the basket. Close the hood and AIR CRISP for 6 minutes, shaking the basket once or twice while they cook.
4. Serve warm.

Grilled Breakfast Burritos

Servings: 4
Cooking Time: 15 Minutes
Ingredients:
- 4 large eggs
- 12 slices bacon, cut into 1-inch pieces
- 1 cup frozen shredded hash browns
- 1 cup shredded Monterey Jack cheese
- 4 (10-inch) flour tortillas
- 2 tablespoons extra-virgin olive oil
- 4 tablespoons sour cream, for topping
- 1 avocado, pitted and diced, for topping

Directions:
1. Insert the Cooking Pot and close the hood. Select AIR CRISP, set the temperature to 390°F, and set the time to 15 minutes. Select START/STOP to begin preheating.
2. While the unit is preheating, in a medium bowl, whisk the eggs. Add the bacon, frozen hash browns, and cheese to the eggs and stir to combine.
3. When the unit beeps to signify it has preheated, pour the egg mixture into the Cooking Pot. Close the hood and cook for 10 minutes.
4. While the eggs are cooking, place the tortillas on top of the Grill Grate.
5. After 10 minutes, open the hood and use a silicone spatula to scramble the eggs and ensure the bacon is cooked. Remove the pot from the unit. Top the center of each tortilla with the scrambled egg mixture. Roll one end of the tortilla over the eggs, fold in the sides, and finish rolling the tortilla. Brush the olive oil over the burritos and place them seam-side down on the Grill Grate. Place the Grill Grate into the unit. Close the hood and cook for the remaining 5 minutes.
6. When cooking is complete, transfer the burritos to plates. Top with the sour cream and avocado and serve.

Cornflakes Toast Sticks

Servings: 4
Cooking Time: 6 Minutes
Ingredients:
- 2 eggs
- ½ cup milk
- ⅛ teaspoon salt
- ½ teaspoon pure vanilla extract
- ¾ cup crushed cornflakes
- 6 slices sandwich bread, each slice cut into 4 strips
- Maple syrup, for dipping
- Cooking spray

Directions:
1. Insert the Crisper Basket and close the hood. Select AIR CRISP, set the temperature to 390°F, and set the time to 6 minutes. Select START/STOP to begin preheating.
2. In a small bowl, beat together the eggs, milk, salt, and vanilla.
3. Put crushed cornflakes on a plate or in a shallow dish.
4. Dip bread strips in egg mixture, shake off excess, and roll in cornflake crumbs.
5. Spray both sides of bread strips with oil.
6. Put bread strips in Crisper Basket in a single layer.
7. Close the hood and AIR CRISP for 6 minutes or until golden brown.

8. Repeat steps 5 and 6 to AIR CRISP remaining French toast sticks.
9. Serve with maple syrup.

Ham And Cheese Cups

Servings:12
Cooking Time: 20 Minutes
Ingredients:
- 12 large eggs
- 3 tablespoons avocado oil
- 12 slices deli ham
- 1 cup shredded cheese of choice
- Salt
- Freshly ground black pepper

Directions:
1. Insert the Grill Grate and close the hood. Select GRILL, set the temperature to HI, and set the time to 20 minutes. Select START/STOP to begin preheating.
2. While the unit is preheating, in a large bowl, beat the eggs. Brush the avocado oil in the bottom and on the sides of two 6-cup muffin tins. Line each muffin cup with a slice of ham. Spoon the eggs evenly into each cup. Top with the shredded cheese and season with salt and pepper.
3. When the unit beeps to signify it has preheated, place one muffin tin on the Grill Grate. Close the hood and grill for 10 minutes.
4. After 10 minutes, open the hood and remove the muffin tin. Place the second muffin tin on the Grill Grate, close the hood, and cook for 10 minutes.
5. When cooking is complete, remove the cups from the tins and serve.

Supersized Family Pizza Omelet

Servings: 4
Cooking Time: 10 Minutes
Ingredients:
- 10 large eggs
- 1 tablespoon Italian seasoning
- ½ cup pizza or marinara sauce
- 1 cup shredded mozzarella cheese
- 2 ounces pepperoni slices (about 24 slices)

Directions:
1. Insert the Cooking Pot and close the hood. Select GRILL, set the temperature to HI, and set the time to 10 minutes. Select START/STOP to begin preheating.
2. While the unit is preheating, in a medium bowl, whisk together the eggs and Italian seasoning.
3. When the unit beeps to signify it has preheated, pour the egg mixture into the Cooking Pot. Close the hood and cook for 5 minutes.
4. Place the Grill Grate next to the unit on top of the counter. After 5 minutes, open the hood and use a spatula to fold the egg sheet in half, then place it on top of the Grill Grate.
5. Place the Grill Grate into the unit. Top the omelet with the pizza sauce, mozzarella cheese, and pepperoni slices. Close the hood and cook for 5 minutes more.
6. When cooking is complete, the cheese will be melted. Remove the omelet from the grill and serve.

Chicken Breakfast Sausages

Servings:8
Cooking Time: 8 To 12 Minutes
Ingredients:
- 1 Granny Smith apple, peeled and finely chopped
- 2 tablespoons apple juice
- 2 garlic cloves, minced
- 1 egg white
- ⅓ cup minced onion
- 3 tablespoons ground almonds
- ⅛ teaspoon freshly ground black pepper
- 1 pound ground chicken breast

Directions:
1. Insert the Crisper Basket and close the hood. Select AIR CRISP, set the temperature to 330ºF, and set the time to 12 minutes. Select START/STOP to begin preheating.
2. Combine all the ingredients except the chicken in a medium mixing bowl and stir well.
3. Add the chicken breast to the apple mixture and mix with your hands until well incorporated.
4. Divide the mixture into 8 equal portions and shape into patties. Arrange the patties in the Crisper Basket. You may need to work in batches depending on the size of your Crisper Basket.
5. Close the hood and AIR CRISP for 8 to 12 minutes, or until a meat thermometer inserted in the center of the chicken reaches at least 165ºF.
6. Remove from the grill to a plate and repeat with the remaining patties.
7. Let the chicken cool for 5 minutes and serve warm.

Blueberry Dump Cake

Servings: 6 To 8
Cooking Time: 25 Minutes
Ingredients:
- 3 cups fresh blueberries
- ½ cup granulated sugar
- 1 (16-ounce) box yellow cake mix
- 8 tablespoons (1 stick) unsalted butter, melted

Directions:
1. Select BAKE, set the temperature to 300°F, and set the time to 25 minutes. Select START/STOP to begin preheating.
2. While the unit is preheating, wash and pat dry the blueberries. Then place them and the sugar into the Cooking Pot and mix to coat the fruit with the sugar.
3. In a large bowl, mix together the cake mix and melted butter. Stir until the cake mix is no longer a powder but crumbly like a streusel. Cover the blueberry-sugar mixture with the cake crumble.
4. When the unit beeps to signify it has preheated, place the Cooking Pot in the unit. Close the hood and bake for 25 minutes.
5. Baking is complete when the fresh blueberries have bubbled and the cake crumble is golden brown. Serve.

Cream Cheese–stuffed French Toast

Servings: 6
Cooking Time: 6 Minutes
Ingredients:
- 2 large eggs
- 1 cup milk
- 1 teaspoon cinnamon
- 1 teaspoon light brown sugar, packed
- 1 teaspoon vanilla extract
- 1 (8-ounce) package whipped cream cheese (flavored or plain)
- 12 slices white bread

Directions:
1. Insert the Grill Grate and close the hood. Select GRILL, set the temperature to HI, and set the time to 6 minutes. Select START/STOP to begin preheating.
2. While the unit is preheating, in a small bowl, whisk together the eggs, milk, cinnamon, brown sugar, and vanilla.
3. Spread a thick layer of cream cheese on one side of 6 bread slices. Top each with the remaining 6 bread slices. Dip the sandwich into the egg mixture, making sure to coat both sides completely.
4. When the unit beeps to signify it has preheated, place the French toast sandwiches on the Grill Grate. Close the hood and grill for 3 minutes.
5. After 3 minutes, open the hood and flip the French toast. Close the hood and continue cooking for 3 minutes more.
6. When cooking is complete, remove the French toast from the grill and serve.

Mushroom And Squash Toast

Servings: 4
Cooking Time: 10 Minutes
Ingredients:
- 1 tablespoon olive oil
- 1 red bell pepper, cut into strips
- 2 green onions, sliced
- 1 cup sliced button or cremini mushrooms
- 1 small yellow squash, sliced
- 2 tablespoons softened butter
- 4 slices bread
- ½ cup soft goat cheese

Directions:
1. Brush the Crisper Basket with the olive oil.
2. Insert the Crisper Basket and close the hood. Select AIR CRISP, set the temperature to 350ºF, and set the time to 7 minutes. Select START/STOP to begin preheating.
3. Put the red pepper, green onions, mushrooms, and squash inside the basket and give them a stir. Close the hood and AIR CRISP for 7 minutes or the vegetables are tender, shaking the basket once throughout the cooking time.
4. Remove the vegetables and set them aside.
5. Spread the butter on the slices of bread and transfer to the basket, butter-side up. Close the hood and AIR CRISP for 3 minutes.
6. Remove the toast from the grill and top with goat cheese and vegetables. Serve warm.

Pb&j

Servings: 4
Cooking Time: 6 Minutes
Ingredients:
- ½ cup cornflakes, crushed
- ¼ cup shredded coconut
- 8 slices oat nut bread or any whole-grain, oversize bread
- 6 tablespoons peanut butter
- 2 medium bananas, cut into ½-inch-thick slices
- 6 tablespoons pineapple preserves
- 1 egg, beaten
- Cooking spray

Directions:
1. Insert the Crisper Basket and close the hood. Select AIR CRISP, set the temperature to 360°F, and set the time to 6 minutes. Select START/STOP to begin preheating.
2. In a shallow dish, mix the cornflake crumbs and coconut.
3. For each sandwich, spread one bread slice with 1½ tablespoons of peanut butter. Top with banana slices. Spread another bread slice with 1½ tablespoons of preserves. Combine to make a sandwich.
4. Using a pastry brush, brush top of sandwich lightly with beaten egg. Sprinkle with about 1½ tablespoons of crumb coating, pressing it in to make it stick. Spray with cooking spray.
5. Turn sandwich over and repeat to coat and spray the other side. Place the sandwiches in the Crisper Basket.
6. Close the hood and AIR CRISP for 6 minutes or until coating is golden brown and crispy.
7. Cut the cooked sandwiches in half and serve warm.

Grilled Egg And Arugula Pizza

Servings: 2
Cooking Time: 8 Minutes
Ingredients:
- 2 tablespoons all-purpose flour, plus more as needed
- ½ store-bought pizza dough
- 1 tablespoon canola oil, divided
- 1 cup fresh ricotta cheese
- 4 large eggs
- Sea salt, to taste
- Freshly ground black pepper, to taste
- 4 cups arugula, torn
- 1 tablespoon extra-virgin olive oil
- 1 teaspoon freshly squeezed lemon juice
- 2 tablespoons grated Parmesan cheese

Directions:
1. Insert the Grill Grate and close the hood. Select GRILL, set the temperature to MAX, and set the time to 7 minutes. Select START/STOP to begin preheating.
2. While the unit is preheating, dust a clean work surface with flour. Place the dough on the floured surface and roll it into a 9-inch round of even thickness. Dust your rolling pin and work surface with additional flour, as needed, to ensure the dough does not stick.
3. Brush the surface of the rolled-out dough evenly with ½ tablespoon of canola oil. Flip the dough over and brush with the remaining ½ tablespoon oil. Poke the dough with a fork 5 or 6 times across its surface to prevent air pockets from forming during cooking.
4. When the unit beeps to signify it has preheated, place the dough on the Grill Grate. Close the hood and GRILL for 4 minutes.
5. After 4 minutes, flip the dough, then spoon teaspoons of ricotta cheese across the surface of the dough, leaving a 1-inch border around the edges.
6. Crack one egg into a ramekin or small bowl. This way you can easily remove any shell that may break into the egg and keep the yolk intact. Imagine the dough is split into four quadrants. Pour one egg into each. Repeat with the remaining 3 eggs. Season the pizza with salt and pepper.
7. Close the hood and continue cooking for the remaining 3 to 4 minutes until the egg whites are firm.
8. Meanwhile, in a medium bowl, toss together the arugula, oil, and lemon juice, and season with salt and pepper.
9. Transfer the pizza to a cutting board and let it cool. Top it with the arugula mixture, drizzle with olive oil, if desired, and sprinkle with Parmesan cheese. Cut into pieces and serve.

Fluffy Pancake Sheet

Servings: 4
Cooking Time: 12 Minutes
Ingredients:
- 3 cups pancake mix
- 1½ cups milk
- 2 eggs
- Nonstick cooking spray
- Unsalted butter, for topping
- Maple syrup, for topping

Directions:
1. Insert the Cooking Pot and close the hood. Select BAKE, set the temperature to 350°F, and set the time to 12 minutes. Select START/STOP to begin preheating.
2. While the unit is preheating, in a large bowl, whisk together the pancake mix, milk, and eggs.
3. When the unit beeps to signify it has preheated, spray the Cooking Pot with cooking spray. Pour the batter into the pot. Close the hood and cook for 12 minutes.
4. When cooking is complete, cut the pancake into squares. Top with the butter and maple syrup and serve.

Everything Bagel Breakfast Bake

Servings: 4
Cooking Time: 25 Minutes
Ingredients:
- 6 large eggs
- 2 cups milk
- ½ cup heavy (whipping) cream
- 4 everything bagels, cut into 1-inch cubes (or bagel flavor of choice)
- 2 cups cherry tomatoes
- 1 pound cream cheese, cut into cubes

Directions:
1. In a large bowl, whisk together the eggs, milk, and heavy cream.
2. Add the bagel cubes to the egg mixture. Set aside to rest for 25 minutes.
3. After 25 minutes, insert the Cooking Pot and close the hood. Select BAKE, set the temperature to 375°F, and set the time to 25 minutes. Select START/STOP to begin preheating.

4. While the unit is preheating, slice the cherry tomatoes into thirds.
5. When the unit beeps to signify it has preheated, pour the bagel mixture into the Cooking Pot. Top with the sliced cherry tomatoes and evenly place the cream cheese cubes over the top. Close the hood and bake for 25 minutes.
6. When cooking is complete, remove the pot from the grill and serve.

Spinach And Mushroom Florentine Hash

Servings: 4
Cooking Time: 15 Minutes
Ingredients:
- 3 cups frozen shredded hash browns
- 5 eggs, divided
- 1 cup shredded cheese of choice
- ½ teaspoon garlic powder
- 8 ounces mushrooms, sliced
- 1 cup fresh spinach

Directions:
1. Select AIR CRISP, set the temperature to 390°F, and set the time to 15 minutes. Select START/STOP to begin preheating.
2. While the unit is preheating, in a large bowl, combine the frozen hash browns, 2 eggs, and the shredded cheese. Transfer the mixture to the Cooking Pot, pressing it into the bottom of the pot in an even layer.
3. When the unit beeps to signify it has preheated, insert the Cooking Pot. Close the hood and cook for 10 minutes.
4. While the hash browns are cooking, in a medium bowl, whisk together the remaining 3 eggs and garlic powder. Stir in the mushrooms and spinach.
5. After 10 minutes, open the hood and pour the egg and veggie mixture on top of the hash brown bed. Close the hood and cook for 5 minutes more.
6. When cooking is complete, the eggs should be set. Serve with optional additional toppings, like sour cream, fresh sliced avocados, and your favorite hot sauce, if you like.

Veggie Frittata

Servings: 4
Cooking Time: 8 To 12 Minutes
Ingredients:
- ½ cup chopped red bell pepper
- ⅓ cup grated carrot
- ⅓ cup minced onion
- 1 teaspoon olive oil
- 1 egg
- 6 egg whites
- ⅓ cup 2% milk
- 1 tablespoon shredded Parmesan cheese

Directions:
1. Select BAKE, set the temperature to 350°F, and set the time to 12 minutes. Select START/STOP to begin preheating.
2. Mix together the red bell pepper, carrot, onion, and olive oil in a baking pan and stir to combine.
3. Place the pan directly in the pot. Close the hood and BAKE for 4 to 6 minutes, or until the veggies are soft. Stir once during cooking.

4. Meantime, whisk together the egg, egg whites, and milk in a medium bowl until creamy.
5. When the veggies are done, pour the egg mixture over the top. Scatter with the Parmesan cheese.
6. Bake for an additional 4 to 6 minutes, or until the eggs are set and the top is golden around the edges.
7. Allow the frittata to cool for 5 minutes before slicing and serving.

Posh Orange Rolls

Servings:8
Cooking Time: 8 Minutes
Ingredients:
- 3 ounces low-fat cream cheese
- 1 tablespoon low-fat sour cream or plain yogurt
- 2 teaspoons sugar
- ¼ teaspoon pure vanilla extract
- ¼ teaspoon orange extract
- 1 can organic crescent roll dough
- ¼ cup chopped walnuts
- ¼ cup dried cranberries
- ¼ cup shredded, sweetened coconut
- Butter-flavored cooking spray
- Orange Glaze:
- ½ cup powdered sugar
- 1 tablespoon orange juice
- ¼ teaspoon orange extract
- Dash of salt

Directions:
1. Cut a circular piece of parchment paper slightly smaller than the bottom of the Crisper Basket. Set aside.
2. In a small bowl, combine the cream cheese, sour cream or yogurt, sugar, and vanilla and orange extracts. Stir until smooth.
3. Insert the Crisper Basket and close the hood. Select AIR CRISP, set the temperature to 300°F, and set the time to 8 minutes. Select START/STOP to begin preheating.
4. Separate crescent roll dough into 8 triangles and divide cream cheese mixture among them. Starting at wide end, spread cheese mixture to within 1 inch of point.
5. Sprinkle nuts and cranberries evenly over cheese mixture.
6. Starting at wide end, roll up triangles, then sprinkle with coconut, pressing in lightly to make it stick. Spray tops of rolls with butter-flavored cooking spray.
7. Put parchment paper in Crisper Basket, and place 4 rolls on top, spaced evenly.
8. Close the hood and AIR CRISP for 8 minutes, until rolls are golden brown and cooked through.
9. Repeat steps 7 and 8 to AIR CRISP remaining 4 rolls. You should be able to use the same piece of parchment paper twice.
10. In a small bowl, stir together ingredients for glaze and drizzle over warm rolls. Serve warm.

Sausage And Cheese Quiche

Servings: 4
Cooking Time: 25 Minutes
Ingredients:
- 12 large eggs
- 1 cup heavy cream
- Salt and black pepper, to taste
- 12 ounces sugar-free breakfast sausage
- 2 cups shredded Cheddar cheese
- Cooking spray

Directions:
1. Select BAKE, set the temperature to 375ºF, and set the time to 25 minutes. Select START/STOP to begin preheating.
2. Coat a casserole dish with cooking spray.
3. Beat together the eggs, heavy cream, salt and pepper in a large bowl until creamy. Stir in the breakfast sausage and Cheddar cheese.
4. Pour the sausage mixture into the prepared casserole dish. Place the dish directly in the pot. Close the hood and BAKE for 25 minutes, or until the top of the quiche is golden brown and the eggs are set.
5. Remove from the grill and let sit for 5 to 10 minutes before serving.

Grit And Ham Fritters

Servings: 6 To 8
Cooking Time: 20 Minutes
Ingredients:
- 4 cups water
- 1 cup quick-cooking grits
- ¼ teaspoon salt
- 2 tablespoons butter
- 2 cups grated Cheddar cheese, divided
- 1 cup finely diced ham
- 1 tablespoon chopped chives
- Salt and freshly ground black pepper, to taste
- 1 egg, beaten
- 2 cups panko bread crumbs
- Cooking spray

Directions:
1. Bring the water to a boil in a saucepan. Whisk in the grits and ¼ teaspoon of salt, and cook for 7 minutes until the grits are soft. Remove the pan from the heat and stir in the butter and 1 cup of the grated Cheddar cheese. Transfer the grits to a bowl and let them cool for 10 to 15 minutes.
2. Stir the ham, chives and the rest of the cheese into the grits and season with salt and pepper to taste. Add the beaten egg and refrigerate the mixture for 30 minutes.
3. Put the panko bread crumbs in a shallow dish. Measure out ¼-cup portions of the grits mixture and shape them into patties. Coat all sides of the patties with the panko bread crumbs, patting them with the hands so the crumbs adhere to the patties. You should have about 16 patties. Spritz both sides of the patties with cooking spray.
4. Insert the Crisper Basket and close the hood. Select AIR CRISP, set the temperature to 400ºF, and set the time to 12 minutes. Select START/STOP to begin preheating.
5. Place the fritters in the basket. Close the hood and AIR CRISP for 8 minutes. Using a flat spatula, flip the fritters over and AIR CRISP for another 4 minutes.

6. Serve hot.

Egg And Sausage Stuffed Breakfast Pockets

Servings: 4
Cooking Time: 23 Minutes
Ingredients:
- 1 package ground breakfast sausage, crumbled
- 3 large eggs, lightly beaten
- ⅓ cup diced red bell pepper
- ⅓ cup thinly sliced scallions (green part only)
- Sea salt, to taste
- Freshly ground black pepper, to taste
- 1 package pizza dough
- All-purpose flour, for dusting
- 1 cup shredded Cheddar cheese
- 2 tablespoons canola oil

Directions:
1. Select ROAST, set the temperature to 375ºF, and set the time to 15 minutes. Select START/STOP to begin preheating.
2. When the unit beeps to signify it has preheated, place the sausage directly in the pot. Close the hood, and ROAST for 10 minutes, checking the sausage every 2 to 3 minutes, breaking apart larger pieces with a wooden spoon.
3. After 10 minutes, pour the eggs, bell pepper, and scallions into the pot. Stir to evenly incorporate with the sausage. Close the hood and let the eggs roast for the remaining 5 minutes, stirring occasionally. Transfer the sausage and egg mixture to a medium bowl to cool slightly. Season with salt and pepper.
4. Insert the Crisper Basket and close the hood. Select AIR CRISP, set the temperature to 350ºF, and set the time to 8 minutes. Select START/STOP to begin preheating.
5. Meanwhile, divide the dough into four equal pieces. Lightly dust a clean work surface with flour. Roll each piece of dough into a 5-inch round of even thickness. Divide the sausage-egg mixture and cheese evenly among each round. Brush the outside edge of the dough with water. Fold the dough over the filling, forming a half circle. Pinch the edges of the dough together to seal in the filling. Brush both sides of each pocket with the oil.
6. When the unit beeps to signify it has preheated, place the breakfast pockets in the basket. Close the hood and AIR CRISP for 6 to 8 minutes, or until golden brown.

Crustless Broccoli Quiche

Servings: 4
Cooking Time: 10 Minutes
Ingredients:
- 1 cup broccoli florets
- ¾ cup chopped roasted red peppers
- 1¼ cups grated Fontina cheese
- 6 eggs
- ¾ cup heavy cream
- ½ teaspoon salt
- Freshly ground black pepper, to taste
- Cooking spray

Directions:
1. Select AIR CRISP, set the temperature to 325ºF, and set the time to 10 minutes. Select START/STOP to begin preheating.

2. Spritz a baking pan with cooking spray
3. Add the broccoli florets and roasted red peppers to the pan and scatter the grated Fontina cheese on top.
4. In a bowl, beat together the eggs and heavy cream. Sprinkle with salt and pepper. Pour the egg mixture over the top of the cheese. Wrap the pan in foil.
5. Place the pan directly in the pot. Close the hood and AIR CRISP for 8 minutes. Remove the foil and continue to cook another 2 minutes until the quiche is golden brown.
6. Rest for 5 minutes before cutting into wedges and serve warm.

Fast Coffee Donuts

Servings: 6
Cooking Time: 6 Minutes
Ingredients:
- ¼ cup sugar
- ½ teaspoon salt
- 1 cup flour
- 1 teaspoon baking powder
- ¼ cup coffee
- 1 tablespoon aquafaba
- 1 tablespoon sunflower oil

Directions:
1. In a large bowl, combine the sugar, salt, flour, and baking powder.
2. Add the coffee, aquafaba, and sunflower oil and mix until a dough is formed. Leave the dough to rest in and the refrigerator.
3. Insert the Crisper Basket and close the hood. Select AIR CRISP, set the temperature to 400ºF, and set the time to 6 minutes. Select START/STOP to begin preheating.
4. Remove the dough from the fridge and divide up, kneading each section into a doughnut.
5. Put the doughnuts in the basket. Close the hood and AIR CRISP for 6 minutes.
6. Serve immediately.

Breakfast Chilaquiles

Servings: 4
Cooking Time: 15 Minutes
Ingredients:
- 4 cups tortilla chips (40 to 50 chips)
- 1 (10- to 14-ounce) can red chile sauce or enchilada sauce
- 6 large eggs
- ¼ cup diced onion, for garnish
- ½ cup crumbled queso fresco, for garnish
- Chopped fresh cilantro, for garnish

Directions:
1. Select GRILL, set the temperature to HI, and set the time to 15 minutes. Select START/STOP to begin preheating.
2. While the unit is preheating, add the tortilla chips to the Cooking Pot and pour the red chile sauce over them.
3. When the unit beeps to signify it has preheated, place the Cooking Pot in the unit. Crack the eggs, one at a time, over the tortilla chips, making sure they're evenly spread out. Close the hood and cook for 15 minutes.
4. Cooking is complete when the egg whites are firm with a runny yellow center. Garnish with the onion, queso fresco, and fresh cilantro, and serve.

Cheesy Breakfast Casserole

Servings: 4
Cooking Time: 14 Minutes
Ingredients:
- 6 slices bacon
- 6 eggs
- Salt and pepper, to taste
- Cooking spray
- ½ cup chopped green bell pepper
- ½ cup chopped onion
- ¾ cup shredded Cheddar cheese

Directions:
1. Place the bacon in a skillet over medium-high heat and cook each side for about 4 minutes until evenly crisp. Remove from the heat to a paper towel-lined plate to drain. Crumble it into small pieces and set aside.
2. Whisk the eggs with the salt and pepper in a medium bowl.
3. Select BAKE, set the temperature to 400ºF, and set the time to 8 minutes. Select START/STOP to begin preheating.
4. Spritz a baking pan with cooking spray.
5. Place the whisked eggs, crumbled bacon, green bell pepper, and onion in the prepared pan. Place the pan directly in the pot. Close the hood and BAKE for 6 minutes.
6. Scatter the Cheddar cheese all over and bake for 2 minutes more.
7. Allow to sit for 5 minutes and serve on plates.

Stuffed Bell Peppers With Italian Maple-glazed Sausage

Servings: 6
Cooking Time: 28 Minutes
Ingredients:
- 2 pounds ground Italian sausage or links
- 1 cup light brown sugar, packed
- 6 bell peppers (any color)
- 1 cup water
- 12 tablespoons (¾ cup) maple syrup, divided

Directions:
1. Insert the Cooking Pot and close the hood. Select GRILL, set the temperature to HI, and set the time to 8 minutes. Select START/STOP to begin preheating.
2. While the unit is preheating, remove the sausage from the casings if using links.
3. When the unit beeps to signify it has preheated, place the sausage and brown sugar in the Cooking Pot. Use a wooden spoon or potato masher to break the sausage apart and mix it with the brown sugar. Close the hood and cook for 8 minutes.
4. While the sausage is cooking, cut the top off each bell pepper and remove the seeds. Then slice the bell peppers in half lengthwise.
5. When cooking is complete, spoon the sausage into each bell pepper cup. Add the water to the Cooking Pot. Place 6 bell pepper halves on the Grill Grate, and place the Grill Grate in the unit.
6. Select GRILL, set the temperature to HI, and set the time to 20 minutes. Select START/STOP and then press the PREHEAT button to skip preheating. Close the hood and cook for 5 minutes.
7. After 5 minutes, open the hood and drizzle 1 tablespoon of maple syrup in each bell pepper cup. Close the hood and

cook 5 minutes more. After 5 minutes, remove the stuffed peppers and place the remaining 6 stuffed peppers on the Grill Grate. Repeat this step to cook.
8. When cooking is complete, remove the peppers from the grill and serve.
9. Adding raw sausage inside a bell pepper will result in a watery mess.

Spinach, Leek And Cheese Frittata

Servings: 2
Cooking Time: 20 To 23 Minutes
Ingredients:
- 4 large eggs
- 4 ounces baby bella mushrooms, chopped
- 1 cup baby spinach, chopped
- ½ cup shredded Cheddar cheese
- ⅓ cup chopped leek, white part only
- ¼ cup halved grape tomatoes
- 1 tablespoon 2% milk
- ¼ teaspoon dried oregano
- ¼ teaspoon garlic powder
- ½ teaspoon kosher salt
- Freshly ground black pepper, to taste
- Cooking spray

Directions:
1. Select BAKE, set the temperature to 300ºF, and set the time to 23 minutes. Select START/STOP to begin preheating.
2. Lightly spritz a baking pan with cooking spray.
3. Whisk the eggs in a large bowl until frothy. Add the mushrooms, baby spinach, cheese, leek, tomatoes, milk, oregano, garlic powder, salt, and pepper and stir until well blended. Pour the mixture into the prepared baking pan.
4. Place the pan directly in the pot. Close the hood and BAKE for 20 to 23 minutes, or until the center is puffed up and the top is golden brown.
5. Let the frittata cool for 5 minutes before slicing to serve.

Bacon And Egg Stuffed Peppers

Servings: 4
Cooking Time: 15 Minutes
Ingredients:
- 1 cup shredded Cheddar cheese
- 4 slices bacon, cooked and chopped
- 4 bell peppers, seeded and tops removed
- 4 large eggs
- Sea salt, to taste
- Freshly ground black pepper, to taste
- Chopped fresh parsley, for garnish

Directions:
1. Insert the Crisper Basket and close the hood. Select AIR CRISP, set the temperature to 390ºF, and set the time to 15 minutes. Select START/STOP to begin preheating.
2. Meanwhile, divide the cheese and bacon between the bell peppers. Crack one of the eggs into each bell pepper, and season with salt and pepper.
3. When the unit beeps to signify it has preheated, place each bell pepper in the basket. Close the hood and AIR CRISP for 10 to 15 minutes, until the egg whites are cooked and the yolks are slightly runny.
4. Remove the peppers from the basket, garnish with parsley, and serve.

Cinnamon Toast With Strawberries

Servings: 4
Cooking Time: 10 Minutes
Ingredients:
- 1 can full-fat coconut milk, refrigerated overnight
- ½ tablespoon powdered sugar
- 1½ teaspoons vanilla extract, divided
- 1 cup halved strawberries
- 1 tablespoon maple syrup, plus more for garnish
- 1 tablespoon brown sugar, divided
- ¾ cup lite coconut milk
- 2 large eggs
- ½ teaspoon ground cinnamon
- 2 tablespoons unsalted butter, at room temperature
- 4 slices challah bread

Directions:
1. Turn the chilled can of full-fat coconut milk upside down (do not shake the can), open the bottom, and pour out the liquid coconut water. Scoop the remaining solid coconut cream into a medium bowl. Using an electric hand mixer, whip the cream for 3 to 5 minutes, until soft peaks form.
2. Add the powdered sugar and ½ teaspoon of the vanilla to the coconut cream, and whip it again until creamy. Place the bowl in the refrigerator.
3. Insert the Grill Grate and close the hood. Select GRILL, set the temperature to MAX, and set the time to 15 minutes. Select START/STOP to begin preheating.
4. While the unit is preheating, combine the strawberries with the maple syrup and toss to coat evenly. Sprinkle evenly with ½ tablespoon of the brown sugar.
5. In a large shallow bowl, whisk together the lite coconut milk, eggs, the remaining 1 teaspoon of vanilla, and cinnamon.
6. When the unit beeps to signify it has preheated, place the strawberries on the Grill Grate. Gently press the fruit down to maximize grill marks. Close the hood and GRILL for 4 minutes without flipping.
7. Meanwhile, butter each slice of bread on both sides. Place one slice in the egg mixture and let it soak for 1 minute. Flip the slice over and soak it for another minute. Repeat with the remaining bread slices. Sprinkle each side of the toast with the remaining ½ tablespoon of brown sugar.
8. After 4 minutes, remove the strawberries from the grill and set aside. Decrease the temperature to HIGH. Place the bread on the Grill Grate; close the hood and GRILL for 4 to 6 minutes until golden and caramelized. Check often to ensure desired doneness.
9. Place the toast on a plate and top with the strawberries and whipped coconut cream. Drizzle with maple syrup, if desired.

Banana Chips With Peanut Butter

Servings: 1
Cooking Time: 8 Hours
Ingredients:
- 2 bananas, sliced into ¼-inch rounds
- 2 tablespoons creamy peanut butter

Directions:
1. In a medium bowl, toss the banana slices with the peanut butter, until well coated. If the peanut butter is too thick and not mixing well, add 1 to 2 tablespoons of water.
6. .

2. Place the banana slices flat on the Crisper Basket. Arrange them in a single layer, without any slices touching each another.
3. Place the basket in the pot and close the hood.
4. Select DEHYDRATE, set the temperature to 135ºF, and set the time to 8 hours. Select START/STOP.
5. When cooking is complete, remove the basket from the pot. Transfer the banana chips to an airtight container and store at room temperature

Sides, Snacks & Appetizers

Avocado Egg Rolls

Servings: 4
Cooking Time: 10 Minutes
Ingredients:
- 4 avocados, pitted and diced
- ½ white onion, diced
- ⅓ cup sun-dried tomatoes, chopped
- 1 (16-ounce) package egg roll wrappers (about 20 wrappers)
- ¼ cup water, for sealing
- 4 tablespoons avocado oil

Directions:
1. Insert the Grill Grate and close the hood. Select GRILL, set the temperature to LO, and set the time to 10 minutes. Select START/STOP to begin preheating.
2. While the unit is preheating, place the diced avocado in a large bowl. Add the onion and sun-dried tomatoes and gently fold together, being careful to not mash the avocado.
3. Place an egg roll wrapper on a flat surface with a corner facing you (like a diamond). Add 2 to 3 tablespoons of the filling in the center of the wrapper. The amount should be about 2½ inches wide. Gently lift the bottom corner of the wrapper over the filling, fold in the sides, and roll away from you to close. Dip your finger into the water and run it over the top corner of the wrapper to seal it. Continue filling, folding, and sealing the rest of the egg rolls.
4. When the unit beeps to signify it has preheated, brush the avocado oil on all sides of the egg rolls. Place the egg rolls on the Grill Grate, seam-side down. Close the hood and grill for 5 minutes.
5. After 5 minutes, open the hood and flip the egg rolls. Give them another brush of avocado oil. Close the hood and cook for 5 minutes more.
6. When cooking is complete, the wrappers will be golden brown. Remove from the grill and serve.

Goat Cheese Bruschetta With Tomatoes

Servings: 4
Cooking Time: 8 Minutes
Ingredients:
- 8 ounces cherry tomatoes (about 35)
- 8 fresh basil leaves
- 1 tablespoon balsamic vinegar
- 1 (8-ounce) baguette
- ½ cup extra-virgin olive oil
- 2 tablespoons garlic powder
- 8 ounces goat cheese (unflavored)

Directions:
1. Insert the Grill Grate and close the hood. Select GRILL, set the temperature to HI, and set the time to 8 minutes. Select START/STOP to begin preheating.
2. While the unit is preheating, quarter the cherry tomatoes. Slice the basil leaves into very thin ribbons. Place the tomatoes and basil in a medium bowl. Add the balsamic vinegar and toss to coat.
3. Slice the baguette into ½-inch slices. In a small bowl, whisk together the olive oil and garlic powder. Brush both sides of the baguette slices with the olive oil mixture.
4. When the unit beeps to signify it has preheated, place half the baguette slices on the Grill Grate in a single layer. Close the hood and cook for 4 minutes. After 4 minutes, remove the baguettes from the grill and set aside on a plate. Place the remaining slices on the Grill Grate. Close the hood and cook for 4 minutes.
5. When cooking is complete, spread a layer of goat cheese on the baguette slices. Top with the tomato-basil mixture and serve.

Dill Pickles

Servings: 4
Cooking Time: 10 Minutes
Ingredients:
- 20 dill pickle slices
- ¼ cup all-purpose flour
- ⅛ teaspoon baking powder
- 3 tablespoons beer or seltzer water
- ⅛ teaspoon sea salt
- 2 tablespoons water, plus more if needed
- 2 tablespoons cornstarch
- 1½ cups panko bread crumbs
- 1 teaspoon paprika
- 1 teaspoon garlic powder
- ¼ teaspoon cayenne pepper
- 2 tablespoons canola oil, divided

Directions:
1. Pat the pickle slices dry, and place them on a dry plate in the freezer.
2. In a medium bowl, stir together the flour, baking powder, beer, salt, and water. The batter should be the consistency of cake batter. If it is too thick, add more water, 1 teaspoon at a time.
3. Place the cornstarch in a small shallow bowl.
4. In a separate large shallow bowl, combine the bread crumbs, paprika, garlic powder, and cayenne pepper.
5. Remove the pickles from the freezer. Dredge each one in cornstarch. Tap off any excess, then coat in the batter. Lastly, coat evenly with the bread crumb mixture.
6. Insert the Crisper Basket and close the hood. Select AIR CRISP, set the temperature to 360ºF, and set the time to 10 minutes. Select START/STOP to begin preheating.
7. When the unit beeps to signify it has preheated, place the breaded pickles in the basket, stacking them if necessary, and gently brush them with 1 tablespoon of oil. Close the hood and AIR CRISP for 5 minutes.
8. After 5 minutes, shake the basket and gently brush the pickles with the remaining 1 tablespoon of oil. Place the basket back in the unit and close the hood to resume cooking.
9. When cooking is complete, serve immediately.

Breaded Green Olives

Servings: 4
Cooking Time: 8 Minutes
Ingredients:
- 1 jar pitted green olives
- ½ cup all-purpose flour
- Salt and pepper, to taste
- ½ cup bread crumbs
- 1 egg
- Cooking spray

Directions:
1. Insert the Crisper Basket and close the hood. Select AIR CRISP, set the temperature to 400ºF, and set the time to 8 minutes. Select START/STOP to begin preheating.
2. Remove the olives from the jar and dry thoroughly with paper towels.
3. In a small bowl, combine the flour with salt and pepper to taste. Place the bread crumbs in another small bowl. In a third small bowl, beat the egg.
4. Spritz the Crisper Basket with cooking spray.
5. Dip the olives in the flour, then the egg, and then the bread crumbs.
6. Place the breaded olives in the basket. It is okay to stack them. Spray the olives with cooking spray. Close the hood and AIR CRISP for 6 minutes. Flip the olives and AIR CRISP for an additional 2 minutes, or until brown and crisp.
7. Cool before serving.

Brussels Sprouts And Bacon

Servings: 4
Cooking Time: 12 Minutes
Ingredients:
- 1 pound Brussels sprouts, trimmed and halved
- 2 tablespoons extra-virgin olive oil
- 1 teaspoon sea salt
- ½ teaspoon freshly ground black pepper
- 6 slices bacon, chopped

Directions:
1. Insert the Crisper Basket and close the hood. Select AIR CRISP, set the temperature to 390ºF, and set the time to 12 minutes. Select START/STOP to begin preheating.
2. Meanwhile, in a large bowl, toss the Brussels sprouts with the olive oil, salt, pepper, and bacon.
3. When the unit beeps to signify it has preheated, add the Brussels sprouts to the basket. Close the hood and AIR CRISP for 10 minutes.
4. After 6 minutes, shake the basket of Brussels sprouts. Place the basket back in the unit and close the hood to resume cooking.
5. After 6 minutes, check for desired crispness. Continue cooking up to 2 more minutes, if necessary.

Crispy Spiced Potatoes

Servings: 4
Cooking Time: 20 Minutes
Ingredients:
- 2 pounds baby red potatoes, quartered
- 2 tablespoons extra-virgin olive oil
- ¼ cup dried onion flakes
- 1 teaspoon dried rosemary
- ½ teaspoon onion powder
- ½ teaspoon garlic powder
- ¼ teaspoon celery powder
- ¼ teaspoon freshly ground black pepper
- ½ teaspoon dried parsley
- ½ teaspoon sea salt

Directions:
1. Insert the Crisper Basket and close the hood. Select AIR CRISP, set the temperature to 390ºF, and set the time to 20 minutes. Select START/STOP to begin preheating.
2. Meanwhile, place all the ingredients in a large bowl and toss until evenly coated.
3. When the unit beeps to signify it has preheated, add the potatoes to the basket. Close the hood and AIR CRISP for 10 minutes.
4. After 10 minutes, shake the basket well. Place the basket back in the unit and close the hood to resume cooking.
5. After 10 minutes, check for desired crispness. Continue cooking up to 5 minutes more, if necessary.

Sweet Potato Chips

Servings:1
Cooking Time: 8 To 10 Hours
Ingredients:
- 1 sweet potato, peeled
- ½ tablespoon avocado oil
- ½ teaspoon sea salt

Directions:
1. Using a mandoline, thinly slice (⅛ inch or less) the sweet potato.
2. In a large bowl, toss the sweet potato slices with the oil until evenly coated. Season with the salt.
3. Place the sweet potato slices flat on the Crisper Basket. Arrange them in a single layer, without any slices touching each another.
4. Place the basket in the pot and close the hood.
5. Select DEHYDRATE, set the temperature to 120ºF, and set the time to 10 hours. Select START/STOP.
6. After 8 hours, check for desired doneness. Continue dehydrating for 2 more hours, if necessary.
7. When cooking is complete, remove the basket from the pot. Transfer the sweet potato chips to an airtight container and store at room temperature.

Easy Muffuletta Sliders With Olives

Servings:8
Cooking Time: 5 To 7 Minutes
Ingredients:
- ¼ pound thinly sliced deli ham
- ¼ pound thinly sliced pastrami
- 4 ounces low-fat Mozzarella cheese, grated
- 8 slider buns, split in half
- Cooking spray
- 1 tablespoon sesame seeds
- Olive Mix:
- ½ cup sliced green olives with pimentos
- ¼ cup sliced black olives
- ¼ cup chopped kalamata olives
- 1 teaspoon red wine vinegar
- ¼ teaspoon basil
- ⅛ teaspoon garlic powder

Directions:
1. Insert the Crisper Basket and close the hood. Select BAKE, set the temperature to 360ºF, and set the time to 7 minutes. Select START/STOP to begin preheating.
2. Combine all the ingredients for the olive mix in a small bowl and stir well.
3. Stir together the ham, pastrami, and cheese in a medium bowl and divide the mixture into 8 equal portions.
4. Assemble the sliders: Top each bottom bun with 1 portion of meat and cheese, 2 tablespoons of olive mix, finished by the remaining buns. Lightly spritz the tops with cooking spray. Scatter the sesame seeds on top.
5. Working in batches, arrange the sliders in the Crisper Basket. Close the hood and BAKE for 5 t0 7 minutes until the cheese melts.
6. Transfer to a large plate and repeat with the remaining sliders.
7. Serve immediately.

Deluxe Cheese Sandwiches

Servings: 4 To 8

Cooking Time: 5 To 6 Minutes
Ingredients:
- 8 ounces Brie
- 8 slices oat nut bread
- 1 large ripe pear, cored and cut into ½-inch-thick slices
- 2 tablespoons butter, melted

Directions:
1. Select BAKE, set the temperature to 360ºF, and set the time to 6 minutes. Select START/STOP to begin preheating. .
2. Make the sandwiches: Spread each of 4 slices of bread with ¼ of the Brie. Top the Brie with the pear slices and remaining 4 bread slices.
3. Brush the melted butter lightly on both sides of each sandwich.
4. Arrange the sandwiches in a baking pan. You may need to work in batches to avoid overcrowding.
5. Place the pan directly in the pot. Close the hood and BAKE for 5 to 6 minutes until the cheese is melted. Repeat with the remaining sandwiches.
6. Serve warm.

Cajun Zucchini Chips

Servings: 4
Cooking Time: 15 To 16 Minutes
Ingredients:
- 2 large zucchini, cut into ⅛-inch-thick slices
- 2 teaspoons Cajun seasoning
- Cooking spray

Directions:
1. Spray the Crisper Basket lightly with cooking spray.
2. Insert the Crisper Basket and close the hood. Select AIR CRISP, set the temperature to 370ºF, and set the time to 16 minutes. Select START/STOP to begin preheating.
3. Put the zucchini slices in a medium bowl and spray them generously with cooking spray.
4. Sprinkle the Cajun seasoning over the zucchini and stir to make sure they are evenly coated with oil and seasoning.
5. Place the slices in a single layer in the Crisper Basket, making sure not to overcrowd. You will need to cook these in several batches.
6. Close the hood and AIR CRISP for 8 minutes. Flip the slices over and AIR CRISP for an additional 7 to 8 minutes, or until they are as crisp and brown as you prefer.
7. Serve immediately.

Herbed Pita Chips

Servings: 4
Cooking Time: 5 To 6 Minutes
Ingredients:
- ¼ teaspoon dried basil
- ¼ teaspoon marjoram
- ¼ teaspoon ground oregano
- ¼ teaspoon garlic powder
- ¼ teaspoon ground thyme
- ¼ teaspoon salt
- 2 whole 6-inch pitas, whole grain or white
- Cooking spray

Directions:
1. Insert the Crisper Basket and close the hood. Select BAKE, set the temperature to 330ºF, and set the time to 6 minutes. Select START/STOP to begin preheating.

2. Mix all the seasonings together.
3. Cut each pita half into 4 wedges. Break apart wedges at the fold.
4. Mist one side of pita wedges with oil. Sprinkle with half of seasoning mix.
5. Turn pita wedges over, mist the other side with oil, and sprinkle with remaining seasonings.
6. Place pita wedges in Crisper Basket. Close the hood and BAKE for 2 minutes.
7. Shake the basket and bake for 2 minutes longer. Shake again, and if needed, bake for 1 or 2 more minutes, or until crisp. Watch carefully because at this point they will cook very quickly.
8. Serve hot.

Crispy Prosciutto-wrapped Asparagus

Servings: 6
Cooking Time: 16 To 24 Minutes
Ingredients:
- 12 asparagus spears, woody ends trimmed
- 24 pieces thinly sliced prosciutto
- Cooking spray

Directions:
1. Insert the Crisper Basket and close the hood. Select AIR CRISP, set the temperature to 360°F, and set the time to 4 minutes. Select START/STOP to begin preheating.
2. Wrap each asparagus spear with 2 slices of prosciutto, then repeat this process with the remaining asparagus and prosciutto.
3. Spray the Crisper Basket with cooking spray, then place 2 to 3 bundles in the basket. Close the hood and AIR CRISP for 4 minutes. Repeat this process with the remaining asparagus bundles.
4. Remove the bundles and allow to cool on a wire rack for 5 minutes before serving.

Garlic Fries

Servings: 4
Cooking Time: 20 Minutes
Ingredients:
- 2 large Idaho or russet potatoes (1½ to 2 pounds)
- 1 head garlic (10 to 12 cloves)
- 4 tablespoons avocado oil, divided
- 1 teaspoon sea salt
- Chopped fresh parsley, for garnish

Directions:
1. Cut the potatoes into ¼-inch-thick slices. Place the slices in a large bowl and cover with cold water. Set aside for 30 minutes. This will ensure the potatoes cook well and crisp up perfectly. While the potatoes are soaking, mince the garlic cloves.
2. Drain the potatoes and pat dry using paper towels. In a large bowl, toss the potato slices with 2 tablespoons of avocado oil.
3. Insert the Cooking Pot and Crisper Basket and close the hood. Select AIR CRISP, set the temperature to 390°F, and set the time to 20 minutes. Select START/STOP to begin preheating.
4. While the unit is preheating, in a small bowl, combine the remaining 2 tablespoons of avocado oil with the minced garlic.

5. When the unit beeps to signify it has preheated, put the fries in the Crisper Basket. Close the hood and cook for 10 minutes.
6. After 10 minutes, open the hood and give the basket a shake to toss the fries. Close the hood and continue cooking for 5 minutes. Open the hood again and give the basket a shake. Close the hood and cook for 5 minutes more.
7. When cooking is complete, the fries will be crispy and golden brown. If you like them extra-crispy, continue cooking to your liking. Transfer the fries to a large bowl and drizzle with the garlic oil. Toss and season with the salt. Garnish with the parsley and serve.

Blistered Lemony Green Beans

Servings: 4
Cooking Time: 10 Minutes
Ingredients:
- 1 pound haricots verts or green beans, trimmed
- 2 tablespoons vegetable oil
- Juice of 1 lemon
- Pinch red pepper flakes
- Flaky sea salt, to taste
- Freshly ground black pepper, to taste

Directions:
1. Insert the Grill Grate and close the hood. Select GRILL, set the temperature to MAX, and set the time to 10 minutes. Select START/STOP to begin preheating.
2. While the unit is preheating, in a medium bowl, toss the green beans in oil until evenly coated.
3. When the unit beeps to signify it has preheated, place the green beans on the Grill Grate. Close the hood and GRILL for 8 to 10 minutes, tossing frequently until blistered on all sides.
4. When cooking is complete, place the green beans on a large serving platter. Squeeze lemon juice over the green beans, top with red pepper flakes, and season with sea salt and black pepper.

Sausage And Mushroom Empanadas

Servings: 4
Cooking Time: 12 Minutes
Ingredients:
- ½ pound Kielbasa smoked sausage, chopped
- 4 chopped canned mushrooms
- 2 tablespoons chopped onion
- ½ teaspoon ground cumin
- ¼ teaspoon paprika
- Salt and black pepper, to taste
- ½ package puff pastry dough, at room temperature
- 1 egg, beaten
- Cooking spray

Directions:
1. Spritz the Crisper Basket with cooking spray.
2. Insert the Crisper Basket and close the hood. Select AIR CRISP, set the temperature to 360°F, and set the time to 12 minutes. Select START/STOP to begin preheating.
3. Combine the sausage, mushrooms, onion, cumin, paprika, salt, and pepper in a bowl and stir to mix well.
4. Make the empanadas: Place the puff pastry dough on a lightly floured surface. Cut circles into the dough with a glass. Place 1 tablespoon of the sausage mixture into the center of each pastry circle. Fold each in half and pinch the

edges to seal. Using a fork, crimp the edges. Brush them with the beaten egg and mist with cooking spray.

5. Place the empanadas in the Crisper Basket. Close the hood and AIR CRISP for 12 minutes until golden brown. Flip the empanadas halfway through the cooking time.

6. Allow them to cool for 5 minutes and serve hot.

Spicy Kale Chips

Servings: 4
Cooking Time: 8 To 12 Minutes
Ingredients:
- 5 cups kale, large stems removed and chopped
- 2 teaspoons canola oil
- ¼ teaspoon smoked paprika
- ¼ teaspoon kosher salt
- Cooking spray

Directions:
1. Insert the Crisper Basket and close the hood. Select AIR CRISP, set the temperature to 390ºF, and set the time to 6 minutes. Select START/STOP to begin preheating.

2. In a large bowl, toss the kale, canola oil, smoked paprika, and kosher salt.

3. Spray the Crisper Basket with cooking spray, then place half the kale in the basket. Close the hood and AIR CRISP for 2 to 3 minutes.

4. Shake the basket and AIR CRISP for 2 to 3 more minutes, or until crispy. Repeat this process with the remaining kale.

5. Remove the kale and allow to cool on a wire rack for 3 to 5 minutes before serving.

Queso Bomb

Servings: 6
Cooking Time: 15 Minutes
Ingredients:
- 1 (1-pound) block easy-melt cheese
- 1 pound ground country breakfast sausage (not links)
- 2 tablespoons minced garlic
- 2 cups shredded Mexican cheese blend or three-cheese blend
- 1 (10-ounce) can diced tomatoes with green chiles
- 1 (10- to 13-ounce) bag tortilla chips

Directions:
1. Insert the Cooking Pot and close the hood. Select GRILL, set the temperature to MED, and set the time to 15 minutes. Select START/STOP to begin preheating.

2. While the unit is preheating, slice the cheese block into 3-inch sections.

3. When the unit beeps to signify it has preheated, place the sausage and garlic in the Cooking Pot. Using a wooden spoon or spatula, break the sausage apart. Close the hood and cook for 5 minutes.

4. After 5 minutes, open the hood and stir the sausage. Add the pieces of easy-melt cheese, then add the shredded cheese blend in an even layer. Pour the diced tomatoes and green chiles with their juices into the pot. Close the hood and cook for 5 minutes.

5. After 5 minutes, stir the sausage and cheese together. Close the hood and cook 5 minutes more.

6. When cooking is complete, the cheese will be fully melted. Serve warm with tortilla chips.

Cheese And Ham Stuffed Baby Bella

Servings: 8
Cooking Time: 12 Minutes
Ingredients:
- 4 ounces Mozzarella cheese, cut into pieces
- ½ cup diced ham
- 2 green onions, chopped
- 2 tablespoons bread crumbs
- ½ teaspoon garlic powder
- ¼ teaspoon ground oregano
- ¼ teaspoon ground black pepper
- 1 to 2 teaspoons olive oil
- 16 fresh Baby Bella mushrooms, stemmed removed

Directions:
1. Process the cheese, ham, green onions, bread crumbs, garlic powder, oregano, and pepper in a food processor until finely chopped.

2. With the food processor running, slowly drizzle in 1 to 2 teaspoons olive oil until a thick paste has formed. Transfer the mixture to a bowl.

3. Evenly divide the mixture into the mushroom caps and lightly press down the mixture.

4. Insert the Crisper Basket and close the hood. Select ROAST, set the temperature to 390ºF, and set the time to 12 minutes. Select START/STOP to begin preheating.

5. Lay the mushrooms in the Crisper Basket in a single layer. You'll need to work in batches to avoid overcrowding.

6. Close the hood and ROAST for 12 minutes until the mushrooms are lightly browned and tender.

7. Remove from the basket to a plate and repeat with the remaining mushrooms.

8. Let the mushrooms cool for 5 minutes and serve warm.

Turkey Bacon-wrapped Dates

Servings:16
Cooking Time: 5 To 7 Minutes
Ingredients:
- 16 whole dates, pitted
- 16 whole almonds
- 6 to 8 strips turkey bacon, cut in half

Directions:
1. Insert the Crisper Basket and close the hood. Select AIR CRISP, set the temperature to 390ºF, and set the time to 7 minutes. Select START/STOP to begin preheating.

2. On a flat work surface, stuff each pitted date with a whole almond.

3. Wrap half slice of bacon around each date and secure it with a toothpick.

4. Place the bacon-wrapped dates in the Crisper Basket. Close the hood and AIR CRISP for 5 to 7 minutes, or until the bacon is cooked to your desired crispiness.

5. Transfer the dates to a paper towel-lined plate to drain. Serve hot.

Cheesy Summer Squash With Red Onion

Servings: 4
Cooking Time: 15 Minutes
Ingredients:
- ½ cup vegetable oil, plus 3 tablespoons
- ¼ cup white wine vinegar
- 1 garlic clove, grated
- 2 summer squash, sliced lengthwise about ¼-inch thick
- 1 red onion, peeled and cut into wedges
- Sea salt, to taste
- Freshly ground black pepper, to taste
- 1 package crumbled feta cheese
- Red pepper flakes, as needed

Directions:
1. Insert the Grill Grate and close the hood. Select GRILL, set the temperature to MAX, and set the time to 15 minutes. Select START/STOP to begin preheating.
2. Meanwhile, in a small bowl, whisk together ½ cup oil, vinegar, and garlic, and set aside.
3. In a large bowl, toss the squash and onion with remaining 3 tablespoons of oil until evenly coated. Season with the salt and pepper.
4. When the unit beeps to signify it has preheated, arrange the squash and onions on the Grill Grate. Close the hood and GRILL for 6 minutes.
5. After 6 minutes, open the hood and flip the squash. Close the hood and GRILL for 6 to 9 minutes more.
6. When vegetables are cooked to desired doneness, remove them from the grill. Arrange the vegetables on a large platter and top with the feta cheese. Drizzle the dressing over the top, and sprinkle with the red pepper flakes. Let stand for 15 minutes before serving.

Grilled Shishito Peppers

Servings: 4
Cooking Time: 10 Minutes
Ingredients:
- 3 cups whole shishito peppers
- 2 tablespoons vegetable oil
- Flaky sea salt, for garnish

Directions:
1. Insert the Grill Grate and close the hood. Select GRILL, set the temperature to MAX, and set the time to 10 minutes. Select START/STOP to begin preheating.
2. While the unit is preheating, in a medium bowl, toss the peppers in the oil until evenly coated.
3. When the unit beeps to signify it has preheated, place the peppers on the Grill Grate. Gently press the peppers down to maximize grill marks. Close the hood and GRILL for 8 to 10 minutes, until they are blistered on all sides.
4. When cooking is complete, place the peppers in a serving dish and top with the flaky sea salt. Serve immediately.

Bacon-wrapped Onion Rings And Spicy Aioli

Servings: 4
Cooking Time: 10 Minutes
Ingredients:
- For the onion rings
- 3 large white onions
- 2 (1-pound) packages thin-sliced bacon
- For the spicy garlic aioli sauce
- 1 cup mayonnaise
- ¼ teaspoon garlic powder
- 1 tablespoon sriracha
- 1 teaspoon freshly squeezed lemon juice

Directions:
1. Insert the Grill Grate and close the hood. Select GRILL, set the temperature to MED, and set the time to 10 minutes. Select START/STOP to begin preheating.
2. While the unit is preheating, cut both ends off the onions. Slice each onion crosswise into thirds and peel off the outer layer of onion skin. Separate the onion rings, keeping two onion layers together to have a stable and firm ring. Wrap each onion ring pair with a slice of bacon. The bacon should slightly overlap itself as you wrap it all the way around the onion ring. Larger rings may need 2 slices of bacon.
3. When the unit beeps to signify it has preheated, place the onion rings on the Grill Grate. Close the hood and grill for 10 minutes. Flipping is not necessary.
4. When cooking is complete, the bacon will be cooked through and starting to crisp. If you prefer the bacon crispier or even close to charred, continue cooking to your liking.
5. While the onion rings are cooking, in a small bowl, whisk together the mayonnaise, garlic powder, sriracha, and lemon juice. Use more or less sriracha depending on your preferred spice level. Serve with the bacon onion rings.

Bacon-wrapped Dates

Servings: 6
Cooking Time: 10 To 14 Minutes
Ingredients:
- 12 dates, pitted
- 6 slices high-quality bacon, cut in half
- Cooking spray

Directions:
1. Insert the Crisper Basket and close the hood. Select BAKE, set the temperature to 360ºF, and set the time to 7 minutes. Select START/STOP to begin preheating.
2. Wrap each date with half a bacon slice and secure with a toothpick.
3. Spray the Crisper Basket with cooking spray, then place 6 bacon-wrapped dates in the basket. Place the pan directly in the pot. Close the hood and BAKE for 5 to 7 minutes or until the bacon is crispy. Repeat this process with the remaining dates.
4. Remove the dates and allow to cool on a wire rack for 5 minutes before serving.

Cheesy Apple Roll-ups

Servings:8
Cooking Time: 4 To 5 Minutes
Ingredients:
- 8 slices whole wheat sandwich bread
- 4 ounces Colby Jack cheese, grated
- ½ small apple, chopped
- 2 tablespoons butter, melted

Directions:
1. Insert the Crisper Basket and close the hood. Select AIR CRISP, set the temperature to 390ºF, and set the time to 5 minutes. Select START/STOP to begin preheating.
2. Remove the crusts from the bread and flatten the slices with a rolling pin. Don't be gentle. Press hard so that bread will be very thin.
3. Top bread slices with cheese and chopped apple, dividing the ingredients evenly.
4. Roll up each slice tightly and secure each with one or two toothpicks.
5. Brush outside of rolls with melted butter.
6. Place in the Crisper Basket. Close the hood and AIR CRISP for 4 to 5 minutes, or until outside is crisp and nicely browned.
7. Serve hot.

Cayenne Sesame Nut Mix

Servings:4
Cooking Time: 2 Minutes
Ingredients:
- 1 tablespoon buttery spread, melted
- 2 teaspoons honey
- ¼ teaspoon cayenne pepper
- 2 teaspoons sesame seeds
- ¼ teaspoon kosher salt
- ¼ teaspoon freshly ground black pepper
- 1 cup cashews
- 1 cup almonds
- 1 cup mini pretzels
- 1 cup rice squares cereal
- Cooking spray

Directions:
1. Select BAKE, set the temperature to 360ºF, and set the time to 2 minutes. Select START/STOP to begin preheating.
2. In a large bowl, combine the buttery spread, honey, cayenne pepper, sesame seeds, kosher salt, and black pepper, then add the cashews, almonds, pretzels, and rice squares, tossing to coat.
3. Spray a baking pan with cooking spray, then pour the mixture into the pan. Place the pan directly in the pot. Close the hood and BAKE for 2 minutes.
4. Remove the sesame mix from the grill and allow to cool in the pan on a wire rack for 5 minutes before serving.

Maple Butter Corn Bread

Servings: 4
Cooking Time: 40 Minutes
Ingredients:
- For the corn bread
- 1 cup all-purpose flour
- 1 cup yellow cornmeal
- 2 teaspoons baking powder

- 1 teaspoon salt
- 1¼ cups milk
- ⅓ cup canola oil
- 1 large egg
- 1 (14.75-ounce) can cream-style sweet corn
- Cooking spray
- For the maple butter
- 1 tablespoon light brown sugar, packed
- 1 tablespoon milk
- 8 tablespoons (1 stick) unsalted butter, at room temperature
- 1 tablespoon maple syrup

Directions:
1. Insert the Cooking Pot and close the hood. Select BAKE, set the temperature to 350°F, and set the time to 40 minutes. Select START/STOP to begin preheating.
2. While the unit is preheating, in a large bowl, combine the flour, cornmeal, baking powder, salt, milk, oil, egg, and sweet corn. Mix until just combined. Grease a 9-by-5-inch loaf pan with cooking spray and pour in the corn bread batter.
3. When the unit beeps to signify it has preheated, place the pan in the Cooking Pot. Close the hood and cook for 40 minutes. If using a metal loaf pan, check the corn bread after 30 minutes, as metal pans may cook faster than glass. Bake until golden brown and the mix is completely baked through.
4. When cooking is complete, the corn bread should be golden brown and a toothpick inserted into the center of the corn bread comes out clean. Remove the pan from the grill and set aside to cool.
5. In a small bowl, whisk together the brown sugar and milk until the sugar is dissolved. Add the butter and continue whisking. Add the maple syrup and continue whisking until fully combined.
6. Cut the corn bread into slices, top with the butter, and serve.

Cuban Sandwiches

Servings:4
Cooking Time: 8 Minutes
Ingredients:
- 8 slices ciabatta bread, about ¼-inch thick
- Cooking spray
- 1 tablespoon brown mustard
- Toppings:
- 6 to 8 ounces thinly sliced leftover roast pork
- 4 ounces thinly sliced deli turkey
- ⅓ cup bread and butter pickle slices
- 2 to 3 ounces Pepper Jack cheese slices

Directions:
1. Insert the Crisper Basket and close the hood. Select AIR CRISP, set the temperature to 390ºF, and set the time to 8 minutes. Select START/STOP to begin preheating.
2. On a clean work surface, spray one side of each slice of bread with cooking spray. Spread the other side of each slice of bread evenly with brown mustard.
3. Top 4 of the bread slices with the roast pork, turkey, pickle slices, cheese, and finish with remaining bread slices. Transfer to the Crisper Basket.
4. Close the hood and AIR CRISP for 8 minutes until golden brown.
5. Cool for 5 minutes and serve warm.

Cheesy Garlic Bread

Servings: 4
Cooking Time: 8 Minutes
Ingredients:
- 1 loaf (about 1 pound) French bread
- 8 tablespoons (1 stick) unsalted butter, at room temperature
- 1 tablespoon minced garlic
- 1 teaspoon garlic powder
- 1½ cups shredded mozzarella cheese
- ½ cup shredded Colby Jack cheese
- 1 teaspoon dried parsley

Directions:
1. Insert the Grill Grate and close the hood. Select GRILL, set the temperature to MED, and set the time to 8 minutes. Select START/STOP to begin preheating.
2. While the unit is preheating, cut the French bread in half lengthwise. In a small bowl, mix together the butter, garlic, and garlic powder until well combined. Spread the garlic butter on both bread halves. Top each half with the mozzarella and Colby Jack cheeses. Sprinkle the dried parsley on top.
3. When the unit beeps to signify it has preheated, place the cheese-topped bread on the Grill Grate. Close the hood and grill for 8 minutes.
4. When cooking is complete, the cheese will be melted and golden brown. Remove the bread from the grill and serve.

Blt With Grilled Heirloom Tomato

Servings: 4
Cooking Time: 10 Minutes
Ingredients:
- 8 slices white bread
- 8 tablespoons mayonnaise
- 2 heirloom tomatoes, sliced ¼-inch thick
- 2 tablespoons canola oil
- Sea salt, to taste
- Freshly ground black pepper, to taste
- 8 slices bacon, cooked
- 8 leaves iceberg lettuce

Directions:
1. Insert the Grill Grate, and close the hood. Select GRILL, set the temperature to MAX, and set the time to 10 minutes. Select START/STOP to begin preheating.
2. While the unit is preheating, spread a thin layer of mayonnaise on one side of each piece of bread.
3. When the unit beeps to signify it has preheated, place the bread, mayonnaise-side down, on the Grill Grate. Close the hood and GRILL for 2 to 3 minutes, until crisp.
4. Meanwhile, remove the watery pulp and seeds from the tomato slices. Brush both sides of the tomatoes with the oil and season with salt and pepper.
5. After 2 to 3 minutes, remove the bread and place the tomatoes on the grill. Close the hood and continue grilling for the remaining 6 to 8 minutes.
6. To assemble, spread a thin layer of mayonnaise on the non-grilled sides of the bread. Layer the tomatoes, bacon, and lettuce on the bread, and top with the remaining slices of bread. Slice each sandwich in half and serve.

Roasted Mixed Nuts

Servings: 6
Cooking Time: 20 Minutes
Ingredients:
- 2 cups mixed nuts (walnuts, pecans, and almonds)
- 2 tablespoons egg white
- 2 tablespoons sugar
- 1 teaspoon paprika
- 1 teaspoon ground cinnamon
- Cooking spray

Directions:
1. Spray the Crisper Basket with cooking spray.
2. Insert the Crisper Basket and close the hood. Select ROAST, set the temperature to 300°F, and set the time to 20 minutes. Select START/STOP to begin preheating.
3. Stir together the mixed nuts, egg white, sugar, paprika, and cinnamon in a small bowl until the nuts are fully coated.
4. Put the nuts in the Crisper Basket. Close the hood and ROAST for 20 minutes. Shake the basket halfway through the cooking time for even cooking.
5. Transfer the nuts to a bowl and serve warm.

Balsamic Broccoli

Servings: 4
Cooking Time: 10 Minutes
Ingredients:
- 4 tablespoons soy sauce
- 4 tablespoons balsamic vinegar
- 2 tablespoons canola oil
- 2 teaspoons maple syrup
- 2 heads broccoli, trimmed into florets
- Red pepper flakes, for garnish
- Sesame seeds, for garnish

Directions:
1. Insert the Grill Grate and close the hood. Select GRILL, set the temperature to MAX, and set the time to 10 minutes. Select START/STOP to begin preheating.
2. While the unit is preheating, in a large bowl, whisk together the soy sauce, balsamic vinegar, oil, and maple syrup. Add the broccoli and toss to coat evenly.
3. When the unit beeps to signify it has preheated, place the broccoli on the Grill Grate. Close the hood and GRILL for 8 to 10 minutes, until charred on all sides.
4. When cooking is complete, place the broccoli on a large serving platter. Garnish with red pepper flakes and sesame seeds. Serve immediately.

Homemade Bbq Chicken Pizza

Servings: 1
Cooking Time: 8 Minutes
Ingredients:
- 1 piece naan bread
- ¼ cup Barbecue sauce
- ¼ cup shredded Monterrey Jack cheese
- ¼ cup shredded Mozzarella cheese
- ½ chicken herby sausage, sliced
- 2 tablespoons red onion, thinly sliced
- Chopped cilantro or parsley, for garnish
- Cooking spray

Directions:

1. Insert the Crisper Basket and close the hood. Select AIR CRISP, set the temperature to 400ºF, and set the time to 8 minutes. Select START/STOP to begin preheating.
2. Spritz the bottom of naan bread with cooking spray, then transfer to the Crisper Basket.
3. Brush with the Barbecue sauce. Top with the cheeses, sausage, and finish with the red onion.
4. Close the hood and AIR CRISP for 8 minutes until the cheese is melted.
5. Garnish with the chopped cilantro or parsley before slicing to serve.

Mushroom And Spinach Calzones

Servings: 4
Cooking Time: 26 To 27 Minutes
Ingredients:
- 2 tablespoons olive oil
- 1 onion, chopped
- 2 garlic cloves, minced
- ¼ cup chopped mushrooms
- 1 pound spinach, chopped
- 1 tablespoon Italian seasoning
- ½ teaspoon oregano
- Salt and black pepper, to taste
- 1½ cups marinara sauce
- 1 cup ricotta cheese, crumbled
- 1 pizza crust
- Cooking spray

Directions:
1. Make the Filling:
2. Heat the olive oil in a pan over medium heat until shimmering.
3. Add the onion, garlic, and mushrooms and sauté for 4 minutes, or until softened.
4. Stir in the spinach and sauté for 2 to 3 minutes, or until the spinach is wilted. Sprinkle with the Italian seasoning, oregano, salt, and pepper and mix well.
5. Add the marinara sauce and cook for about 5 minutes, stirring occasionally, or until the sauce is thickened.
6. Remove the pan from the heat and stir in the ricotta cheese. Set aside.
7. Make the Calzones:
8. Spritz the Crisper Basket with cooking spray.
9. Insert the Crisper Basket and close the hood. Select AIR CRISP, set the temperature to 375ºF, and set the time to 15 minutes. Select START/STOP to begin preheating.
10. Roll the pizza crust out with a rolling pin on a lightly floured work surface, then cut it into 4 rectangles.
11. Spoon ¼ of the filling into each rectangle and fold in half. Crimp the edges with a fork to seal. Mist them with cooking spray.
12. Place the calzones in the Crisper Basket. Close the hood and AIR CRISP for 15 minutes, flipping once, or until the calzones are golden brown and crisp.
13. Transfer the calzones to a paper towel-lined plate and serve.

Creamy Artichoke Dip With Pita Chips

Servings: 4
Cooking Time: 15 Minutes
Ingredients:
- 8 ounces cream cheese, at room temperature
- 1 (13-ounce) can marinated artichoke quarters, drained and coarsely chopped
- ½ cup sour cream
- ½ cup grated Parmesan cheese
- ¼ teaspoon garlic powder
- 2 cups shredded mozzarella
- 1 (6-ounce) package mini pita bread rounds
- Extra-virgin olive oil
- Chopped fresh chives, for garnish

Directions:
1. Insert the Cooking Pot and close the hood. Select GRILL, set the temperature to MED, and set the time to 15 minutes. Select START/STOP to begin preheating.
2. While the unit is preheating, place the cream cheese, artichokes, sour cream, Parmesan cheese, garlic powder, and mozzarella cheese in a 9-by-5-inch loaf pan. Stir until well combined.
3. When the unit beeps to signify it has preheated, place the pan in the Cooking Pot. Close the hood and cook for 5 minutes.
4. After 5 minutes, open the hood and stir the dip with a wooden spoon, holding onto the loaf pan with grill mitts. Close the hood and cook for 7 minutes more.
5. Meanwhile, place the Grill Grate next to the Foodi™ Grill. Put the pita rounds in a large bowl and drizzle with the olive oil. Toss to coat. Place the pita rounds on the Grill Grate.
6. After 7 minutes, open the hood. Remove the pan of artichoke dip from the Cooking Pot. Place the Grill Grate into the unit. Close the hood and cook for the remaining 3 minutes.
7. Cooking is complete when the pita chips are warm and crispy. Garnish the dip with the fresh chives and serve.

Caramelized Peaches

Servings: 4
Cooking Time: 10 To 13 Minutes
Ingredients:
- 2 tablespoons sugar
- ¼ teaspoon ground cinnamon
- 4 peaches, cut into wedges
- Cooking spray

Directions:
1. Lightly spray the Crisper Basket with cooking spray.
2. Insert the Crisper Basket and close the hood. Select AIR CRISP, set the temperature to 350ºF, and set the time to 13 minutes. Select START/STOP to begin preheating.
3. Toss the peaches with the sugar and cinnamon in a medium bowl until evenly coated.
4. Arrange the peaches in the Crisper Basket in a single layer. Lightly mist the peaches with cooking spray. You may need to work in batches to avoid overcrowding.
5. Close the hood and AIR CRISP for 5 minutes. Flip the peaches and AIR CRISP for another 5 to 8 minutes, or until the peaches are caramelized.
6. Repeat with the remaining peaches.
7. Let the peaches cool for 5 minutes and serve warm.

Jalapeño Poppers

Servings: 4
Cooking Time: 10 Minutes
Ingredients:
- 8 jalapeños
- 4 ounces cream cheese, at room temperature
- ¼ cup grated Parmesan cheese
- ¼ cup shredded cheddar cheese
- ½ teaspoon garlic powder
- 8 slices thin-cut bacon

Directions:
1. Insert the Grill Grate and close the hood. Select GRILL, set the temperature to HI, and set the time to 10 minutes. Select START/STOP to begin preheating.
2. While the unit is preheating, slice the jalapeños in half lengthwise and scoop out the seeds and membranes.
3. In a small bowl, combine the cream cheese, Parmesan cheese, cheddar cheese, and garlic powder. Scoop the cheese mixture evenly into each jalapeño half.
4. Slice the bacon in half lengthwise so you have 16 strips. Wrap each jalapeño half with a bacon slice, starting from the bottom end and wrapping around until it reaches the top of the jalapeño.
5. When the unit beeps to signify it has preheated, place the jalapeños on the Grill Grate, filling-side up. Close the hood and grill for 10 minutes.
6. When cooking is complete, the bacon will be cooked and beginning to crisp. If you prefer your bacon crispier or charred, continue cooking to your liking. Remove the poppers from the grill and serve.

Cheesy Steak Fries

Servings: 5
Cooking Time: 20 Minutes
Ingredients:
- 1 bag frozen steak fries
- Cooking spray
- Salt and pepper, to taste
- ½ cup beef gravy
- 1 cup shredded Mozzarella cheese
- 2 scallions, green parts only, chopped

Directions:
1. Insert the Crisper Basket and close the hood. Select AIR CRISP, set the temperature to 400ºF, and set the time to 20 minutes. Select START/STOP to begin preheating.
2. Place the frozen steak fries in the basket. Close the hood and AIR CRISP for 10 minutes. Shake the basket and spritz the fries with cooking spray. Sprinkle with salt and pepper. AIR CRISP for an additional 8 minutes.
3. Pour the beef gravy into a medium, microwave-safe bowl. Microwave for 30 seconds, or until the gravy is warm.
4. Sprinkle the fries with the cheese. Close the hood and AIR CRISP for an additional 2 minutes, until the cheese is melted.
5. Transfer the fries to a serving dish. Drizzle the fries with gravy and sprinkle the scallions on top for a green garnish. Serve.

Grilled Carrots With Honey Glazed

Servings: 4
Cooking Time: 10 Minutes
Ingredients:
- 6 medium carrots, peeled and cut lengthwise
- 1 tablespoon canola oil
- 2 tablespoons unsalted butter, melted
- ¼ cup brown sugar, melted
- ¼ cup honey
- ⅛ teaspoon sea salt

Directions:
1. Insert the Grill Grate and close the hood. Select GRILL, set the temperature to MAX, and set the time to 10 minutes. Select START/STOP to begin preheating.
2. In a large bowl, toss the carrots and oil until well coated.
3. When the unit beeps to signify it has preheated, place carrots on the center of the Grill Grate. Close the hood and GRILL for 5 minutes.
4. Meanwhile, in a small bowl, whisk together the butter, brown sugar, honey, and salt.
5. After 5 minutes, open the hood and baste the carrots with the glaze. Using tongs, turn the carrots and baste the other side. Close the hood and GRILL for another 5 minutes.
6. When cooking is complete, serve immediately.

Grilled Blooming Onion

Servings: 4
Cooking Time: 12 Minutes
Ingredients:
- 2 large yellow onions
- 1 cup milk
- 2 large eggs
- 1 teaspoon paprika
- 1 teaspoon cayenne pepper
- 1 teaspoon garlic powder
- 1 teaspoon onion powder
- 2 cups all-purpose flour
- Salt
- Freshly ground black pepper
- Nonstick cooking spray

Directions:
1. Insert the Grill Grate and close the hood. Select GRILL, set the temperature to LO, and set the time to 12 minutes. Select START/STOP to begin preheating.
2. While the unit is preheating, cut off both ends of the onions, keeping the root end as intact as possible. Peel off the outer layer of skin. With the root facing up, begin cutting your petals Starting from ¼ inch below the root end (do not cut through the root), cut downward to slit the onion into 4 equal sections, and then again in between each cut so there are 8 equal sections, and then again to make 16 petals. Turn the onion upside down so the root is now on the bottom, and the petals should begin to open.
3. In a large bowl, whisk together the milk and eggs. Carefully place the blooming onion in the mixture to soak.
4. In a separate large bowl, combine the paprika, cayenne pepper, garlic powder, onion powder, and flour. Season with salt and pepper. Transfer the blooming onion to the bowl with the seasonings. Using your hands, carefully sift some of the mixture into the cracks of the onion, making sure the petals are coated well. Shake off any excess.
5. When the unit beeps to signify it has preheated, generously spray the onion with cooking spray and place it, petals facing up, on the Grill Grate. Close the hood and grill for 10 minutes.

6. After 10 minutes, open the hood and check for crispiness and if the onion is browned to your liking. To continue cooking, generously spray the onion with more cooking spray. Close the hood and continue cooking for 2 minutes more, or until the onions have browned and crisped up to your desired doneness. Remove the onion from the grill and serve.

Breaded Artichoke Hearts

Servings: 14
Cooking Time: 8 Minutes
Ingredients:
- 14 whole artichoke hearts, packed in water
- 1 egg
- ½ cup all-purpose flour
- ⅓ cup panko bread crumbs
- 1 teaspoon Italian seasoning
- Cooking spray

Directions:
1. Insert the Crisper Basket and close the hood. Select AIR CRISP, set the temperature to 380ºF, and set the time to 8 minutes. Select START/STOP to begin preheating.
2. Squeeze excess water from the artichoke hearts and place them on paper towels to dry.
3. In a small bowl, beat the egg. In another small bowl, place the flour. In a third small bowl, combine the bread crumbs and Italian seasoning, and stir.
4. Spritz the Crisper Basket with cooking spray.
5. Dip the artichoke hearts in the flour, then the egg, and then the bread crumb mixture.
6. Place the breaded artichoke hearts in the Crisper Basket. Spray them with cooking spray.
7. Close the hood and AIR CRISP for 8 minutes, or until the artichoke hearts have browned and are crisp, flipping once halfway through.
8. Let cool for 5 minutes before serving.

One-pot Nachos

Servings: 4
Cooking Time: 10 Minutes
Ingredients:
- 1 pound ground beef
- 1 (1-ounce) packet taco seasoning mix
- 1 (16-ounce) can refried beans
- 1 (14.5-ounce) can diced tomatoes, drained
- 2 cups sour cream
- 3 cups shredded Mexican cheese blend
- 2 cups shredded iceberg lettuce
- 1 cup sliced black olives
- Sliced scallions, both white and green parts, for garnish
- 1 (10- to 13-ounce) bag tortilla chips

Directions:
1. Insert the Cooking Pot and close the hood. Select GRILL, set the temperature to MED, and set the time to 10 minutes. Select START/STOP to begin preheating.
2. When the unit beeps to signify it has preheated, place the ground beef in the Cooking Pot and sprinkle it with the taco seasoning. Using a wooden spoon or spatula, break apart the ground beef. Close the hood and cook for 5 minutes.
3. After 5 minutes, open the hood and stir the ground beef to mix a little more with the taco seasoning. Evenly spread the ground beef across the bottom of the pot. Add the refried beans in an even layer over the meat, then an even layer of the diced tomatoes. Close the hood and cook for 5 minutes more.
4. When cooking is complete, remove the Cooking Pot from the unit and place it on a heatproof surface. Add an even layer each of sour cream, shredded cheese, shredded lettuce, and olives on top. Garnish with scallions and serve with the tortilla chips.

Buttermilk Marinated Chicken Wings

Servings: 4
Cooking Time: 17 To 19 Minutes
Ingredients:
- 2 pounds chicken wings
- Marinade:
- 1 cup buttermilk
- ½ teaspoon salt
- ½ teaspoon black pepper
- Coating:
- 1 cup flour
- 1 cup panko bread crumbs
- 2 tablespoons poultry seasoning
- 2 teaspoons salt
- Cooking spray

Directions:
1. Whisk together all the ingredients for the marinade in a large bowl.
2. Add the chicken wings to the marinade and toss well. Transfer to the refrigerator to marinate for at least an hour.
3. Spritz the Crisper Basket with cooking spray.
4. Insert the Crisper Basket and close the hood. Select AIR CRISP, set the temperature to 360ºF, and set the time to 19 minutes. Select START/STOP to begin preheating.
5. Thoroughly combine all the ingredients for the coating in a shallow bowl.
6. Remove the chicken wings from the marinade and shake off any excess. Roll them in the coating mixture.
7. Place the chicken wings in the Crisper Basket in a single layer. Mist the wings with cooking spray. You'll need to work in batches to avoid overcrowding.
8. Close the hood and AIR CRISP for 17 to 19 minutes, or until the wings are crisp and golden brown on the outside. Flip the wings halfway through the cooking time.
9. Remove from the basket to a plate and repeat with the remaining wings.
10. Serve hot.

Garlicky And Lemony Artichokes

Servings: 4
Cooking Time: 10 Minutes
Ingredients:
- Juice of ½ lemon
- ½ cup canola oil
- 3 garlic cloves, chopped
- Sea salt, to taste
- Freshly ground black pepper, to taste
- 2 large artichokes, trimmed and halved

Directions:
1. Insert the Grill Grate and close the hood. Select GRILL, set the temperature to MAX, and set the time to 10 minutes. Select START/STOP to begin preheating.

2. While the unit is preheating, in a medium bowl, combine the lemon juice, oil, and garlic. Season with salt and pepper, then brush the artichoke halves with the lemon-garlic mixture.

3. When the unit beeps to signify it has preheated, place the artichokes on the Grill Grate, cut side down. Gently press them down to maximize grill marks. Close the hood and GRILL for 8 to 10 minutes, occasionally basting generously with the lemon-garlic mixture throughout cooking, until blistered on all sides.

Zucchini And Potato Tots

Servings: 4
Cooking Time: 20 Minutes
Ingredients:
- 1 large zucchini, grated
- 1 medium baked potato, skin removed and mashed
- ¼ cup shredded Cheddar cheese
- 1 large egg, beaten
- ½ teaspoon kosher salt
- Cooking spray

Directions:
1. Select AIR CRISP, set the temperature to 390ºF, and set the time to 10 minutes. Select START/STOP to begin preheating.
2. Wrap the grated zucchini in a paper towel and squeeze out any excess liquid, then combine the zucchini, baked potato, shredded Cheddar cheese, egg, and kosher salt in a large bowl.
3. Spray a baking pan with cooking spray, then place individual tablespoons of the zucchini mixture in the pan. Place the pan directly in the pot. Close the hood and AIR CRISP for 10 minutes. Repeat this process with the remaining mixture.
4. Remove the tots and allow to cool on a wire rack for 5 minutes before serving.

Mozzarella Sticks

Servings: 4
Cooking Time: 8 Minutes
Ingredients:
- 2 large eggs
- 2 cups plain bread crumbs
- 2 tablespoons Italian seasoning
- 10 to 12 mozzarella cheese sticks
- Marinara sauce, for dipping

Directions:
1. In a large bowl, whisk the eggs. In a separate large bowl, combine the bread crumbs and Italian seasoning.
2. Dip each cheese stick in the egg and then dip it in the bread crumbs to evenly coat. Place the breaded mozzarella sticks on a baking sheet or flat tray, then freeze for 30 minutes.
3. Insert the Grill Grate and close the hood. Select GRILL, set the temperature to MED, and set the time to 8 minutes. Select START/STOP to begin preheating.
4. When the unit beeps to signify it has preheated, open the hood and place the mozzarella sticks on the Grill Grate. Close the hood and grill for 8 minutes.
5. When cooking is complete, the mozzarella sticks will be golden brown and crispy. If you prefer browner mozzarella sticks, continue cooking to your liking. Serve with the marinara sauce on the side.

French Fries

Servings: 4
Cooking Time: 25 Minutes
Ingredients:
- 1 pound russet or Idaho potatoes, cut in 2-inch strips
- 3 tablespoons canola oil

Directions:
1. Place the potatoes in a large bowl and cover them with cold water. Let soak for 30 minutes. Drain well, then pat with a paper towel until very dry.
2. Insert the Crisper Basket and close the hood. Select AIR CRISP, set the temperature to 390ºF, and set the time to 25 minutes. Select START/STOP to begin preheating.
3. Meanwhile, in a large bowl, toss the potatoes with the oil.
4. When the unit beeps to signify it has preheated, add the potatoes to the basket. Close the hood and AIR CRISP for 10 minutes.
5. After 10 minutes, shake the basket well. Place the basket back in the unit and close the hood to resume cooking.
6. After 10 minutes, check for desired crispness. Continue cooking up to 5 minutes more, if necessary.
7. When cooking is complete, serve immediately with your favorite dipping sauce.

Bruschetta With Tomato And Basil

Servings: 6
Cooking Time: 6 Minutes
Ingredients:
- 4 tomatoes, diced
- ⅓ cup shredded fresh basil
- ¼ cup shredded Parmesan cheese
- 1 tablespoon balsamic vinegar
- 1 tablespoon minced garlic
- 1 teaspoon olive oil
- 1 teaspoon salt
- 1 teaspoon freshly ground black pepper
- 1 loaf French bread, cut into 1-inch-thick slices
- Cooking spray

Directions:
1. Insert the Crisper Basket and close the hood. Select BAKE, set the temperature to 250ºF, and set the time to 3 minutes. Select START/STOP to begin preheating.
2. Mix together the tomatoes and basil in a medium bowl. Add the cheese, vinegar, garlic, olive oil, salt, and pepper and stir until well incorporated. Set aside.
3. Spritz the Crisper Basket with cooking spray. Working in batches, lay the bread slices in the basket in a single layer. Spray the slices with cooking spray.
4. Close the hood and BAKE for 3 minutes until golden brown.
5. Remove from the basket to a plate. Repeat with the remaining bread slices.
6. Top each slice with a generous spoonful of the tomato mixture and serve.

Rosemary Baked Cashews

Servings:2
Cooking Time: 3 Minutes
Ingredients:
- 2 sprigs of fresh rosemary
- 1 teaspoon olive oil
- 1 teaspoon kosher salt
- ½ teaspoon honey
- 2 cups roasted and unsalted whole cashews
- Cooking spray

Directions:
1. Insert the Crisper Basket and close the hood. Select BAKE, set the temperature to 300ºF, and set the time to 3 minutes. Select START/STOP to begin preheating.
2. In a medium bowl, whisk together the chopped rosemary, olive oil, kosher salt, and honey. Set aside.
3. Spray the Crisper Basket with cooking spray, then place the cashews and the whole rosemary sprig in the basket. Close the hood and BAKE for 3 minutes.
4. Remove the cashews and rosemary from the grill, then discard the rosemary and add the cashews to the olive oil mixture, tossing to coat.
5. Allow to cool for 15 minutes before serving.

Candied Brussels Sprouts With Bacon

Servings: 4
Cooking Time: 20 Minutes
Ingredients:
- 2 pounds Brussels sprouts, ends trimmed
- 2 tablespoons avocado oil
- ¼ cup light brown sugar, packed
- 8 ounces thick-cut bacon, cut into bite-size pieces
- 3 tablespoons maple syrup

Directions:
1. Insert the Crisper Basket and close the hood. Select AIR CRISP, set the temperature to 390°F, and set the time to 20 minutes. Select START/STOP to begin preheating.
2. While the unit is preheating, put the Brussels sprouts in a large bowl, drizzle with the avocado oil, and toss to coat.
3. In a medium bowl, rub the brown sugar into the bacon pieces.
4. When the unit beeps to signify it has preheated, place the Brussels sprouts in the Crisper Basket and sprinkle the bacon bits on top. Close the hood and cook for 10 minutes.
5. After 10 minutes, open the hood and flip the Brussels sprouts. Drizzle the maple syrup over the sprouts. Close the hood and cook for 10 minutes more. If you like, you can turn the Brussels sprouts a second time when there are 5 minutes of cooking time remaining.
6. When cooking is complete, remove the Brussels sprouts from the grill and serve. If you want your Brussels sprouts crispier and more browned, continue cooking to your liking.

Crispy Cod Fingers

Servings: 4
Cooking Time: 12 Minutes
Ingredients:
- 2 eggs
- 2 tablespoons milk
- 2 cups flour
- 1 cup cornmeal
- 1 teaspoon seafood seasoning
- Salt and black pepper, to taste
- 1 cup bread crumbs
- 1 pound cod fillets, cut into 1-inch strips

Directions:
1. Insert the Crisper Basket and close the hood. Select AIR CRISP, set the temperature to 400ºF, and set the time to 12 minutes. Select START/STOP to begin preheating.
2. Beat the eggs with the milk in a shallow bowl. In another shallow bowl, combine the flour, cornmeal, seafood seasoning, salt, and pepper. On a plate, place the bread crumbs.
3. Dredge the cod strips, one at a time, in the flour mixture, then in the egg mixture, finally in the bread crumb to coat evenly.
4. Arrange the cod strips in the Crisper Basket. Close the hood and AIR CRISP for 12 minutes until crispy.
5. Transfer the cod strips to a paper towel-lined plate and serve warm.

Cheesy Crab Toasts

Servings:15
Cooking Time: 5 Minutes
Ingredients:
- 1 can flaked crab meat, well drained
- 3 tablespoons light mayonnaise
- ¼ cup shredded Parmesan cheese
- ¼ cup shredded Cheddar cheese
- 1 teaspoon Worcestershire sauce
- ½ teaspoon lemon juice
- 1 loaf artisan bread, French bread, or baguette, cut into ⅜-inch-thick slices

Directions:
1. Insert the Crisper Basket and close the hood. Select BAKE, set the temperature to 360ºF, and set the time to 5 minutes. Select START/STOP to begin preheating.
2. In a large bowl, stir together all the ingredients except the bread slices.
3. On a clean work surface, lay the bread slices. Spread ½ tablespoon of crab mixture onto each slice of bread.
4. Arrange the bread slices in the Crisper Basket in a single layer. You'll need to work in batches to avoid overcrowding.
5. Close the hood and BAKE for 5 minutes until the tops are lightly browned.
6. Transfer to a plate and repeat with the remaining bread slices.
7. Serve warm.

Twice Air-crisped Potatoes

Servings: 4
Cooking Time: 40 Minutes
Ingredients:
- 4 medium Idaho or russet potatoes
- Extra-virgin olive oil
- Kosher salt
- 8 tablespoons (1 stick) unsalted butter, at room temperature
- ½ cup sour cream
- 1 cup shredded cheddar cheese
- Freshly ground black pepper

Directions:

1. Insert the Crisper Basket and close the hood. Select AIR CRISP, set the temperature to 400°F, and set the time to 40 minutes. Select START/STOP to begin preheating.
2. While the unit is preheating, rinse and scrub the potatoes. Poke each potato several times with a fork. Brush a generous amount of olive oil over the potatoes and season well with salt.
3. When the unit beeps to signify it has preheated, place the potatoes in the Crisper Basket. Close the hood and cook for 30 minutes.
4. After 30 minutes, open the hood and remove the potatoes. Place on a plate and set aside.
5. Slice the potatoes in half lengthwise. Use a fork to carefully scoop out the insides of the potatoes without damaging the skins. Put the potato flesh in a large bowl. Add the butter, sour cream, and cheddar cheese. Using a spatula, carefully fold the mixture until the butter melts. Scoop the filling into the potato skins. Season each potato half with salt and pepper.
6. Place the loaded potatoes back into the Crisper Basket. Close the hood and cook for 10 minutes more.
7. When cooking is complete, the potato skins will be crispy and the cheese will be melted and infused into the potatoes. Remove the potatoes from the grill and serve.

Sweet Potato Fries With Honey-butter Sauce

Servings: 4
Cooking Time: 20 Minutes
Ingredients:
- For the sweet potato fries

- 2 medium sweet potatoes, cut into ¼-inch-thick slices
- 3 teaspoons avocado oil
- 1 teaspoon salt
- ½ teaspoon paprika
- ½ teaspoon garlic powder
- ¼ teaspoon freshly ground black pepper
- For the honey butter
- 1 tablespoon honey
- 1 teaspoon powdered sugar
- 8 tablespoons (1 stick) salted butter, at room temperature

Directions:
1. Insert the Crisper Basket and close the hood. Select AIR CRISP, set the temperature to 400°F, and set the time to 20 minutes. Select START/STOP to begin preheating.
2. In a large bowl, drizzle the sweet potatoes with the avocado oil and toss to coat. In a small bowl, mix together the salt, paprika, garlic powder, and pepper. Sprinkle the seasoning over the sweet potatoes and toss gently to coat.
3. When the unit beeps to signify it has preheated, place the sweet potato fries in the Crisper Basket. Close the hood and cook for 10 minutes.
4. After 10 minutes, open the hood and shake the basket. Close the hood and cook for 5 minutes more. Open the hood again and shake the basket. If the fries are to your desired crispness, then remove them. If not, close the hood and cook up to 5 minutes more.
5. In a small bowl, whisk together the honey and powdered sugar until the sugar is dissolved. Add the butter and continue whisking. Serve alongside the fries

Meats

Crispy Fish Sticks

Servings: 4
Cooking Time: 10 Minutes
Ingredients:
- 1 pound cod fillets
- ¼ cup all-purpose flour
- 1 large egg
- 1 teaspoon Dijon mustard
- ½ cup bread crumbs
- 1 tablespoon dried parsley
- 1 teaspoon paprika
- ½ teaspoon freshly ground black pepper
- Nonstick cooking spray

Directions:

1. Insert the Crisper Basket, and close the hood. Select AIR CRISP, set the temperature to 390°F, and set the time to 10 minutes. Select START/STOP to begin preheating.
2. While the unit is preheating, cut the fish fillets into ¾- to 1-inch-wide strips.
3. Place the flour on a plate. In a medium shallow bowl, whisk together the egg and Dijon mustard. In a separate medium shallow bowl, combine the bread crumbs, dried parsley, paprika, and black pepper.
4. One at a time, dredge the cod strips in the flour, shaking off any excess, then coat them in the egg mixture. Finally, dredge them in the bread crumb mixture, and coat on all sides.
5. When the unit beeps to signify it has preheated, spray the basket with the cooking spray. Place the cod fillet strips in the basket, and coat them with the cooking spray. Close the hood, and AIR CRISP for 10 minutes.
6. Remove the fish sticks from the basket and serve.

Tonkatsu

Servings: 4
Cooking Time: 10 Minutes Per Batch
Ingredients:
- ⅔ cup all-purpose flour
- 2 large egg whites
- 1 cup panko breadcrumbs
- 4 center-cut boneless pork loin chops (about ½ inch thick)
- Cooking spray

Directions:
1. Spritz the Crisper Basket with cooking spray.
2. Insert the Crisper Basket and close the hood. Select AIR CRISP, set the temperature to 375ºF, and set the time to 10 minutes. Select START/STOP to begin preheating.
3. Pour the flour in a bowl. Whisk the egg whites in a separate bowl. Spread the breadcrumbs on a large plate.
4. Dredge the pork loin chops in the flour first, press to coat well, then shake the excess off and dunk the chops in the eggs whites, and then roll the chops over the breadcrumbs. Shake the excess off.
5. Arrange the pork chops in batches in a single layer in the basket and spritz with cooking spray.
6. Close the hood and AIR CRISP for 10 minutes or until the pork chops are lightly browned and crunchy. Flip the chops halfway through. Repeat with remaining chops.
7. Serve immediately.

Crispy Crab And Fish Cakes

Servings: 4
Cooking Time: 10 To 12 Minutes
Ingredients:
- 8 ounces imitation crab meat
- 4 ounces leftover cooked fish (such as cod, pollock, or haddock)
- 2 tablespoons minced celery
- 2 tablespoons minced green onion
- 2 tablespoons light mayonnaise
- 1 tablespoon plus 2 teaspoons Worcestershire sauce
- ¾ cup crushed saltine cracker crumbs
- 2 teaspoons dried parsley flakes
- 1 teaspoon prepared yellow mustard
- ½ teaspoon garlic powder
- ½ teaspoon dried dill weed, crushed
- ½ teaspoon Old Bay seasoning
- ½ cup panko bread crumbs
- Cooking spray

Directions:
1. Insert the Crisper Basket and close the hood. Select BAKE, set the temperature to 390ºF, and set the time to 12 minutes. Select START/STOP to begin preheating.
2. Pulse the crab meat and fish in a food processor until finely chopped.
3. Transfer the meat mixture to a large bowl, along with the celery, green onion, mayo, Worcestershire sauce, cracker crumbs, parsley flakes, mustard, garlic powder, dill weed, and Old Bay seasoning. Stir to mix well.
4. Scoop out the meat mixture and form into 8 equal-sized patties with your hands.

5. Place the panko bread crumbs on a plate. Roll the patties in the bread crumbs until they are evenly coated on both sides. Spritz the patties with cooking spray.
6. Put the patties in the Crisper Basket. Close the hood and BAKE for 10 to 12 minutes, flipping them halfway through, or until they are golden brown and cooked through.
7. Divide the patties among four plates and serve.

Crispy Catfish Strips

Servings: 4
Cooking Time: 16 To 18 Minutes
Ingredients:
- 1 cup buttermilk
- 5 catfish fillets, cut into 1½-inch strips
- Cooking spray
- 1 cup cornmeal
- 1 tablespoon Creole, Cajun, or Old Bay seasoning

Directions:
1. Pour the buttermilk into a shallow baking pan. Place the catfish in the dish and refrigerate for at least 1 hour to help remove any fishy taste.
2. Insert the Crisper Basket and close the hood. Select AIR CRISP, set the temperature to 400ºF, and set the time to 18 minutes. Select START/STOP to begin preheating.
3. Spray the Crisper Basket lightly with cooking spray.
4. In a shallow bowl, combine cornmeal and Creole seasoning.
5. Shake any excess buttermilk off the catfish. Place each strip in the cornmeal mixture and coat completely. Press the cornmeal into the catfish gently to help it stick.
6. Place the strips in the Crisper Basket in a single layer. Lightly spray the catfish with cooking spray. You may need to cook the catfish in more than one batch.
7. Close the hood and AIR CRISP for 8 minutes. Turn the catfish strips over and lightly spray with cooking spray. AIR CRISP until golden brown and crispy, for 8 to 10 more minutes.
8. Serve warm.

Easy Shrimp And Vegetable Paella

Servings: 4
Cooking Time: 14 To 17 Minutes
Ingredients:
- 1 package frozen cooked rice, thawed
- 1 jar artichoke hearts, drained and chopped
- ¼ cup vegetable broth
- ½ teaspoon dried thyme
- ½ teaspoon turmeric
- 1 cup frozen cooked small shrimp
- ½ cup frozen baby peas
- 1 tomato, diced

Directions:
1. Select BAKE, set the temperature to 340ºF, and set the time to 17 minutes. Select START/STOP to begin preheating.
2. Mix together the cooked rice, chopped artichoke hearts, vegetable broth, thyme, and turmeric in a baking pan and stir to combine.
3. Place the pan directly in the pot. Close the hood and BAKE for 9 minutes, or until the rice is heated through.
4. Remove the pan from the grill and fold in the shrimp, baby peas, and diced tomato and mix well.

5. Return to the grill and continue baking for 5 to 8 minutes, or until the shrimp are done and the paella is bubbling.
6. Cool for 5 minutes before serving.

Rib Eye Steak With Rosemary Butter
Servings: 4
Cooking Time: 10 Minutes
Ingredients:
- 4 garlic cloves, minced
- 1 teaspoon salt
- 4 tablespoons (½ stick) unsalted butter, at room temperature
- ½ tablespoon chopped fresh rosemary (about 2 sprigs)
- 4 (1-pound) bone-in rib eye steaks
Directions:
1. Plug the thermometer into the unit. Insert the Grill Grate and close the hood. Select GRILL, set the temperature to HI, then select PRESET. Use the arrows to the right to select BEEF, then choose MED (6) or desired doneness. Insert the Smart Thermometer into the thickest part of one of the steaks. Select START/STOP to begin preheating.
2. While the unit is preheating, in a small bowl, combine the garlic, salt, butter, and rosemary to form a butter paste.
3. When the unit beeps to signify it has preheated, place the steaks on the Grill Grate. Close the hood to begin cooking.
4. When the grill indicates it is time to flip, open the hood, flip the steaks, and add 1 tablespoon of the rosemary butter on top of each steak. Close the hood and cook until the Smart Thermometer indicates your desired internal temperature has been reached.
5. When cooking is complete, remove the steaks from the grill and let rest for 5 minutes before slicing against the grain. Serve.

Blackened Shrimp Tacos
Servings: 4
Cooking Time: 10 To 15 Minutes
Ingredients:
- 12 ounces medium shrimp, deveined, with tails off
- 1 teaspoon olive oil
- 1 to 2 teaspoons Blackened seasoning
- 8 corn tortillas, warmed
- 1 bag coleslaw mix
- 2 limes, cut in half
- Cooking spray
Directions:
1. Insert the Crisper Basket and close the hood. Select AIR CRISP, set the temperature to 400ºF, and set the time to 15 minutes. Select START/STOP to begin preheating.
2. Spray the Crisper Basket lightly with cooking spray.
3. Dry the shrimp with a paper towel to remove excess water.
4. In a medium bowl, toss the shrimp with olive oil and Blackened seasoning.
5. Place the shrimp in the Crisper Basket. Close the hood and AIR CRISP for 5 minutes. Shake the basket, lightly spray with cooking spray, and cook until the shrimp are cooked through and starting to brown, 5 to 10 more minutes.

6. Fill each tortilla with the coleslaw mix and top with the blackened shrimp. Squeeze fresh lime juice over top and serve.

Classic Walliser Schnitzel
Servings: 2
Cooking Time: 14 Minutes
Ingredients:
- ½ cup pork rinds
- ½ tablespoon fresh parsley
- ½ teaspoon fennel seed
- ½ teaspoon mustard
- ⅓ tablespoon cider vinegar
- 1 teaspoon garlic salt
- ⅓ teaspoon ground black pepper
- 2 eggs
- 2 pork schnitzel, halved
- Cooking spray
Directions:
1. Spritz the Crisper Basket with cooking spray.
2. Insert the Crisper Basket and close the hood. Select AIR CRISP, set the temperature to 350ºF, and set the time to 14 minutes. Select START/STOP to begin preheating.
3. Put the pork rinds, parsley, fennel seeds, and mustard in a food processor. Pour in the vinegar and sprinkle with salt and ground black pepper. Pulse until well combined and smooth.
4. Pour the pork rind mixture in a large bowl. Whisk the eggs in a separate bowl.
5. Dunk the pork schnitzel in the whisked eggs, then dunk in the pork rind mixture to coat well. Shake the excess off.
6. Arrange the schnitzel in the basket and spritz with cooking spray. Close the hood and AIR CRISP for 14 minutes or until golden and crispy. Flip the schnitzel halfway through.
7. Serve immediately.

Garlic Herb Crusted Lamb
Servings: 6
Cooking Time: 1 Hour
Ingredients:
- ¼ cup red wine vinegar
- 3 garlic cloves, minced
- 1 tablespoon garlic powder
- 1 tablespoon paprika
- 1 tablespoon ground cumin
- 1 tablespoon dried parsley
- 1 tablespoon dried thyme
- 1 tablespoon dried oregano
- 1 teaspoon salt
- ½ teaspoon freshly ground black pepper
- Juice of ½ lemon
- 1 (3-pound) boneless leg of lamb
Directions:
1. In a large bowl, mix together the vinegar, garlic, garlic powder, paprika, cumin, parsley, thyme, oregano, salt, pepper, and lemon juice until well combined—the marinade will turn into a thick paste. Add the leg of lamb and massage the marinade into the meat. Coat the lamb with the marinade and let sit for at least 30 minutes. If marinating for longer, cover and refrigerate.

2. Plug the thermometer into the unit. Insert the Grill Grate and close the hood. Select GRILL, set the temperature to LO, and set the time to 30 minutes. Insert the Smart Thermometer into the thickest part of the meat. Select START/STOP to begin preheating.

3. When the unit beeps to signify it has preheated, place the lamb on the Grill Grate. Select the BEEF/LAMB preset and choose MEDIUM-WELL or according to your desired doneness. Close the hood and cook for 30 minutes.

4. After 30 minutes, which is the maximum time for the LO setting, select GRILL again, set the temperature to LO, and set the time to 30 minutes. Select START/STOP and press PREHEAT to skip preheating. Cook until the Smart Thermometer indicates that the desired internal temperature has been reached.

5. When cooking is complete, remove the lamb from the grill and serve.

Rosemary And Garlic Lamb Pitas

Servings: 6
Cooking Time: 12 Minutes
Ingredients:
- For the lamb
- ¼ cup extra-virgin olive oil
- 1 tablespoon garlic powder
- 2 garlic cloves, minced
- 2 teaspoons onion powder
- Juice of ½ lemon
- ¼ teaspoon nutmeg
- 2 tablespoons fresh rosemary
- 1 teaspoon salt
- 2 pounds boneless lamb, thinly sliced
- 6 pitas
- For the tzatziki sauce
- 2 cups Greek yogurt
- 1 tablespoon garlic powder
- ¼ teaspoon onion powder
- 2 teaspoons salt
- 2 tablespoons fresh dill
- 2 tablespoons freshly squeezed lemon juice
- ⅛ teaspoon freshly ground black pepper
- 1 tablespoon extra-virgin olive oil
- 1 cucumber, seeded and diced

Directions:
1. In a large bowl, whisk together the olive oil, garlic powder, minced garlic, onion powder, lemon juice, nutmeg, rosemary, and salt. Add the lamb and massage the mixture into the meat. Cover and marinate for 30 minutes.

2. Insert the Grill Grate and close the hood. Select GRILL, set the temperature to HI, and set the time to 12 minutes. Select START/STOP to begin preheating.

3. When the unit beeps to signify it has preheated, place the lamb slices on the Grill Grate in a single layer. Close the hood and cook for 6 minutes.

4. After 6 minutes, open the hood and flip the meat. Close the hood and cook for 6 minutes more.

5. While the lamb is cooking, in a medium bowl, combine the yogurt, garlic powder, onion powder, salt, dill, lemon juice, pepper, and olive oil. Add the cucumber and mix well.

6. Serve the lamb inside warm pita pockets and top with tzatziki sauce.

Peppercorn Beef Tenderloin

Servings: 6 To 8
Cooking Time: 30 Minutes
Ingredients:
- ¾ cup tricolored peppercorns or black peppercorns, crushed
- 2 garlic cloves, minced
- 2 tablespoons avocado oil
- 1 tablespoon kosher salt
- ¼ cup yellow mustard or horseradish
- 1 (3-pound) beef tenderloin, trimmed

Directions:
1. In a small bowl, combine the crushed peppercorns, garlic, avocado oil, salt, and mustard. Using a basting brush, coat the tenderloin all over with the mustard mixture. Then press the mixture into the meat with your hands.

2. Plug the thermometer into the unit. Insert the Grill Grate and close the hood. Select ROAST, set the temperature to 400°F, then select PRESET. Use the arrows to the right to select BEEF. The unit will default to WELL to cook to a safe temperature. Insert the Smart Thermometer into the thickest part of the loin. Select START/STOP to begin preheating.

3. When the unit beeps to signify it has preheated, place the tenderloin on the Grill Grate. (If the Splatter Shield is touching the tenderloin when you close the hood, use grill mitts to remove the Grill Grate and place the tenderloin in the Cooking Pot instead.) Close the hood and cook until the Smart Thermometer indicates your desired internal temperature has been reached.

4. When cooking is complete, remove the tenderloin and let rest for 10 minutes before slicing and serving.

5. You will want to tuck the thin (tail) end under the center and tie it with kitchen twine or butcher's twine every 2 inches to make a uniform size to get the perfect level of doneness throughout. You can also ask your butcher to tie it for you.

Beef Steak Fajitas

Servings: 4
Cooking Time: 25 Minutes
Ingredients:
- ¼ cup avocado oil
- 2 tablespoons soy sauce
- Juice of 2 limes
- 1 tablespoon chili powder
- 1 teaspoon onion powder
- 1 teaspoon garlic powder
- 1 teaspoon ground cumin
- 1 teaspoon paprika
- 2 teaspoons salt
- 2 pounds hanger steak
- 1 green bell pepper, cut into strips
- 1 red bell pepper, cut into strips
- 1 yellow bell pepper, cut into strips
- 1 white onion, sliced
- 8 to 10 (10-inch) flour tortillas
- 1. In a large bowl, whisk together the avocado oil, soy sauce, lime juice, chili powder, onion powder, garlic powder, cumin, paprika, and salt. Add the hanger steak, making sure it is fully covered with the marinade. Marinate for at least 15

minutes. Or, if you want to marinate the meat overnight, combine the marinade ingredients in a resealable bag, add the steak, massage the marinade into the steak, seal, and refrigerate. (If marinating overnight, also store the bell peppers and onion in a separate resealable bag in the refrigerator.)

Directions:

1. Plug the thermometer into the unit. Insert the Grill Grate and close the hood. Select GRILL, set the temperature to HI, then select PRESET. Use the arrows to the right to select BEEF, then choose desired doneness. Insert the Smart Thermometer into the thickest part of the steak. Select START/STOP to begin preheating.

2. When the unit beeps to signify it has preheated, place the steak on the Grill Grate. Close the hood to begin cooking. The Foodi™ Grill will tell you when to flip the steak and when the internal temperature has been reached (15 minutes is for well-done steak).

3. When cooking is complete, use grill mitts to remove the Grill Grate and steak. Let the steak rest while the vegetables cook.

4. Put the bell peppers and onion in the Cooking Pot. Select GRILL, set the temperature to HI, and set the time to 10 minutes. Select START/STOP and then press PREHEAT to skip preheating. Close the hood and cook for 5 minutes.

5. After 5 minutes, open the hood and stir the peppers and onion with a wooden spoon. Close the hood and cook for 5 minutes more.

6. When cooking is complete, thinly slice the steak against the grain. Serve in the tortillas with the bell peppers and onion. Garnish with your favorite toppings, such as shredded cheese, pico de gallo, sour cream, and guacamole.

Carne Asada Tacos

Servings: 4
Cooking Time: 15 Minutes

Ingredients:
- For the tacos
- ¼ cup avocado oil
- ¼ cup soy sauce
- ¼ cup orange juice
- 3 tablespoons white wine vinegar
- 3 tablespoons minced garlic
- Juice of 2 limes
- 1 teaspoon ground cumin
- 1 teaspoon salt
- 1 teaspoon freshly ground black pepper
- 1 teaspoon onion powder
- ½ cup chopped fresh cilantro
- 2 pounds skirt steak at least 1 inch thick
- 10 corn tortillas
- For the creamy cilantro sauce
- ¼ cup mayonnaise
- ¼ cup sour cream
- ¼ cup minced fresh cilantro, including stems
- Juice of 1 lime wedge, or more as desired
- ¼ teaspoon paprika
- ¼ teaspoon onion powder

Directions:

1. In a large bowl, whisk together the avocado oil, soy sauce, orange juice, vinegar, garlic, lime juice, cumin, salt, pepper, onion powder, and cilantro. Add the steak, making

sure it is fully coated with the marinade. Set aside to marinate for 15 minutes.

2. Plug the thermometer into the unit. Insert the Grill Grate and close the hood. Select GRILL, set the temperature to HI, then select PRESET. Use the arrows to the right to select BEEF, then choose desired doneness. Insert the Smart Thermometer into the thickest part of the steak. Select START/STOP to begin preheating.

3. When the unit beeps to signify it has preheated, place the steak on the Grill Grate. Close the hood to begin cooking. The Foodi™ Grill will tell you when to flip the steak and when the desired internal temperature has been reached (15 minutes is for well-done steak).

4. While the steak is cooking, in a small bowl, combine the mayonnaise, sour cream, cilantro, lime juice, paprika, and onion powder.

5. When cooking is complete, remove the steak from the grill. Let it rest for 10 minutes before slicing against the grain. Serve in the tortillas and dress with the creamy cilantro sauce.

Spicy Pork Chops With Carrots And Mushrooms

Servings: 4
Cooking Time: 15 To 18 Minutes

Ingredients:
- 2 carrots, cut into sticks
- 1 cup mushrooms, sliced
- 2 garlic cloves, minced
- 2 tablespoons olive oil
- 1 pound boneless pork chops
- 1 teaspoon dried oregano
- 1 teaspoon dried thyme
- 1 teaspoon cayenne pepper
- Salt and ground black pepper, to taste
- Cooking spray

Directions:

1. Spritz the Crisper Basket with cooking spray.

2. Insert the Crisper Basket and close the hood. Select AIR CRISP, set the temperature to 360ºF, and set the time to 18 minutes. Select START/STOP to begin preheating.

3. In a mixing bowl, toss together the carrots, mushrooms, garlic, olive oil and salt until well combined.

4. Add the pork chops to a different bowl and season with oregano, thyme, cayenne pepper, salt and black pepper.

5. Lower the vegetable mixture in the prepared Crisper Basket. Place the seasoned pork chops on top. Close the hood and AIR CRISP for 15 to 18 minutes, or until the pork is well browned and the vegetables are tender, flipping the pork and shaking the basket once halfway through.

6. Transfer the pork chops to the serving dishes and let cool for 5 minutes. Serve warm with vegetable on the side.

Mushroom And Beef Meatloaf

Servings: 4
Cooking Time: 25 Minutes

Ingredients:
- 1 pound ground beef
- 1 egg, beaten
- 1 mushrooms, sliced
- 1 tablespoon thyme
- 1 small onion, chopped

- 3 tablespoons bread crumbs
- Ground black pepper, to taste

Directions:
1. Select BAKE, set the temperature to 400ºF, and set the time to 25 minutes. Select START/STOP to begin preheating.
2. Put all the ingredients into a large bowl and combine entirely.
3. Transfer the meatloaf mixture into the loaf pan. Place the pan directly in the pot.
4. Close the hood and BAKE for 25 minutes.
5. Slice up before serving.

Barbecue Pork Ribs

Servings: 4
Cooking Time: 30 Minutes
Ingredients:
- 1 tablespoon barbecue dry rub
- 1 teaspoon mustard
- 1 tablespoon apple cider vinegar
- 1 teaspoon sesame oil
- 1 pound pork ribs, chopped

Directions:
1. Combine the dry rub, mustard, apple cider vinegar, and sesame oil, then coat the ribs with this mixture. Refrigerate the ribs for 20 minutes.
2. Insert the Crisper Basket and close the hood. Select AIR CRISP, set the temperature to 360ºF, and set the time to 30 minutes. Select START/STOP to begin preheating.
3. When the ribs are ready, place them in the basket. Close the hood and AIR CRISP for 15 minutes. Flip them and AIR CRISP on the other side for a further 15 minutes.
4. Serve immediately.

Lamb Rack With Pistachio

Servings: 2
Cooking Time: 20 Minutes
Ingredients:
- ½ cup finely chopped pistachios
- 1 teaspoon chopped fresh rosemary
- 3 tablespoons panko breadcrumbs
- 2 teaspoons chopped fresh oregano
- 1 tablespoon olive oil
- Salt and freshly ground black pepper, to taste
- 1 lamb rack, bones fat trimmed and frenched
- 1 tablespoon Dijon mustard

Directions:
1. Insert the Crisper Basket and close the hood. Select AIR CRISP, set the temperature to 380ºF, and set the time to 12 minutes. Select START/STOP to begin preheating.
2. Put the pistachios, rosemary, breadcrumbs, oregano, olive oil, salt, and black pepper in a food processor. Pulse to combine until smooth.
3. Rub the lamb rack with salt and black pepper on a clean work surface, then place it in the basket.
4. Close the hood and AIR CRISP for 12 minutes or until lightly browned. Flip the lamb halfway through the cooking time.
5. Transfer the lamb to a plate and brush with Dijon mustard on the fat side, then sprinkle with the pistachios mixture over the lamb rack to coat well.

6. Put the lamb rack back to the basket. Close the hood and AIR CRISP for 8 more minutes or until the internal temperature of the rack reaches at least 145ºF.
7. Remove the lamb rack from the grill with tongs and allow to cool for 5 minutes before sling to serve.

Blackened Salmon

Servings: 4
Cooking Time: 5 To 7 Minutes
Ingredients:
- Salmon:
- 1 tablespoon sweet paprika
- ½ teaspoon cayenne pepper
- 1 teaspoon garlic powder
- 1 teaspoon dried oregano
- 1 teaspoon dried thyme
- ¾ teaspoon kosher salt
- ⅛ teaspoon freshly ground black pepper
- Cooking spray
- 4 wild salmon fillets
- Cucumber-Avocado Salsa:
- 2 tablespoons chopped red onion
- 1½ tablespoons fresh lemon juice
- 1 teaspoon extra-virgin olive oil
- ¼ teaspoon plus ⅛ teaspoon kosher salt
- Freshly ground black pepper, to taste
- 4 Persian cucumbers, diced
- 6 ounces Hass avocado, diced

Directions:
1. For the salmon: In a small bowl, combine the paprika, cayenne, garlic powder, oregano, thyme, salt, and black pepper. Spray both sides of the fish with oil and rub all over. Coat the fish all over with the spices.
2. For the cucumber-avocado salsa: In a medium bowl, combine the red onion, lemon juice, olive oil, salt, and pepper. Let stand for 5 minutes, then add the cucumbers and avocado.
3. Insert the Crisper Basket and close the hood. Select AIR CRISP, set the temperature to 400ºF, and set the time to 7 minutes. Select START/STOP to begin preheating.
4. Working in batches, arrange the salmon fillets skin side down in the Crisper Basket. Close the hood and AIR CRISP for 5 to 7 minutes, or until the fish flakes easily with a fork, depending on the thickness of the fish.
5. Serve topped with the salsa.

Uncle's Famous Tri-tip

Servings: 6 To 8
Cooking Time: 20 Minutes
Ingredients:
- ¼ cup avocado oil
- ½ cup red wine vinegar
- ¼ cup light brown sugar, packed
- 4 tablespoons honey mustard
- 1 tablespoon garlic powder
- 1 tablespoon onion powder
- 1 tablespoon paprika
- 1 tablespoon salt
- 1 tablespoon freshly ground black pepper
- 3 pounds tri-tip

Directions:

1. In a large resealable bag, combine the avocado oil, red wine vinegar, brown sugar, honey mustard, garlic powder, onion powder, paprika, salt, and pepper. Add the tri-tip, seal, and massage the mixture into the meat. Refrigerate overnight.
2. About 20 minutes before grilling, remove the bag from the refrigerator so the marinade becomes liquid again at room temperature.
3. Plug the thermometer into the unit. Insert the Grill Grate and close the hood. Select GRILL, set the temperature to MED, and select PRESET. Use the arrows to the right to select BEEF, then choose desired doneness. Insert the Smart Thermometer into the thickest part of the meat. Select START/STOP to begin preheating.
4. When the unit beeps to signify it has preheated, place the tri-tip on the Grill Grate, fat-side up. Close the hood to begin cooking.
5. When the Foodi™ Grill indicates it is time to flip, open the hood and flip the tri-tip. Close the hood and continue cooking until the Smart Thermometer indicates your desired internal temperature has been reached.
6. When cooking is complete, remove the tri-tip from the grill. Let rest for 10 minutes before slicing against the grain. Serve.

Steak And Lettuce Salad

Servings: 4 To 6
Cooking Time: 16 Minutes
Ingredients:
- 4 skirt steaks
- Sea salt, to taste
- Freshly ground black pepper, to taste
- 6 cups chopped romaine lettuce
- ¾ cup cherry tomatoes, halved
- ¼ cup blue cheese, crumbled
- 1 cup croutons
- 2 avocados, peeled and sliced
- 1 cup blue cheese dressing

Directions:
1. Insert the Grill Grate and close the hood. Select GRILL, set the temperature to HIGH, and set the time to 8 minutes. Select START/STOP to begin preheating.
2. Season the steaks on both sides with the salt and pepper.
3. When the unit beeps to signify it has preheated, place 2 steaks on the Grill Grate. Gently press the steaks down to maximize grill marks. Close the hood and GRILL for 4 minutes. After 4 minutes, flip the steaks, close the hood, and GRILL for an additional 4 minutes.
4. Remove the steaks from the grill and transfer to them a cutting board. Tent with aluminum foil.
5. Repeat step 3 with the remaining 2 steaks.
6. While the second set of steaks is cooking, assemble the salad by tossing together the lettuce, tomatoes, blue cheese crumbles, and croutons. Top with the avocado slices.
7. Once the second set of steaks has finished cooking, slice all four of the steaks into thin strips, and place on top of the salad. Drizzle with the blue cheese dressing and serve.

Hamburger Steak With Mushroom Gravy

Servings: 4
Cooking Time: 18 Minutes

Ingredients:
- For the hamburger steaks
- 1 cup plain bread crumbs
- 2 tablespoons Worcestershire sauce
- 1 teaspoon onion powder
- 1 teaspoon garlic powder
- 1 large egg
- 1 teaspoon granulated sugar
- 1 teaspoon salt
- ¼ teaspoon freshly ground black pepper
- 1 pound ground beef
- For the mushroom gravy
- 2 cups beef broth
- 4 tablespoons (½ stick) unsalted butter
- 8 ounces white mushrooms, sliced
- 1 tablespoon Worcestershire sauce
- 4 tablespoons all-purpose flour
- Salt
- Freshly ground black pepper

Directions:
1. Insert the Grill Grate and close the hood. Select GRILL, set the temperature to HI, and set the time to 10 minutes. Select START/STOP to begin preheating.
2. While the unit is preheating, in a large bowl, combine the bread crumbs, Worcestershire sauce, onion powder, garlic powder, egg, sugar, salt, and pepper. Add the ground beef in chunks and loosely mix until just combined. Form the mixture into 4 equal-sized patties.
3. When the unit beeps to signify it has preheated, place the beef patties on the Grill Grate. Close the hood and grill for 5 minutes.
4. While the patties are cooking, gather and measure the ingredients for the gravy.
5. After 5 minutes, open the hood and flip the burgers. Close the hood and cook for 5 minutes more.
6. When cooking is complete, use grill mitts to remove the Grill Grate and burgers from the unit.
7. Add the beef broth, butter, mushrooms, and Worcestershire sauce to the Cooking Pot. Select GRILL, set the temperature to HI, and set the time to 8 minutes. Select START/STOP and then press the PREHEAT button to skip preheating. Close the hood and cook for 4 minutes.
8. After 4 minutes, open the hood and stir in the flour. Mix well. Close the hood and cook for 4 minutes more.
9. When cooking is complete, the sauce will be thickened and the butter will be completely melted. Season with salt and pepper. Pour the mushroom gravy over the hamburger steaks and serve.

Korean-style Steak Tips

Servings: 4
Cooking Time: 13 Minutes
Ingredients:
- 4 garlic cloves, minced
- ½ apple, peeled and grated
- 3 tablespoons sesame oil
- 3 tablespoons brown sugar
- ⅓ cup soy sauce
- 1 teaspoon freshly ground black pepper
- Sea salt
- 1½ pounds beef tips

Directions:
1. In a medium bowl, combine the garlic, apple, sesame oil, sugar, soy sauce, pepper, and salt until well mixed.
2. Place the beef tips in a large shallow bowl and pour the marinade over them. Cover and refrigerate for 30 minutes.
3. Insert the Grill Grate and close the hood. Select GRILL, set the temperature to MEDIUM, and set the time to 13 minutes. Select START/STOP to begin preheating.
4. When the unit beeps to signify it has preheated, place the steak tips on the Grill Grate. Close the hood and GRILL for 11 minutes.
5. Cooking is complete to medium doneness when the internal temperature of the meat reaches 145ºF on a food thermometer. If desired, GRILL for up to 2 minutes more.
6. Remove the steak, and set it on a cutting board to rest for 5 minutes. Serve.

Herb And Pesto Stuffed Pork Loin
Servings: 8
Cooking Time: 15 Minutes
Ingredients:
- 1 (4-pound) boneless center-cut pork loin
- ½ cup avocado oil
- ½ cup grated Parmesan cheese
- 2 tablespoons finely chopped fresh basil
- 1 tablespoon finely chopped fresh parsley
- 1 tablespoon chopped fresh chives
- ½ teaspoon finely chopped fresh rosemary
- 5 garlic cloves, minced

Directions:
1. Butterfly the pork loin. You can use the same method as you would for a chicken breast or steak (see here), but because a pork loin is thicker, you can perform this double butterfly technique: Place the boneless, trimmed loin on a cutting board. One-third from the bottom of the loin, slice horizontally from the side (parallel to the cutting board), stopping about ½ inch from the opposite side, and open the flap like a book. Make another horizontal cut from the thicker side of the loin to match the thickness of the first cut, stopping again ½ inch from the edge. Open up the flap to create a rectangular piece of flat meat.
2. Plug the thermometer into the unit. Insert the Grill Grate and close the hood. Select GRILL, set the temperature to MED, and select PRESET. Use the arrows to the right to select PORK. The unit will default to WELL to cook pork to a safe temperature. Select START/STOP to begin preheating.
3. While the unit is preheating, in a small bowl, combine the avocado oil, Parmesan cheese, basil, parsley, chives, rosemary, and garlic. Spread the pesto sauce evenly over the cut side of each tenderloin. Starting from a longer side, roll up the pork tightly over the filling. Use toothpicks to secure the ends. Insert the Smart Thermometer into the thickest part of the meat.
4. When the unit beeps to signify it has preheated, place the loin on the Grill Grate. Close the hood to begin cooking.
5. When the Foodi™ Grill indicates it's time to flip, open the hood and flip the loin. Close the hood to continue cooking.
6. When cooking is complete, the Smart Thermometer will indicate that the internal temperature has been reached. Open the hood and remove the loin. Let the meat rest for 10 minutes before slicing in between the toothpicks. Serve.

Beef And Vegetable Cubes
Servings: 4
Cooking Time: 17 Minutes
Ingredients:
- 2 tablespoons olive oil
- 1 tablespoon apple cider vinegar
- 1 teaspoon fine sea salt
- ½ teaspoons ground black pepper
- 1 teaspoon shallot powder
- ¾ teaspoon smoked cayenne pepper
- ½ teaspoons garlic powder
- ¼ teaspoon ground cumin
- 1 pound top round steak, cut into cubes
- 4 ounces broccoli, cut into florets
- 4 ounces mushrooms, sliced
- 1 teaspoon dried basil
- 1 teaspoon celery seeds

Directions:
1. Massage the olive oil, vinegar, salt, black pepper, shallot powder, cayenne pepper, garlic powder, and cumin into the cubed steak, ensuring to coat each piece evenly.
2. Allow to marinate for a minimum of 3 hours.
3. Insert the Crisper Basket and close the hood. Select AIR CRISP, set the temperature to 365ºF, and set the time to 12 minutes. Select START/STOP to begin preheating.
4. Put the beef cubes in the Crisper Basket. Close the hood and AIR CRISP for 12 minutes.
5. When the steak is cooked through, place it in a bowl.
6. Wipe the grease from the basket and pour in the vegetables. Season them with basil and celery seeds.
7. Increase the temperature of the grill to 400ºF and AIR CRISP for 5 to 6 minutes. When the vegetables are hot, serve them with the steak.

Teriyaki Pork And Mushroom Rolls
Servings: 6
Cooking Time: 8 Minutes
Ingredients:
- 4 tablespoons brown sugar
- 4 tablespoons mirin
- 4 tablespoons soy sauce
- 1 teaspoon almond flour
- 2-inch ginger, chopped
- 6 pork belly slices
- 6 ounces Enoki mushrooms

Directions:
1. Mix the brown sugar, mirin, soy sauce, almond flour, and ginger together until brown sugar dissolves.
2. Take pork belly slices and wrap around a bundle of mushrooms. Brush each roll with teriyaki sauce. Chill for half an hour.
3. Insert the Crisper Basket and close the hood. Select AIR CRISP, set the temperature to 350ºF, and set the time to 8 minutes. Select START/STOP to begin preheating.
4. Add marinated pork rolls to the basket.
5. Close the hood and AIR CRISP for 8 minutes. Flip the rolls halfway through.
6. Serve immediately.

Char Siew

Servings: 4 To 6
Cooking Time: 20 Minutes
Ingredients:
- 1 strip of pork shoulder butt with a good amount of fat marbling
- Olive oil, for brushing the pan
- Marinade:
- 1 teaspoon sesame oil
- 4 tablespoons raw honey
- 1 teaspoon low-sodium dark soy sauce
- 1 teaspoon light soy sauce
- 1 tablespoon rose wine
- 2 tablespoons Hoisin sauce

Directions:
1. Combine all the marinade ingredients together in a Ziploc bag. Put pork in bag, making sure all sections of pork strip are engulfed in the marinade. Chill for 3 to 24 hours.
2. Take out the strip 30 minutes before planning to roast.
3. Select ROAST, set the temperature to 350ºF, and set the time to 20 minutes. Select START/STOP to begin preheating.
4. Put foil on the pot and brush with olive oil. Put marinated pork strip onto prepared pot.
5. Close the hood and ROAST for 20 minutes.
6. Glaze with marinade every 5 to 10 minutes.
7. Remove strip and leave to cool a few minutes before slicing.
8. Serve immediately.

Smoked Beef

Servings: 8
Cooking Time: 45 Minutes
Ingredients:
- 2 pounds roast beef, at room temperature
- 2 tablespoons extra-virgin olive oil
- 1 teaspoon sea salt flakes
- 1 teaspoon ground black pepper
- 1 teaspoon smoked paprika
- Few dashes of liquid smoke
- 2 jalapeño peppers, thinly sliced

Directions:
1. Select ROAST, set the temperature to 330ºF, and set the time to 45 minutes. Select START/STOP to begin preheating.
2. With kitchen towels, pat the beef dry.
3. Massage the extra-virgin olive oil, salt, black pepper, and paprika into the meat. Cover with liquid smoke.
4. Put the beef in the pot. Close the hood and ROAST for 30 minutes. Flip the roast over and allow to roast for another 15 minutes.
5. When cooked through, serve topped with sliced jalapeños.

Coconut Breaded Shrimp

Servings: 4
Cooking Time: 15 Minutes
Ingredients:
- ½ cup all-purpose flour
- 2 teaspoons freshly ground black pepper
- ½ teaspoon sea salt
- 2 large eggs
- ¾ cup unsweetened coconut flakes
- ¼ cup panko bread crumbs
- 24 peeled, deveined shrimp
- Nonstick cooking spray
- Sweet chili sauce, for serving

Directions:
1. Insert the Crisper Basket and close the hood. Select AIR CRISP, set the temperature to 400ºF, and set the time to 8 minutes. Select START/STOP to begin preheating.
2. While the unit is preheating, in a medium shallow bowl, mix together the flour, black pepper, and salt. In a second medium shallow bowl, whisk the eggs. In a third, combine the coconut flakes and bread crumbs.
3. Dredge each shrimp in the flour mixture, then in the egg. Press each shrimp into the coconut mixture on both sides, leaving the tail uncoated.
4. When the unit beeps to signify it has preheated, place half of the shrimp into the basket and coat them with the cooking spray. Close the hood and AIR CRISP for 7 minutes.
5. Remove the cooked shrimp and add the remaining uncooked shrimp to the basket. Spray them with the cooking spray, close the hood, and AIR CRISP for 7 minutes.
6. Serve with sweet chili sauce.

Grilled Kalbi Beef Short Ribs

Servings: 4
Cooking Time: 10 Minutes
Ingredients:
- ½ cup soy sauce
- ¼ cup water
- ½ cup light brown sugar, packed
- ¼ cup honey
- 2 tablespoons sesame oil
- ½ teaspoon onion powder
- 1 teaspoon garlic powder
- 1 teaspoon peeled minced fresh ginger
- 3 pounds short ribs
- 1 scallion, both white and green parts, sliced, for garnish
- Sesame seeds, for garnish

Directions:
1. In a large bowl, combine the soy sauce, water, brown sugar, honey, sesame oil, onion powder, garlic powder, and minced ginger until the sugar is dissolved. Place the short ribs in the bowl and massage the marinade into the meat. Set aside to marinate for at least 30 minutes. If marinating for longer, cover and refrigerate.
2. Insert the Grill Grate and close the hood. Select GRILL, set the temperature to HI, and set the time to 10 minutes. Select START/STOP to begin preheating.
3. When the unit beeps to signify it has preheated, place the short ribs on the Grill Grate. Close the hood and cook for 5 minutes.
4. After 5 minutes, open the hood and flip the short ribs. Close the hood and cook for 5 minutes more.
5. When cooking is complete, remove the short ribs from the grill and garnish with the scallions and sesame seeds. Serve.

Goat Cheese Shrimp

Servings: 2
Cooking Time: 7 To 8 Minutes
Ingredients:
- 1 pound shrimp, deveined
- 1½ tablespoons olive oil
- 1½ tablespoons balsamic vinegar
- 1 tablespoon coconut aminos
- ½ tablespoon fresh parsley, roughly chopped
- Sea salt flakes, to taste
- 1 teaspoon Dijon mustard
- ½ teaspoon smoked cayenne pepper
- ½ teaspoon garlic powder
- Salt and ground black peppercorns, to taste
- 1 cup shredded goat cheese

Directions:
1. Insert the Crisper Basket and close the hood. Select AIR CRISP, set the temperature to 385ºF, and set the time to 8 minutes. Select START/STOP to begin preheating.
2. Except for the cheese, stir together all the ingredients in a large bowl until the shrimp are evenly coated.
3. Arrange the shrimp in the Crisper Basket. Close the hood and AIR CRISP for 7 to 8 minutes, shaking the basket halfway through, or until the shrimp are pink and cooked through.
4. Serve the shrimp with the shredded goat cheese sprinkled on top.

Cheesy Jalapeño Popper Burgers

Servings: 4
Cooking Time: 9 Minutes
Ingredients:
- 2 jalapeño peppers, seeded, stemmed, and minced
- ½ cup shredded Cheddar cheese
- 4 ounces cream cheese, at room temperature
- 4 slices bacon, cooked and crumbled
- 2 pounds ground beef
- ½ teaspoon chili powder
- ¼ teaspoon paprika
- ¼ teaspoon freshly ground black pepper
- 4 hamburger buns
- 4 slices pepper Jack cheese
- Lettuce, sliced tomato, and sliced red onion, for topping (optional)

Directions:
1. Insert the Grill Grate and close the hood. Select GRILL, set the temperature to HIGH, and set the time to 9 minutes. Select START/STOP to begin preheating.
2. In a medium bowl, combine the peppers, Cheddar cheese, cream cheese, and bacon until well combined.
3. Form the ground beef into 8¼-inch-thick patties. Spoon some of the filling mixture onto four of the patties, then place a second patty on top of each to make four burgers. Use your fingers to pinch the edges of the patties together to seal in the filling. Reshape the patties with your hands as needed.
4. Combine the chili powder, paprika, and pepper in a small bowl. Sprinkle the mixture onto both sides of the burgers.
5. When the units beeps to signify it has preheated, place the burgers on the Grill Grate. Close the hood and GRILL

for 4 minutes without flipping. Cooking is complete when the internal temperature of the beef reaches at least 145ºF on a food thermometer. If needed, GRILL for up to 5 more minutes.
6. Place the burgers on the hamburger buns and top with pepper Jack cheese. Add lettuce, tomato, and red onion, if desired.

Filet Mignon With Blue Cheese Butter

Servings: 4
Cooking Time: 10 Minutes
Ingredients:
- 4 garlic cloves, minced
- 4 tablespoons (½ stick) unsalted butter
- 3 tablespoons blue cheese crumbles
- 4 (6-ounce) filet mignon steaks
- Avocado oil

Directions:
1. Plug the thermometer into the unit. Insert the Grill Grate and close the hood. Select GRILL, set the temperature to HI, then select PRESET. Use the arrows to the right to select BEEF, then choose MED (6) or desired doneness. Insert the Smart Thermometer into the thickest part of one of the steaks. Select START/STOP to begin preheating.
2. While the unit is preheating, in a small bowl, combine the garlic, butter, and blue cheese. Mix well to form a buttery paste.
3. Drizzle the steaks with avocado oil on both sides.
4. When the unit beeps to signify it has preheated, place the filets mignons on the Grill Grate. Close the hood to begin cooking.
5. When the Foodi™ Grill tells you to, flip the steaks, then add 1 tablespoon of the blue cheese butter on top of each steak. Close the hood and continue cooking until the Smart Thermometer indicates the desired internal temperature has been reached.
6. When cooking is complete, remove the steaks from the grill. Let them rest for about 5 minutes before serving.
7. Add your favorite seasonings, like fresh parsley, rosemary, thyme, and garlic, and you'll have a flavorful butter that's ready for you anytime!

Bacon Burger Meatballs

Servings: 4
Cooking Time: 20 Minutes
Ingredients:
- 1 white onion, diced
- 1 pound thick-cut bacon (12 to 16 slices), cooked and crumbled
- 8 ounces cream cheese, at room temperature
- 4 tablespoons minced garlic
- ¼ cup ketchup
- ¼ cup yellow mustard
- ¼ cup gluten-free Worcestershire sauce
- 3 eggs
- 2 pounds ground beef

Directions:
1. In a large bowl, mix together the onion, bacon crumbles, cream cheese, garlic, ketchup, mustard, Worcestershire sauce, and eggs. Add the ground beef and, using your hands, mix the ingredients together until just combined, being

careful to not overmix. Form the mixture into 1½- to 2-inch meatballs. This should make 20 to 22 meatballs.

2. Insert the Grill Grate and close the hood. Select GRILL, set the temperature to MED, and set the time to 20 minutes. Select START/STOP to begin preheating.

3. When the unit beeps to signify it has preheated, place the meatballs on the Grill Grate. Close the hood and cook for 10 minutes.

4. After 10 minutes, open the hood and flip the meatballs. Close the hood and cook for 10 minutes more.

5. When cooking is complete, remove the meatballs from the grill and serve.

Vegetable And Fish Tacos

Servings: 4
Cooking Time: 9 To 12 Minutes
Ingredients:
- 1 pound white fish fillets
- 2 teaspoons olive oil
- 3 tablespoons freshly squeezed lemon juice, divided
- 1½ cups chopped red cabbage
- 1 large carrot, grated
- ½ cup low-sodium salsa
- ⅓ cup low-fat Greek yogurt
- 4 soft low-sodium whole-wheat tortillas

Directions:
1. Insert the Crisper Basket and close the hood. Select AIR CRISP, set the temperature to 400ºF, and set the time to 12 minutes. Select START/STOP to begin preheating.

2. Brush the fish with the olive oil and sprinkle with 1 tablespoon of lemon juice. Close the hood and AIR CRISP for 9 to 12 minutes, or until the fish just flakes when tested with a fork.

3. Meanwhile, in a medium bowl, stir together the remaining 2 tablespoons of lemon juice, the red cabbage, carrot, salsa, and yogurt.

4. When the fish is cooked, remove it from the Crisper Basket and break it up into large pieces.

5. Offer the fish, tortillas, and the cabbage mixture, and let each person assemble a taco.

6. Serve immediately.

Garlic Scallops

Servings: 4
Cooking Time: 10 To 15 Minutes
Ingredients:
- 2 teaspoons olive oil
- 1 packet dry zesty Italian dressing mix
- 1 teaspoon minced garlic
- 16 ounces small scallops, patted dry
- Cooking spray

Directions:
1. Insert the Crisper Basket and close the hood. Select AIR CRISP, set the temperature to 400ºF, and set the time to 15 minutes. Select START/STOP to begin preheating.

2. Spray the Crisper Basket lightly with cooking spray.

3. In a large zip-top plastic bag, combine the olive oil, Italian dressing mix, and garlic.

4. Add the scallops, seal the zip-top bag, and coat the scallops in the seasoning mixture.

5. Place the scallops in the Crisper Basket and lightly spray with cooking spray.

6. Close the hood and AIR CRISP for 5 minutes, shake the basket, and AIR CRISP for 5 to 10 more minutes, or until the scallops reach an internal temperature of 120ºF.

7. Serve immediately.

Pork Spareribs With Peanut Sauce

Servings: 6
Cooking Time: 30 Minutes
Ingredients:
- 2 (2- to 3-pound) racks St. Louis–style spareribs
- Sea salt
- ½ cup crunchy peanut butter
- 1 tablespoon rice vinegar
- 2 tablespoons hoisin sauce
- 1 tablespoon honey
- 2 tablespoons soy sauce
- 1 teaspoon garlic powder

Directions:
1. Plug the thermometer into the unit. Insert the Grill Grate and close the hood. Select GRILL, set the temperature to MED, and select PRESET. Use the arrows to the right to select PORK. The unit will default to WELL to cook the pork to a safe temperature. Insert the Smart Thermometer into the thickest part of the meat between two bones, making sure it does not touch bone. Select START/STOP to begin preheating.

2. When the unit beeps to signify it has preheated, place the racks of ribs on the Grill Grate. Close the hood to begin cooking.

3. When the Foodi™ Grill indicates it's time to flip, open the hood and flip the racks. Then close the hood to continue cooking.

4. While the ribs are cooking, in a small bowl, combine the peanut butter, vinegar, hoisin sauce, honey, soy sauce, and garlic powder and mix until well blended.

5. When cooking is complete, the Smart Thermometer will indicate that the desired internal temperature has been reached. Open the hood and remove the ribs. Either pour the sauce over the ribs or divide the sauce between individual bowls for dipping. Serve.

Roasted Cod With Sesame Seeds

Servings:1
Cooking Time: 7 To 9 Minutes
Ingredients:
- 1 tablespoon reduced-sodium soy sauce
- 2 teaspoons honey
- Cooking spray
- 6 ounces fresh cod fillet
- 1 teaspoon sesame seeds

Directions:
1. Insert the Crisper Basket and close the hood. Select ROAST, set the temperature to 360ºF, and set the time to 10 minutes. Select START/STOP to begin preheating.

2. In a small bowl, combine the soy sauce and honey.

3. Spray the Crisper Basket with cooking spray, then place the cod in the basket, brush with the soy mixture, and sprinkle sesame seeds on top.

4. Close the hood and ROAST for 7 to 9 minutes, or until opaque.

5. Remove the fish and allow to cool on a wire rack for 5 minutes before serving.

Citrus Pork Loin Roast

Servings: 8
Cooking Time: 45 Minutes
Ingredients:
- 1 tablespoon lime juice
- 1 tablespoon orange marmalade
- 1 teaspoon coarse brown mustard
- 1 teaspoon curry powder
- 1 teaspoon dried lemongrass
- 2 pound boneless pork loin roast
- Salt and ground black pepper, to taste
- Cooking spray

Directions:
1. Insert the Crisper Basket and close the hood. Select AIR CRISP, set the temperature to 360°F, and set the time to 45 minutes. Select START/STOP to begin preheating.
2. Mix the lime juice, marmalade, mustard, curry powder, and lemongrass.
3. Rub mixture all over the surface of the pork loin. Season with salt and pepper.
4. Spray the Crisper Basket with cooking spray and place pork roast diagonally in the basket.
5. Close the hood and AIR CRISP for 45 minutes, until the internal temperature reaches at least 145°F.
6. Wrap roast in foil and let rest for 10 minutes before slicing.
7. Serve immediately.

Easy Beef Schnitzel

Servings: 1
Cooking Time: 12 Minutes
Ingredients:
- ½ cup friendly bread crumbs
- 2 tablespoons olive oil
- Pepper and salt, to taste
- 1 egg, beaten
- 1 thin beef schnitzel

Directions:
1. Insert the Crisper Basket and close the hood. Select AIR CRISP, set the temperature to 350°F, and set the time to 12 minutes. Select START/STOP to begin preheating.
2. In a shallow dish, combine the bread crumbs, oil, pepper, and salt.
3. In a second shallow dish, place the beaten egg.
4. Dredge the schnitzel in the egg before rolling it in the bread crumbs.
5. Put the coated schnitzel in the Crisper Basket. Close the hood and AIR CRISP for 12 minutes. Flip the schnitzel halfway through.
6. Serve immediately.

Breaded Scallops

Servings: 4
Cooking Time: 6 To 8 Minutes
Ingredients:
- 1 egg
- 3 tablespoons flour
- 1 cup bread crumbs
- 1 pound fresh scallops
- 2 tablespoons olive oil
- Salt and black pepper, to taste

Directions:
1. Insert the Crisper Basket and close the hood. Select AIR CRISP, set the temperature to 360°F, and set the time to 8 minutes. Select START/STOP to begin preheating.
2. In a bowl, lightly beat the egg. Place the flour and bread crumbs into separate shallow dishes.
3. Dredge the scallops in the flour and shake off any excess. Dip the flour-coated scallops in the beaten egg and roll in the bread crumbs.
4. Brush the scallops generously with olive oil and season with salt and pepper, to taste.
5. Arrange the scallops in the Crisper Basket. Close the hood and AIR CRISP for 6 to 8 minutes, or until the scallops are firm and reach an internal temperature of just 145°F on a meat thermometer. Shake the basket halfway through the cooking time.
6. Let the scallops cool for 5 minutes and serve.

Smoky Paprika Pork And Vegetable Kabobs

Servings: 4
Cooking Time: 15 Minutes
Ingredients:
- 1 pound pork tenderloin, cubed
- 1 teaspoon smoked paprika
- Salt and ground black pepper, to taste
- 1 green bell pepper, cut into chunks
- 1 zucchini, cut into chunks
- 1 red onion, sliced
- 1 tablespoon oregano
- Cooking spray

Directions:
1. Spritz the Crisper Basket with cooking spray.
2. Insert the Crisper Basket and close the hood. Select AIR CRISP, set the temperature to 350°F, and set the time to 15 minutes. Select START/STOP to begin preheating.
3. Add the pork to a bowl and season with the smoked paprika, salt and black pepper. Thread the seasoned pork cubes and vegetables alternately onto the soaked skewers.
4. Arrange the skewers in the prepared Crisper Basket and spray with cooking spray.
5. Close the hood and AIR CRISP for 15 minutes, or until the pork is well browned and the vegetables are tender, flipping once halfway through.
6. Transfer the skewers to the serving dishes and sprinkle with oregano. Serve hot.

Coconut Chili Fish Curry

Servings: 4
Cooking Time: 20 To 22 Minutes
Ingredients:
- 2 tablespoons sunflower oil, divided
- 1 pound fish, chopped
- 1 ripe tomato, pureéd
- 2 red chilies, chopped
- 1 shallot, minced
- 1 garlic clove, minced
- 1 cup coconut milk
- 1 tablespoon coriander powder
- 1 teaspoon red curry paste
- ½ teaspoon fenugreek seeds

- Salt and white pepper, to taste

Directions:

1. Insert the Crisper Basket and close the hood. Select AIR CRISP, set the temperature to 380ºF, and set the time to 10 minutes. Select START/STOP to begin preheating.
2. Coat the Crisper Basket with 1 tablespoon of sunflower oil.
3. Place the fish in the basket. Close the hood and AIR CRISP for 10 minutes. Flip the fish halfway through the cooking time.
4. When done, transfer the cooked fish to a baking pan greased with the remaining 1 tablespoon of sunflower oil. Stir in the remaining ingredients and return to the grill.
5. Reduce the temperature to 350ºF and AIR CRISP for another 10 to 12 minutes until heated through.
6. Cool for 5 to 8 minutes before serving.

Baby Back Ribs In Gochujang Marinade

Servings: 4
Cooking Time: 22 Minutes

Ingredients:

- ¼ cup gochujang paste
- ¼ cup soy sauce
- ¼ cup freshly squeezed orange juice
- 2 tablespoons apple cider vinegar
- 2 tablespoons sesame oil
- 6 garlic cloves, minced
- 1½ tablespoons brown sugar
- 1 tablespoon grated fresh ginger
- 1 teaspoon salt
- 4 baby back ribs

Directions:

1. In a medium bowl, add the gochujang paste, soy sauce, orange juice, vinegar, oil, garlic, sugar, ginger, and salt, and stir to combine.
2. Place the baby back ribs on a baking sheet and coat all sides with the sauce. Cover with aluminum foil and refrigerate for 6 hours.
3. Insert the Grill Grate and close the hood. Select GRILL, set the temperature to MEDIUM, and set the time to 22 minutes. Select START/STOP to begin preheating.
4. When the unit beeps to signify it has preheated, place the ribs on the Grill Grate. Close the hood and GRILL for 11 minutes. After 11 minutes, flip the ribs, close the hood, and GRILL for an additional 11 minutes.
5. When cooking is complete, serve immediately.

Chimichurri Skirt Steak

Servings: 6 To 8
Cooking Time: 15 Minutes

Ingredients:

- 1 cup finely chopped fresh cilantro
- 1 cup finely chopped fresh parsley
- 1 shallot, finely chopped
- 3 garlic cloves, minced
- 2 teaspoons red wine vinegar
- ½ cup extra-virgin olive oil
- 2 (2-pound) skirt steaks
- Salt

Directions:

1. Plug the thermometer into the unit. Insert the Grill Grate and close the hood. Select GRILL, set the temperature to HI, then select PRESET. Use the arrows to the right to select BEEF, then choose MED (6) or desired doneness. Insert the Smart Thermometer into the thickest part of one of the steaks. Select START/STOP to begin preheating.
2. While the unit is preheating, in a small bowl, combine the cilantro, parsley, shallot, garlic, red wine vinegar, and olive oil. Mix well and set aside.
3. When the unit beeps to signify it has preheated, season the steaks with salt, then place them on the Grill Grate. Close the hood to begin cooking. The Foodi™ Grill will tell you when to flip the steak and when the desired internal temperature has been reached.
4. When cooking is complete, remove the steaks. Let them rest for 10 minutes before slicing against the grain. Spoon the chimichurri sauce over the top and serve.

Lemony Shrimp And Zucchini

Servings: 4
Cooking Time: 7 To 8 Minutes

Ingredients:

- 1¼ pounds extra-large raw shrimp, peeled and deveined
- 2 medium zucchini, halved lengthwise and cut into ½-inch-thick slices
- 1½ tablespoons olive oil
- ½ teaspoon garlic salt
- 1½ teaspoons dried oregano
- ⅛ teaspoon crushed red pepper flakes (optional)
- Juice of ½ lemon
- 1 tablespoon chopped fresh mint
- 1 tablespoon chopped fresh dill

Directions:

1. Insert the Crisper Basket and close the hood. Select AIR CRISP, set the temperature to 350ºF, and set the time to 8 minutes. Select START/STOP to begin preheating.
2. In a large bowl, combine the shrimp, zucchini, oil, garlic salt, oregano, and pepper flakes (if using) and toss to coat.
3. Working in batches, arrange a single layer of the shrimp and zucchini in the Crisper Basket. Close the hood and AIR CRISP for 7 to 8 minutes, shaking the basket halfway, until the zucchini is golden and the shrimp are cooked through.
4. Transfer to a serving dish and tent with foil while you AIR CRISP the remaining shrimp and zucchini.
5. Top with the lemon juice, mint, and dill and serve.

Crackling Pork Roast

Servings: 8
Cooking Time: 1 Hour 30 Minutes

Ingredients:

- 1 (3- to 4-pound) boneless pork shoulder, rind on
- Kosher salt

Directions:

1. Pat the roast dry with a paper towel. Using a sharp knife, score the rind, creating a diamond pattern on top. Season generously with salt. Place it in the refrigerator, uncovered, overnight to brine.
2. Plug the thermometer into the unit. Insert the Cooking Pot and close the hood. Select ROAST, set the temperature to 350ºF, then select PRESET. Use the arrows to the right to select PORK. The unit will default to WELL to cook pork to a safe temperature. Insert the Smart Thermometer into the

thickest part of the meat. Select START/STOP to begin preheating.

3. When the unit beeps to signify it has preheated, place the roast in the Cooking Pot. Close the hood to begin cooking.

4. When cooking is complete, the Smart Thermometer will indicate that the desired temperature has been reached. Remove the pork and let it rest for 10 minutes before slicing.

Grilled Salmon In Lemony Sriracha Glaze

Servings: 4
Cooking Time: 8 Minutes
Ingredients:

- 1 cup sriracha
- Juice of 2 lemons
- ¼ cup honey
- 4 skinless salmon fillets
- Chives, chopped, for garnish

Directions:

1. Place the sriracha, lemon juice, and honey in a large resealable plastic bag or container. Add the salmon fillets and coat evenly. Refrigerate for 30 minutes.

2. Insert the Grill Grate and close the hood. Select GRILL, set the temperature to MAX, and set the time to 8 minutes. Select START/STOP to begin preheating.

3. When the unit beeps to signify it has preheated, place the fillets on the Grill Grate, gently pressing them down to maximize grill marks. Close the hood and GRILL for 6 minutes. (There is no need to flip the fish during cooking.)

4. After 6 minutes, check the fillets for doneness; the internal temperature should read at least 140ºF on a food thermometer. If necessary, close the hood and continue cooking up to 2 minutes more.

5. When cooking is complete, remove the fillets from the grill. Plate, and garnish with the chives.

Pork Chops With Creamy Mushroom Sauce

Servings: 6
Cooking Time: 10 Minutes
Ingredients:

- 1 cup heavy (whipping) cream
- ½ cup chicken broth
- 1 tablespoon cornstarch
- 1 teaspoon garlic powder
- 6 (6-ounce) boneless pork chops
- 8 ounces mushrooms, sliced

Directions:

1. Insert the Grill Grate and close the hood. Select GRILL, set the temperature to HI, and set the time to 10 minutes. Select START/STOP to begin preheating.

2. While the unit is preheating, in a medium bowl, whisk together the heavy cream, chicken broth, cornstarch, and garlic powder.

3. When the unit beeps to signify it has preheated, place the pork chops on the Grill Grate. Close the hood and grill for 5 minutes.

4. After 5 minutes, open the hood and use grill mitts to remove the Grill Grate and the chops. Pour the cream mixture into the Cooking Pot. Put the Grill Grate back into

the unit and flip the pork chops. Close the hood and cook for 5 minutes more.

5. When cooking is complete, remove the pork chops from the grill. Use grill mitts to remove the Grill Grate from the unit and stir the cream mixture. Add the sliced mushrooms, close the hood, and let sit for 5 minutes. Pour the creamy mushroom sauce over the pork chops and serve.

Swedish Beef Meatballs

Servings: 8
Cooking Time: 12 Minutes
Ingredients:

- 1 pound ground beef
- 1 egg, beaten
- 2 carrots, shredded
- 2 bread slices, crumbled
- 1 small onion, minced
- ½ teaspoons garlic salt
- Pepper and salt, to taste
- 1 cup tomato sauce
- 2 cups pasta sauce

Directions:

1. Insert the Crisper Basket and close the hood. Select AIR CRISP, set the temperature to 400ºF, and set the time to 7 minutes. Select START/STOP to begin preheating.

2. In a bowl, combine the ground beef, egg, carrots, crumbled bread, onion, garlic salt, pepper and salt.

3. Divide the mixture into equal amounts and shape each one into a small meatball.

4. Put them in the Crisper Basket. Close the hood and AIR CRISP for 7 minutes.

5. Transfer the meatballs to an oven-safe dish and top with the tomato sauce and pasta sauce.

6. Set the dish into the pot and allow to AIR CRISP at 320ºF for 5 more minutes. Serve hot.

Rack Of Lamb Chops With Rosemary

Servings: 2
Cooking Time: 14 Minutes
Ingredients:

- 3 tablespoons extra-virgin olive oil
- 1 garlic clove, minced
- 1 tablespoon fresh rosemary, chopped
- ½ rack lamb
- Sea salt, to taste
- Freshly ground black pepper, to taste

Directions:

1. Combine the oil, garlic, and rosemary in a large bowl. Season the rack of lamb with the salt and pepper, then place the lamb in the bowl, using tongs to turn and coat fully in the oil mixture. Cover and refrigerate for 2 hours.

2. Insert the Grill Grate and close the hood. Select GRILL, set the temperature to HIGH, and set the time to 14 minutes. Select START/STOP to begin preheating.

3. When the unit beeps to signify it has preheated, place the lamb on the Grill Grate. Close the hood and GRILL for 6 minutes. After 6 minutes, flip the lamb and continue grilling for 6 minutes more.

4. Cooking is complete when the internal temperature of the lamb reaches 145ºF on a food thermometer. If needed, GRILL for up to 2 minutes more.

Pepperoni And Bell Pepper Pockets

Servings: 4
Cooking Time: 8 Minutes
Ingredients:

- 4 bread slices, 1-inch thick
- Olive oil, for misting
- 24 slices pepperoni
- 1 ounce roasted red peppers, drained and patted dry
- 1 ounce Pepper Jack cheese, cut into 4 slices

Directions:

1. Insert the Crisper Basket and close the hood. Select AIR CRISP, set the temperature to 360ºF, and set the time to 8 minutes. Select START/STOP to begin preheating.
2. Spray both sides of bread slices with olive oil.
3. Stand slices upright and cut a deep slit in the top to create a pocket (almost to the bottom crust, but not all the way through).
4. Stuff each bread pocket with 6 slices of pepperoni, a large strip of roasted red pepper, and a slice of cheese.
5. Put bread pockets in Crisper Basket, standing up. Close the hood and AIR CRISP for 8 minutes, until filling is heated through and bread is lightly browned.
6. Serve hot.

Crab Ratatouille With Eggplant And Tomatoes

Servings: 4
Cooking Time: 11 To 14 Minutes
Ingredients:

- 1½ cups peeled and cubed eggplant
- 2 large tomatoes, chopped
- 1 red bell pepper, chopped
- 1 onion, chopped
- 1 tablespoon olive oil
- ½ teaspoon dried basil
- ½ teaspoon dried thyme
- Pinch salt
- Freshly ground black pepper, to taste
- 1½ cups cooked crab meat

Directions:

1. Select ROAST, set the temperature to 400ºF., and set the time to 15 minutes. Select START/STOP to begin preheating.
2. In the pot, stir together the eggplant, tomatoes, bell pepper, onion, olive oil, basil and thyme. Season with salt and pepper.
3. Close the hood and ROAST for 9 minutes.
4. Add the crab meat and stir well and roast for another 2 to 5 minutes, or until the vegetables are softened and the ratatouille is bubbling.
5. Serve warm.

Mozzarella Meatball Sandwiches With Basil

Servings: 4
Cooking Time: 10 Minutes
Ingredients:

- 12 frozen meatballs
- 8 slices Mozzarella cheese
- 4 sub rolls, halved lengthwise
- ½ cup marinara sauce, warmed
- 12 fresh basil leaves

Directions:

1. Insert the Crisper Basket and close the hood. Select AIR CRISP, set the temperature to 350ºF, and set the time to 10 minutes. Select START/STOP to begin preheating.
2. When the unit beeps to signify it has preheated, place the meatballs in the basket. Close the hood and AIR CRISP for 5 minutes.
3. After 5 minutes, shake the basket of meatballs. Place the basket back in the unit and close the hood to resume cooking.
4. While the meatballs are cooking, place two slices of Mozzarella cheese on each sub roll. Use a spoon to spread the marinara sauce on top of the cheese slices. Press three leaves of basil into the sauce on each roll.
5. When cooking is complete, place three meatballs on each sub roll. Serve immediately.

Coffee-rubbed Steak

Servings: 4
Cooking Time: 10 Minutes
Ingredients:

- ¼ cup finely ground coffee
- 2 tablespoons chili powder
- 2 tablespoons paprika
- 1 tablespoon sea salt
- 1 teaspoon freshly ground black pepper
- 1 teaspoon garlic powder
- 1 teaspoon onion powder
- ¼ cup light brown sugar, packed
- 4 (1-inch-thick) New York strip steaks
- Avocado oil

Directions:

1. Plug the thermometer into the unit. Insert the Grill Grate and close the hood. Select GRILL, set the temperature to HI, then select PRESET. Use the arrows to the right to select BEEF, then choose MED (6) or desired doneness. Insert the Smart Thermometer into the thickest part of one of the steaks. Select START/STOP to begin preheating.
2. While the unit is preheating, in a small bowl, combine the coffee, chili powder, paprika, salt, pepper, garlic powder, onion powder, and brown sugar. Mix well.
3. On a large plate, drizzle the steaks with avocado oil on both sides, and generously rub and pat down the coffee mixture on both sides of the steaks.
4. When the unit beeps to signify it has preheated, place the steaks on the Grill Grate. Close the hood to begin cooking. The Foodi™ Grill will tell you when to flip the steak and when the desired internal temperature has been reached.
5. When cooking is complete, remove the steaks from the grill. Let them rest for about 5 minutes before slicing against the grain, then serve.

Homemade Teriyaki Pork Ribs

Servings: 4
Cooking Time: 30 Minutes
Ingredients:
- ¼ cup soy sauce
- ¼ cup honey
- 1 teaspoon garlic powder
- 1 teaspoon ground dried ginger
- 4 boneless country-style pork ribs
- Cooking spray

Directions:
1. Spritz the Crisper Basket with cooking spray.
2. Insert the Crisper Basket and close the hood. Select AIR CRISP, set the temperature to 350ºF, and set the time to 30 minutes. Select START/STOP to begin preheating.
3. Make the teriyaki sauce: combine the soy sauce, honey, garlic powder, and ginger in a bowl. Stir to mix well.
4. Brush the ribs with half of the teriyaki sauce, then arrange the ribs in the basket. Spritz with cooking spray. You may need to work in batches to avoid overcrowding.
5. Close the hood and AIR CRISP for 30 minutes or until the internal temperature of the ribs reaches at least 145ºF. Brush the ribs with remaining teriyaki sauce and flip halfway through.
6. Serve immediately.

Sausage Ratatouille

Servings: 4
Cooking Time: 25 Minutes
Ingredients:
- 4 pork sausages
- Ratatouille:
- 2 zucchinis, sliced
- 1 eggplant, sliced
- 15 ounces tomatoes, sliced
- 1 red bell pepper, sliced
- 1 medium red onion, sliced
- 1 cup canned butter beans, drained
- 1 tablespoon balsamic vinegar
- 2 garlic cloves, minced
- 1 red chili, chopped
- 2 tablespoons fresh thyme, chopped
- 2 tablespoons olive oil

Directions:
1. Insert the Crisper Basket and close the hood. Select AIR CRISP, set the temperature to 390ºF, and set the time to 10 minutes. Select START/STOP to begin preheating.
2. Place the sausages in the basket. Close the hood and AIR CRISP for 10 minutes or until the sausage is lightly browned. Flip the sausages halfway through.
3. Meanwhile, make the ratatouille: arrange the vegetable slices on the a baking pan alternatively, then add the remaining ingredients on top.
4. Transfer the sausage to a plate. Place the pan directly in the pot. Close the hood and BAKE for 15 minutes or until the vegetables are tender.
5. Serve the ratatouille with the sausage on top.

Potato And Prosciutto Salad

Servings: 8
Cooking Time: 7 Minutes

Ingredients:
- Salad:
- 4 pounds potatoes, boiled and cubed
- 15 slices prosciutto, diced
- 2 cups shredded Cheddar cheese
- Dressing:
- 15 ounces sour cream
- 2 tablespoons mayonnaise
- 1 teaspoon salt
- 1 teaspoon black pepper
- 1 teaspoon dried basil

Directions:
1. Select AIR CRISP, set the temperature to 350ºF, and set the time to 7 minutes. Select START/STOP to begin preheating.
2. Put the potatoes, prosciutto, and Cheddar in a baking pan. Place the pan directly in the pot. Close the hood and AIR CRISP for 7 minutes.
3. In a separate bowl, mix the sour cream, mayonnaise, salt, pepper, and basil using a whisk.
4. Coat the salad with the dressing and serve.

Italian Sausage And Peppers

Servings: 4
Cooking Time: 10 Minutes
Ingredients:
- 1 green bell pepper
- 1 large red onion
- 1 pound ground Italian sausage (not links)
- 1 tablespoon garlic, minced
- 2 tablespoons white wine vinegar

Directions:
1. Insert the Cooking Pot and close the hood. Select GRILL, set the temperature to HI, and set the time to 10 minutes. Select START/STOP to begin preheating.
2. While the unit is preheating, cut the bell pepper into strips and slice the red onion.
3. When the unit beeps to signify it has preheated, place the sausage, garlic, and vinegar in the Cooking Pot. Slowly break apart the sausage using a wooden spoon or a spatula. Close the hood and cook for 5 minutes.
4. After 5 minutes, open the hood and stir the sausage. Add the bell pepper and onion. Close the hood and cook for 5 minutes more.
5. When cooking is complete, stir the sausage, pepper, and onion again. Serve.

Apple-glazed Pork

Servings: 4
Cooking Time: 19 Minutes
Ingredients:
- 1 sliced apple
- 1 small onion, sliced
- 2 tablespoons apple cider vinegar, divided
- ½ teaspoon thyme
- ½ teaspoon rosemary
- ¼ teaspoon brown sugar
- 3 tablespoons olive oil, divided
- ¼ teaspoon smoked paprika
- 4 pork chops
- Salt and ground black pepper, to taste

Directions:
1. Select BAKE, set the temperature to 350ºF, and set the time to 4 minutes. Select START/STOP to begin preheating.
2. Combine the apple slices, onion, 1 tablespoon of vinegar, thyme, rosemary, brown sugar, and 2 tablespoons of olive oil in a baking pan. Stir to mix well.
3. Place the pan directly in the pot. Close the hood and BAKE for 4 minutes.
4. Meanwhile, combine the remaining vinegar and olive oil, and paprika in a large bowl. Sprinkle with salt and ground black pepper. Stir to mix well. Dredge the pork in the mixture and toss to coat well.
5. Remove the baking pan from the grill and put in the pork. Place the pan directly in the pot. Close the hood and AIR CRISP for 10 minutes to lightly brown the pork. Flip the pork chops halfway through.
6. Remove the pork from the grill and baste with baked apple mixture on both sides. Put the pork back to the grill and AIR CRISP for an additional 5 minutes. Flip halfway through.
7. Serve immediately.

Cajun-style Salmon Burgers

Servings: 4
Cooking Time: 10 To 15 Minutes
Ingredients:
- 4 cans pink salmon in water, any skin and bones removed, drained
- 2 eggs, beaten
- 1 cup whole-wheat bread crumbs
- 4 tablespoons light mayonnaise
- 2 teaspoons Cajun seasoning
- 2 teaspoons dry mustard
- 4 whole-wheat buns
- Cooking spray
Directions:
1. In a medium bowl, mix the salmon, egg, bread crumbs, mayonnaise, Cajun seasoning, and dry mustard. Cover with plastic wrap and refrigerate for 30 minutes.
2. Insert the Crisper Basket and close the hood. Select AIR CRISP, set the temperature to 360ºF, and set the time to 15 minutes. Select START/STOP to begin preheating.
3. Spray the Crisper Basket lightly with cooking spray.
4. Shape the mixture into four ½-inch-thick patties about the same size as the buns.
5. Place the salmon patties in the Crisper Basket in a single layer and lightly spray the tops with cooking spray. You may need to cook them in batches.
6. Close the hood and AIR CRISP for 6 to 8 minutes. Turn the patties over and lightly spray with cooking spray. AIR CRISP until crispy on the outside, for 4 to 7 more minutes.
7. Serve on whole-wheat buns.

Miso-glazed Cod With Bok Choy

Servings: 4
Cooking Time: 17 Minutes
Ingredients:
- 4 cod fillets
- ¼ cup miso
- 3 tablespoons brown sugar
- 1 teaspoon sesame oil, divided
- 1 tablespoon white wine or mirin

- 2 tablespoons soy sauce
- ¼ teaspoon red pepper flakes
- 1 pound baby bok choy, halved lengthwise
Directions:
1. Place the cod, miso, brown sugar, ¾ teaspoon of sesame oil, and white wine in a large resealable plastic bag or container. Move the fillets around to coat evenly with the marinade. Refrigerate for 30 minutes.
2. Insert the Grill Grate and close the hood. Select GRILL, set the temperature to MAX, and set the time to 8 minutes. Select START/STOP to begin preheating.
3. When the unit beeps to signify it has preheated, place the fillets on the Grill Grate. Gently press them down to maximize grill marks. Close the hood and GRILL for 8 minutes. (There is no need to flip the fish during grilling.)
4. While the cod grills, in a small bowl, whisk together the remaining ¼ teaspoon of sesame oil, soy sauce, and red pepper flakes. Brush the bok choy halves with the soy sauce mixture on all sides.
5. Remove the cod from the grill and set aside on a cutting board to rest. Tent with aluminum foil to keep warm.
6. Close the hood of the grill. Select GRILL, set the temperature to MAX, and set the time to 9 minutes. Select START/STOP to begin preheating to grill the bok choy.
7. When the unit beeps to signify it has preheated, place the bok choy on the Grill Grate, cut-side down. Close the hood and GRILL for 9 minutes. (There is no need to flip the bok choy during grilling.)
8. Remove the bok choy from the grill, plate with the cod, and serve.

Tuna And Cucumber Salad

Servings: 4
Cooking Time: 6 Minutes
Ingredients:
- 2 tablespoons rice wine vinegar
- ¼ teaspoon sea salt, plus additional for seasoning
- ½ teaspoon freshly ground black pepper, plus additional for seasoning
- 6 tablespoons extra-virgin olive oil
- 1½ pounds ahi tuna, cut into four strips
- 2 tablespoons sesame oil
- 1 bag baby greens
- ½ English cucumber, sliced
Directions:
1. Insert the Grill Grate, and close the hood. Select GRILL, set the temperature to MAX, and set the time to 6 minutes. Select START/STOP to begin preheating.
2. Meanwhile, in a small bowl, whisk together the rice vinegar, ¼ teaspoon of salt, and ½ teaspoon of pepper. Slowly pour in the oil while whisking, until the vinaigrette is fully combined.
3. Season the tuna with salt and pepper, and drizzle with the sesame oil.
4. When the unit beeps to signify it has preheated, place the tuna strips on the Grill Grate. Close the hood, and GRILL for 4 to 6 minutes. (There is no need to flip during cooking.)
5. While the tuna cooks, divide the baby greens and cucumber slices evenly among four plates or bowls.

6. When cooking is complete, top each salad with one tuna strip. Drizzle the vinaigrette over the top, and serve immediately.

Crispy Pork Tenderloin

Servings: 6
Cooking Time: 10 Minutes
Ingredients:
- 2 large egg whites
- 1½ tablespoons Dijon mustard
- 2 cups crushed pretzel crumbs
- 1½ pounds pork tenderloin, cut into ¼-pound sections
- Cooking spray

Directions:
1. Spritz the Crisper Basket with cooking spray.
2. Insert the Crisper Basket and close the hood. Select AIR CRISP, set the temperature to 350ºF, and set the time to 10 minutes. Select START/STOP to begin preheating.
3. Whisk the egg whites with Dijon mustard in a bowl until bubbly. Pour the pretzel crumbs in a separate bowl.
4. Dredge the pork tenderloin in the egg white mixture and press to coat. Shake the excess off and roll the tenderloin over the pretzel crumbs.
5. Arrange the well-coated pork tenderloin in batches in a single layer in the Crisper Basket and spritz with cooking spray.
6. Close the hood and AIR CRISP for 10 minutes or until the pork is golden brown and crispy. Flip the pork halfway through. Repeat with remaining pork sections.
7. Serve immediately.

Korean Bbq Beef

Servings: 4
Cooking Time: 5 Minutes
Ingredients:
- ⅓ cup soy sauce
- 2 tablespoons sesame oil
- 2½ tablespoons brown sugar
- 3 garlic cloves, minced
- ½ teaspoon freshly ground black pepper
- 1 pound rib eye steak, thinly sliced
- 2 scallions, thinly sliced, for garnish
- Toasted sesame seeds, for garnish

Directions:
1. In a small bowl, whisk together the soy sauce, sesame oil, brown sugar, garlic, and black pepper until fully combined.
2. Place the beef into a large shallow bowl, and pour the sauce over the slices. Cover and refrigerate for 1 hour.
3. Insert the Grill Grate and close the hood. Select GRILL, set the temperature to MEDIUM, and set the time to 5 minutes. Select START/STOP to begin preheating.
4. When the unit beeps to signify it has preheated, place the beef onto the Grill Grate. Close the hood and GRILL for 4 minutes without flipping.
5. After 4 minutes, check the steak for desired doneness, grilling for up to 1 minute more, if desired.
6. When cooking is complete, top with scallions and sesame seeds and serve immediately.

Stuffed-onion Burgers

Servings: 6

Cooking Time: 15 Minutes
Ingredients:
- 2 large red onions
- 1 teaspoon onion powder
- 1 teaspoon garlic powder
- 2 teaspoons sea salt
- 2 teaspoons freshly ground black pepper
- 4 tablespoons gluten-free Worcestershire sauce
- 2 pounds ground beef

Directions:
1. Cut both ends off the onions. Slice each onion crosswise into thirds and peel off the papery outer skin. Separate the outer two rings (keeping the pair together) from each third for a stable and firm onion ring wrapper.
2. Insert the Grill Grate and close the hood. Select GRILL, set the temperature to HI, and set the time to 15 minutes. Select START/STOP to begin preheating.
3. In a large bowl, combine the onion powder, garlic powder, salt, pepper, and Worcestershire sauce. Add the ground beef in chunks and loosely mix. Form the mixture into 6 equal-size patties. Stuff the burger patties into the onion rings and make a small indentation in the middle of each patty with your thumb.
4. When the unit beeps to signify it has preheated, place the patties on the Grill Grate. Close the hood and grill for 7 minutes, 30 seconds.
5. After 7 minutes, 30 seconds, open the hood and flip the burgers. Close the hood and cook for 7 minutes, 30 seconds more for medium-well burgers. If you prefer your burgers more well-done, continue cooking to your liking.
6. When cooking is complete, remove the burgers from the grill and serve.

Bacon-wrapped Sausage With Tomato Relish

Servings: 4
Cooking Time: 32 Minutes
Ingredients:
- 8 pork sausages
- 8 bacon strips
- Relish:
- 8 large tomatoes, chopped
- 1 small onion, peeled
- 1 clove garlic, peeled
- 1 tablespoon white wine vinegar
- 3 tablespoons chopped parsley
- 1 teaspoon smoked paprika
- 2 tablespoons sugar
- Salt and ground black pepper, to taste

Directions:
1. Purée the tomatoes, onion, and garlic in a food processor until well mixed and smooth.
2. Pour the purée in a saucepan and drizzle with white wine vinegar. Sprinkle with salt and ground black pepper. Simmer over medium heat for 10 minutes.
3. Add the parsley, paprika, and sugar to the saucepan and cook for 10 more minutes or until it has a thick consistency. Keep stirring during the cooking. Refrigerate for an hour to chill.

4. Insert the Crisper Basket and close the hood. Select AIR CRISP, set the temperature to 350ºF, and set the time to 12 minutes. Select START/STOP to begin preheating.
5. Wrap the sausage with bacon strips and secure with toothpicks, then place them in the basket.
6. Close the hood and AIR CRISP for 12 minutes or until the bacon is crispy and browned. Flip the bacon-wrapped sausage halfway through.
7. Transfer the bacon-wrapped sausage on a plate and baste with the relish or just serve with the relish alongside.

Honey-caramelized Pork Tenderloin

Servings: 4
Cooking Time: 15 To 20 Minutes
Ingredients:
- 2 tablespoons honey
- 1 tablespoon soy sauce
- ½ teaspoon garlic powder
- ½ teaspoon sea salt
- 1 pork tenderloin
Directions:
1. Insert the Grill Grate and close the hood. Select GRILL, set the temperature to MEDIUM, and set the time to 20 minutes. Select START/STOP to begin preheating.
2. Meanwhile, in a small bowl, combine the honey, soy sauce, garlic powder, and salt.
3. When the unit beeps to signify it has preheated, place the pork tenderloin on the Grill Grate. Baste all sides with the honey glaze. Close the hood and GRILL for 8 minutes. After 8 minutes, flip the pork tenderloin and baste with any remaining glaze. Close the hood and GRILL for 7 minutes more.
4. Cooking is complete when the internal temperature of the pork reaches 145ºF on a food thermometer. If needed, GRILL for up to 5 minutes more.
5. Remove the pork, and set it on a cutting board to rest for 5 minutes. Slice and serve.

Fast Lamb Satay

Servings: 2
Cooking Time: 8 Minutes
Ingredients:
- ¼ teaspoon cumin
- 1 teaspoon ginger
- ½ teaspoons nutmeg
- Salt and ground black pepper, to taste
- 2 boneless lamb steaks
- Cooking spray
Directions:
1. Combine the cumin, ginger, nutmeg, salt and pepper in a bowl.
2. Cube the lamb steaks and massage the spice mixture into each one.
3. Leave to marinate for 10 minutes, then transfer onto metal skewers.
4. Insert the Crisper Basket and close the hood. Select AIR CRISP, set the temperature to 400ºF, and set the time to 8 minutes. Select START/STOP to begin preheating.
5. Place the skewers in the basket and spritz with cooking spray. Close the hood and AIR CRISP for 8 minutes.
6. Take care when removing them from the grill and serve.

Paprika Shrimp

Servings: 4
Cooking Time: 10 Minutes
Ingredients:
- 1 pound tiger shrimp
- 2 tablespoons olive oil
- ½ tablespoon old bay seasoning
- ¼ tablespoon smoked paprika
- ¼ teaspoon cayenne pepper
- A pinch of sea salt
Directions:
1. Insert the Crisper Basket and close the hood. Select AIR CRISP, set the temperature to 380ºF, and set the time to 10 minutes. Select START/STOP to begin preheating.
2. Toss all the ingredients in a large bowl until the shrimp are evenly coated.
3. Arrange the shrimp in the Crisper Basket. Close the hood and AIR CRISP for 10 minutes, shaking the basket halfway through, or until the shrimp are pink and cooked through.
4. Serve hot.

Ranch And Cheddar Pork Chops

Servings: 6
Cooking Time: 10 Minutes
Ingredients:
- 8 ounces cream cheese, at room temperature
- 1 tablespoon ranch seasoning mix
- ½ cup shredded cheddar cheese
- 6 (6-ounce) boneless pork chops
Directions:
1. Insert the Grill Grate and close the hood. Select GRILL, set the temperature to HI, and set the time to 10 minutes. Select START/STOP to begin preheating.
2. While the unit is preheating, in a small bowl, combine the cream cheese, ranch seasoning, and cheddar cheese.
3. When the unit beeps to signify it has preheated, place the pork chops on the Grill Grate. Close the hood and grill for 5 minutes.
4. After 5 minutes, open the hood and flip the chops. Then top each with the ranch-cheese mixture. Close the hood and cook for 5 minutes more.
5. When cooking is complete, remove the chops from the grill and serve.

Grilled Pork Banh Mi

Servings: 6
Cooking Time: 15 Minutes
Ingredients:
- 3 tablespoons light brown sugar, packed
- 1 tablespoon soy sauce
- 3 tablespoons minced garlic
- Juice of 2 limes
- 1 shallot, finely minced
- 2 pounds pork tenderloin, cut into 1-inch-thick slices
- 1 daikon radish, cut into thin strips
- 1 large carrot, cut into thin strips
- 3 tablespoons rice vinegar
- ½ teaspoon kosher salt
- 1 teaspoon granulated sugar
- 6 sandwich-size baguettes

- Mayonnaise
- 1 cucumber, thinly sliced
- Fresh cilantro
- 1 jalapeño, sliced

Directions:
1. In a large bowl, combine the brown sugar, soy sauce, garlic, lime juice, shallot, and pork tenderloin slices. Marinate for at least 30 minutes. If marinating for longer, cover and refrigerate.
2. Insert the Cooking Pot and close the hood. Select GRILL, set the temperature to HI, and set the time to 15 minutes. Select START/STOP to begin preheating.
3. While the unit is preheating, in a medium bowl, combine the daikon, carrot, rice vinegar, salt, and sugar.
4. When the unit beeps to signify it has preheated, place the pork in the Cooking Pot. Feel free to add a little bit of the marinade to the pot. Close the hood and cook for 8 minutes.
5. After 8 minutes, open the hood and stir the pork. Close the hood and cook for 7 minutes more.
6. When cooking is complete, slice open each baguette and spread mayonnaise on both sides. Add a layer each of pork, pickled daikon and carrot, cucumber, cilantro, and jalapeño slices and serve.

Garlic Shrimp With Parsley

Servings: 4
Cooking Time: 5 Minutes

Ingredients:
- 18 shrimp, shelled and deveined
- 2 garlic cloves, peeled and minced
- 2 tablespoons extra-virgin olive oil
- 2 tablespoons freshly squeezed lemon juice
- ½ cup fresh parsley, coarsely chopped
- 1 teaspoon onion powder
- 1 teaspoon lemon-pepper seasoning
- ½ teaspoon hot paprika
- ½ teaspoon salt
- ¼ teaspoon cumin powder

Directions:
1. Toss all the ingredients in a mixing bowl until the shrimp are well coated.
2. Cover and allow to marinate in the refrigerator for 30 minutes.
3. Insert the Crisper Basket and close the hood. Select AIR CRISP, set the temperature to 400ºF, and set the time to 5 minutes. Select START/STOP to begin preheating.
4. Arrange the shrimp in the Crisper Basket. Close the hood and AIR CRISP for 5 minutes, or until the shrimp are pink on the outside and opaque in the center.
5. Remove from the basket and serve warm.

Pulled Pork Sandwiches

Servings: 6 To 8
Cooking Time: 1 Hour 30 Minutes

Ingredients:
- 1 tablespoon onion powder
- 1 tablespoon garlic powder
- 1 tablespoon salt
- 1 teaspoon freshly ground black pepper
- 1 teaspoon ground cumin
- 1 teaspoon ground cayenne pepper

- 3 tablespoons light brown sugar, packed
- 1 tablespoon granulated sugar
- 3 to 4 pounds pork shoulder, cut into 3 or 4 equal pieces
- 3 tablespoons unsalted butter, sliced
- 3 tablespoons honey
- 4 tablespoons barbecue sauce
- Hamburger buns or sandwich bread

Directions:
1. Plug the thermometer into the unit. Insert the Grill Grate and close the hood. Select ROAST, set the temperature to 350°F, and set the time to 90 minutes. Select START/STOP to begin preheating.
2. While the unit is preheating, in a small bowl, combine the onion powder, garlic powder, salt, black pepper, cumin, cayenne pepper, brown sugar, and granulated sugar. Rub the mixture on all sides of the pork pieces. Insert the Smart Thermometer into the thickest part of the meat.
3. When the unit beeps to signify it has preheated, place the pork on the Grill Grate. Manually select the temperature setting to reach 165°F. Close the hood and cook for 45 minutes or until the Smart Thermometer indicates the temperature has been reached.
4. When cooking is complete, open the hood and remove the Smart Thermometer. Use grill mitts to remove the Grill Grate and pork shoulder. Place the pork pieces on top of a large piece of aluminum foil. Top with the butter slices and drizzle with the honey and barbecue sauce. Close the foil over the pork and crimp it to seal.
5. Place the foil-wrapped pork in the Cooking Pot. Carefully pierce the foil to reinsert the Smart Thermometer in the thickest part of the meat. Manually select the temperature setting to reach 200°F. Close the hood and cook for 45 minutes.
6. When cooking is complete, the Smart Thermometer will indicate that the desired temperature has been reached. Open the hood and use grill mitts to remove the foil-wrapped pork. Let the meat rest in the foil for 30 minutes. Once it has rested, shred the pork using two forks and place some meat on top of a bun, topped with more barbecue sauce, if desired. Serve.

Bacon-wrapped Stuffed Sausage

Servings: 4
Cooking Time: 15 Minutes

Ingredients:
- 1 pound ground Italian sausage (not links)
- 1 cup fresh spinach leaves
- ⅓ cup sun-dried tomatoes, drained
- ½ cup shredded provolone cheese
- 14 slices thin-sliced bacon

Directions:
1. Cut off the two corners (small cuts) of a gallon-size resealable plastic bag. (This makes the next part easier.) Place the sausage in the bag, then press the meat until it is evenly flat and fills the entire bag. Using scissors, cut the side seams of the bag, then peel back the top and flip the flattened sausage onto a sheet of parchment paper. Gently pull back and remove the plastic bag.
2. Layer the spinach leaves, sun-dried tomatoes, and provolone cheese evenly across the bottom half of the sausage. Lift up the end of the wax paper, rolling the sausage over the stuffing, and slowly peel back the wax

paper as you continue rolling, leaving the sausage roll on the last bit of wax paper.

3. Insert the Grill Grate and close the hood. Select GRILL, set the temperature to HI, and set the time to 15 minutes. Select START/STOP to begin preheating.

4. While the unit is preheating, on a new piece of wax paper, place 7 bacon slices side by side but not touching each other. Place another bacon slice across the 7 slices, weaving it over and under them, creating a basket-weave pattern. Repeat this with the remaining 6 bacon slices. Once the bacon is woven together, carefully place the sausage roll on the bottom portion of the bacon weave. Then, lifting the end of the wax paper under the bacon, roll it up tightly, until the bacon is wrapped around the stuffed sausage.

5. When the unit beeps to signify it has preheated, place the bacon-wrapped sausage roll on the Grill Grate. Close the hood and grill for 8 minutes.

6. After 8 minutes, open the hood and flip the sausage roll. Close the hood and cook for 7 minutes more.

7. When cooking is complete, open the hood and check the sausage roll. If you prefer your bacon crispier, continue cooking to your liking. Remove the sausage from the grill and serve.

Crispy Cod Cakes With Salad Greens
Servings: 4
Cooking Time: 12 Minutes
Ingredients:
- 1 pound cod fillets, cut into chunks
- ⅓ cup packed fresh basil leaves
- 3 cloves garlic, crushed
- ½ teaspoon smoked paprika
- ¼ teaspoon salt
- ¼ teaspoon pepper
- 1 large egg, beaten
- 1 cup panko bread crumbs
- Cooking spray
- Salad greens, for serving

Directions:
1. In a food processor, pulse cod, basil, garlic, smoked paprika, salt, and pepper until cod is finely chopped, stirring occasionally. Form into 8 patties, about 2 inches in diameter. Dip each first into the egg, then into the panko, patting to adhere. Spray with oil on one side.

2. Insert the Crisper Basket and close the hood. Select AIR CRISP, set the temperature to 400ºF, and set the time to 12 minutes. Select START/STOP to begin preheating.

3. Working in batches, place half the cakes in the basket, oil-side down; spray with oil. Close the hood and AIR CRISP for 12 minutes, until golden brown and cooked through.

4. Serve cod cakes with salad greens.

Sweet And Tangy Beef
Servings: 4
Cooking Time: 12 Minutes
Ingredients:
- For the beef
- 2 pounds top sirloin steak, thinly sliced
- 1 tablespoon cornstarch
- 3 tablespoons avocado oil
- 3 tablespoons soy sauce

- 2 tablespoons oyster sauce
- 1 tablespoon peeled minced fresh ginger
- 1 tablespoon sesame oil
- ½ teaspoon salt
- 1 onion, coarsely chopped
- 1 red bell pepper, coarsely chopped
- For the sweet and tangy sauce
- ½ cup water
- 2 tablespoons ketchup
- 2 tablespoons oyster sauce
- 2 tablespoons light brown sugar, packed
- 1 teaspoon salt
- 1 teaspoon sesame oil
- 1 tablespoon white vinegar
- 1 tablespoon Worcestershire sauce

Directions:
1. Insert the Cooking Pot and close the hood. Select GRILL, set the temperature to HI, and set the time to 12 minutes. Select START/STOP to begin preheating.

2. In a large bowl, combine the beef, cornstarch, avocado oil, soy sauce, oyster sauce, ginger, sesame oil, and salt. Mix well so the beef slices are fully coated.

3. When the unit beeps to signify it has preheated, transfer the beef to the Cooking Pot. Close the hood and cook for 6 minutes.

4. While the beef is cooking, in a small bowl, combine the water, ketchup, oyster sauce, brown sugar, salt, sesame oil, vinegar, and Worcestershire sauce. Stir until the sugar is dissolved.

5. After 6 minutes, open the hood and stir the beef. Add the onion and red bell pepper to the Cooking Pot. Close the hood and cook for 2 minutes. After 2 minutes, open the hood and add the sauce to the pot. Close the hood and cook for 4 minutes more.

6. When cooking is complete, spoon the beef and sauce over white rice, if desired. Serve.

Fired Shrimp With Mayonnaise Sauce
Servings: 4
Cooking Time: 7 Minutes
Ingredients:
- Shrimp
- 12 jumbo shrimp
- ½ teaspoon garlic salt
- ¼ teaspoon freshly cracked mixed peppercorns
- Sauce:
- 4 tablespoons mayonnaise
- 1 teaspoon grated lemon rind
- 1 teaspoon Dijon mustard
- 1 teaspoon chipotle powder
- ½ teaspoon cumin powder

Directions:
1. Insert the Crisper Basket and close the hood. Select AIR CRISP, set the temperature to 395ºF, and set the time to 7 minutes. Select START/STOP to begin preheating.

2. In a medium bowl, season the shrimp with garlic salt and cracked mixed peppercorns.

3. Place the shrimp in the Crisper Basket. Close the hood and AIR CRISP for 5 minutes. Flip the shrimp and cook for another 2 minutes until they are pink and no longer opaque.

4. Meanwhile, stir together all the ingredients for the sauce in a small bowl until well mixed.
5. Remove the shrimp from the basket and serve alongside the sauce.

Green Curry Beef

Servings: 4
Cooking Time: 12 Minutes
Ingredients:
- 1 yellow onion
- 1 red bell pepper
- 2 pounds sirloin steak
- 1 tablespoon minced garlic
- 1 tablespoon light brown sugar, packed
- 2 tablespoons green curry paste
- 1 teaspoon salt
- ½ teaspoon freshly ground black pepper
- Juice of ½ lime
- 1 (13-ounce) can full-fat unsweetened coconut milk
- 2 tablespoons fish sauce (optional)
- 1 cup fresh Thai basil or sweet basil

Directions:
1. Insert the Cooking Pot and close the hood. Select GRILL, set the temperature to MED, and set the time to 12 minutes. Select START/STOP to begin preheating.
2. While the unit is preheating, dice the onion, slice the red bell pepper, and thinly slice the steak into bite-size strips.
3. When the unit beeps to signify it has preheated, place the onion and garlic in the Cooking Pot. Then add the beef and stir with a wooden spoon. Close the hood and cook for 4 minutes.
4. After 4 minutes, open the hood and add the brown sugar, green curry paste, salt, pepper, lime juice, coconut milk, and fish sauce (if using). Close the hood and cook for 4 minutes. After 4 minutes, open the hood and stir the curry. Close the hood and cook for 4 minutes more.
5. When cooking is complete, open the hood, add the basil, and stir one more time. Close the hood and let the coconut curry sit for 5 minutes before serving.

Beef And Scallion Rolls

Servings: 4
Cooking Time: 10 Minutes
Ingredients:
- 1 pound skirt steak, very thinly sliced (12 slices)
- Salt
- Freshly ground black pepper
- 6 scallions, both white and green parts, halved lengthwise
- 2 tablespoons cornstarch
- ¼ cup water
- ¼ cup soy sauce
- 2 tablespoons light brown sugar, packed
- 1 teaspoon peeled minced fresh ginger
- 1 teaspoon garlic powder

Directions:
1. Insert the Grill Grate and close the hood. Select GRILL, set the temperature to HI, and set the time to 10 minutes. Select START/STOP to begin preheating.
2. While the unit is preheating, season each steak slice with salt and pepper. With one of the longer sides of a steak slice closest to you, place a scallion length at the bottom, and roll away from you to wrap the scallion. Sprinkle cornstarch on the outer layer of the rolled-up steak. Repeat for the remaining steak slices, scallions, and cornstarch.
3. In a small bowl, mix together the water, soy sauce, brown sugar, ginger, and garlic until the sugar is dissolved.
4. When the unit beeps to signify it has preheated, dip each beef roll in the soy sauce mixture and place it on the Grill Grate, seam-side down. Close the hood and grill for 5 minutes.
5. After 5 minutes, open the hood and flip the beef rolls. Brush each roll with the marinade. Close the hood and cook for 5 minutes more.
6. When cooking is complete, remove the beef rolls from the grill and serve.

Spiced Flank Steak

Servings: 2
Cooking Time: 8 Minutes
Ingredients:
- 1 tablespoon chili powder
- 1 teaspoon dried oregano
- 2 teaspoons ground cumin
- 1 teaspoon sea salt
- ¼ teaspoon freshly ground black pepper
- 2 flank steaks

Directions:
1. Insert the Grill Grate and close the hood. Select GRILL, set the temperature to HIGH, and set the time to 8 minutes. Select START/STOP to begin preheating.
2. In a small bowl, mix together the chili powder, oregano, cumin, salt, and pepper. Use your hands to rub the spice mixture on all sides of the steaks.
3. When the unit beeps to signify it has preheated, place the steaks on the Grill Grate. Gently press the steaks down to maximize grill marks. Close the hood and GRILL for 4 minutes. After 4 minutes, flip the steaks, close the hood, and GRILL for 4 minutes more.
4. Remove the steaks from the grill, and transfer them to a cutting board. Let rest for 5 minutes before slicing and serving.

Honey Barbecue Meat Loaf

Servings: 6
Cooking Time: 15 Minutes
Ingredients:
- 1 white onion, diced
- 1 cup plain bread crumbs
- 4 tablespoons minced garlic
- 2 tablespoons Worcestershire sauce
- ½ cup barbecue sauce, divided
- 2 tablespoons honey
- 2 large eggs
- 2 pounds ground beef

Directions:
1. Plug the thermometer into the unit. Insert the Grill Grate and close the hood. Select GRILL, set the temperature to MED, then select PRESET. Use the arrows to the right to select BEEF. The unit will default to WELL to cook beef to a safe temperature. Select START/STOP to begin preheating.
2. While the unit is preheating, in a large bowl, combine the onion, bread crumbs, garlic, Worcestershire sauce, ¼ cup

of barbecue sauce, honey, and eggs. Add the ground beef in chunks and loosely mix, then form the meat into a loaf about 3 inches high and 6 to 8 inches long. Insert the Smart Thermometer into the loaf.

3. When the unit beeps to signify it has preheated, place the meat loaf on the Grill Grate. Close the hood and grill until the Smart Thermometer indicates the internal temperature is 145°F.

4. When it does, open the hood and brush on the remaining ¼ cup of barbecue sauce. Close the hood and continue cooking until the Smart Thermometer indicates the meat loaf has reached 160°F.

5. When cooking is complete, remove the meat loaf from the grill and serve.

Sizzling Pork Sisig

Servings: 6 To 8
Cooking Time: 50 Minutes
Ingredients:
- 3 pounds pork shoulder or pork belly, cut into 1-inch-thick slices
- 2 tablespoons soy sauce
- 2 tablespoons rice vinegar
- 2 tablespoons fish sauce
- Juice of 1 lemon, divided
- 1 tablespoon garlic powder
- ¼ teaspoon peeled minced fresh ginger
- 1 small red onion, diced
- 2 red Thai chiles, sliced

Directions:
1. Insert the Cooking Pot and close the hood. Select ROAST, set the temperature to 350°F, and set the time to 30 minutes. Select START/STOP to begin preheating.

2. When the unit beeps to signify it has preheated, place the pork in the Cooking Pot. Close the hood and cook for 15 minutes.

3. After 15 minutes, open the hood and flip the pork. Close the hood and cook for 15 minutes more.

4. When cooking is complete, remove the pork and set aside to cool.

5. While the pork is cooling, prepare the sauce. In a small bowl, combine the soy sauce, vinegar, fish sauce, juice of ½ lemon, garlic powder, and ginger. Place the diced onion and sliced chiles in a separate small bowl and set aside. Once the pork has cooled down enough to handle, cut the pork into ½-inch cubes.

6. Wash and dry the Cooking Pot. Then insert the Cooking Pot and close the hood. Select GRILL, set the temperature to HI, and set the time to 20 minutes. Select START/STOP to begin preheating.

7. When the unit beeps to signify it has preheated, place the pork in the Cooking Pot. Close the hood and cook for 10 minutes.

8. After 10 minutes, open the hood, stir the pork, and pour in the sauce. Close the hood and cook for 10 minutes more.

9. When cooking is complete, transfer the pork and sauce to a bowl. Add the onion and chiles on top and squeeze the juice of the remaining ½ lemon over the top. Serve.

Lime-honey Salmon With Mango Salsa

Servings: 4
Cooking Time: 8 Minutes
Ingredients:

- 2 tablespoons unsalted butter, melted
- ⅓ cup honey
- 1 tablespoon soy sauce
- Juice of 3 limes, divided
- Grated zest of ½ lime
- 3 garlic cloves, minced and divided
- 4 skinless salmon fillets
- 1 mango, peeled and diced
- 1 avocado, peeled and diced
- ½ tomato, diced
- ½ red onion, diced
- 1 jalapeño pepper, seeded, stemmed, and diced
- 1 tablespoon extra-virgin olive oil
- Sea salt, to taste
- Freshly ground black pepper, to taste

Directions:
1. Place the butter, honey, soy sauce, juice of 2 limes, lime zest, and 2 minced garlic cloves in a large resealable plastic bag or container. Add the salmon fillets and coat evenly with the marinade. Refrigerate for 30 minutes.

2. While the salmon is marinating, in a large bowl, combine the mango, avocado, tomato, onion, remaining minced garlic clove, jalapeño, remaining juice of 1 lime, oil, salt, and pepper. Cover and refrigerate.

3. Insert the Grill Grate and close the hood. Select GRILL, set the temperature to MAX, and set the time to 8 minutes. Select START/STOP to begin preheating.

4. When the unit beeps to signify it has preheated, place the fillets on the Grill Grate, gently pressing them down to maximize grill marks. Close the hood and GRILL for 6 minutes. (There is no need to flip the fish during grilling.)

5. After 6 minutes, check the fillets for doneness; the internal temperature should read at least 140°F on a food thermometer. If necessary, close the hood and continue cooking up to 2 minutes more.

6. When cooking is complete, top the fillets with salsa and serve immediately.

Vietnamese Pork Chops

Servings: 2
Cooking Time: 12 Minutes
Ingredients:
- 1 tablespoon chopped shallot
- 1 tablespoon chopped garlic
- 1 tablespoon fish sauce
- 3 tablespoons lemongrass
- 1 teaspoon soy sauce
- 1 tablespoon brown sugar
- 1 tablespoon olive oil
- 1 teaspoon ground black pepper
- 2 pork chops

Directions:
1. Combine shallot, garlic, fish sauce, lemongrass, soy sauce, brown sugar, olive oil, and pepper in a bowl. Stir to mix well.

2. Put the pork chops in the bowl. Toss to coat well. Place the bowl in the refrigerator to marinate for 2 hours.

3. Insert the Crisper Basket and close the hood. Select AIR CRISP, set the temperature to 400ºF, and set the time to 12 minutes. Select START/STOP to begin preheating.

4. Remove the pork chops from the bowl and discard the marinade. Transfer the chops into the basket.
5. Close the hood and AIR CRISP for 12 minutes or until lightly browned. Flip the pork chops halfway through the cooking time.
6. Remove the pork chops from the basket and serve hot.

Cheesy Beef Meatballs

Servings: 6
Cooking Time: 18 Minutes
Ingredients:
- 1 pound ground beef
- ½ cup grated Parmesan cheese
- 1 tablespoon minced garlic
- ½ cup Mozzarella cheese
- 1 teaspoon freshly ground pepper

Directions:
1. Insert the Crisper Basket and close the hood. Select AIR CRISP, set the temperature to 400ºF, and set the time to 18 minutes. Select START/STOP to begin preheating.
2. In a bowl, mix all the ingredients together.
3. Roll the meat mixture into 5 generous meatballs. Transfer to the basket.
4. Close the hood and AIR CRISP for 18 minutes.
5. Serve immediately.

Spicy Orange Shrimp

Servings: 4
Cooking Time: 10 To 15 Minutes
Ingredients:
- ⅓ cup orange juice
- 3 teaspoons minced garlic
- 1 teaspoon Old Bay seasoning
- ¼ to ½ teaspoon cayenne pepper
- 1 pound medium shrimp, peeled and deveined, with tails off
- Cooking spray

Directions:
1. In a medium bowl, combine the orange juice, garlic, Old Bay seasoning, and cayenne pepper.
2. Dry the shrimp with paper towels to remove excess water.
3. Add the shrimp to the marinade and stir to evenly coat. Cover with plastic wrap and place in the refrigerator for 30 minutes so the shrimp can soak up the marinade.
4. Insert the Crisper Basket and close the hood. Select AIR CRISP, set the temperature to 400ºF, and set the time to 15 minutes. Select START/STOP to begin preheating.
5. Spray the Crisper Basket lightly with cooking spray.
6. Place the shrimp into the Crisper Basket. Close the hood and AIR CRISP for 5 minutes. Shake the basket and lightly spray with olive oil. AIR CRISP until the shrimp are opaque and crisp, 5 to 10 more minutes.
7. Serve immediately.

Breaded Calamari With Lemon

Servings: 4
Cooking Time: 12 Minutes
Ingredients:
- 2 large eggs
- 2 garlic cloves, minced
- ½ cup cornstarch
- 1 cup bread crumbs
- 1 pound calamari rings
- Cooking spray
- 1 lemon, sliced

Directions:
1. In a small bowl, whisk the eggs with minced garlic. Place the cornstarch and bread crumbs into separate shallow dishes.
2. Dredge the calamari rings in the cornstarch, then dip in the egg mixture, shaking off any excess, finally roll them in the bread crumbs to coat well. Let the calamari rings sit for 10 minutes in the refrigerator.
3. Insert the Crisper Basket and close the hood. Select AIR CRISP, set the temperature to 390ºF, and set the time to 12 minutes. Select START/STOP to begin preheating.
4. Spritz the Crisper Basket with cooking spray.
5. Put the calamari rings in the basket. Close the hood and AIR CRISP for 12 minutes until cooked through. Shake the basket halfway through the cooking time.
6. Serve the calamari rings with the lemon slices sprinkled on top.

Tomato And Lamb Stew

Servings: 6
Cooking Time: 1 Hour
Ingredients:
- 2 tablespoons unsalted butter
- 1 yellow onion, diced
- 4 garlic cloves, minced
- 2 pounds lamb shoulder roast, cut into 1-inch cubes
- 3 cups beef broth
- 1 large potato, cubed
- 1 medium carrot, sliced
- 3 bay leaves
- Salt
- Freshly ground black pepper
- 1 (8-ounce) can tomato sauce
- 1 red bell pepper, chopped
- 1 green bell pepper, chopped

Directions:
1. Insert the Cooking Pot and close the hood. Select ROAST, set the temperature to 350°F, and set the time to 1 hour. Select START/STOP to begin preheating.
2. When the unit beeps to signify it has preheated, place the butter, onion, and garlic in the Cooking Pot. Then add the lamb and stir with a wooden spoon. Close the hood and cook for 10 minutes.
3. After 10 minutes, open the hood and add the beef broth, potato, carrot, and bay leaves, and then season with salt and pepper. Stir to combine. Close the hood and cook for 20 minutes.
4. After 20 minutes, open the hood and stir in the tomato sauce. Close the hood and cook for 10 minutes. After 10 minutes, open the hood and stir. Close the hood and cook for 10 minutes. After 10 minutes, open the hood and add the bell peppers. Close the hood and cook for 10 minutes more.
5. When cooking is complete, open the hood, stir the stew, and remove the bay leaves. Transfer to bowls and serve.

Garlicky Shrimp Caesar Salad

Servings: 4
Cooking Time: 5 Minutes
Ingredients:
- 1 pound fresh jumbo shrimp
- Juice of ½ lemon
- 3 garlic cloves, minced
- Sea salt, to taste
- Freshly ground black pepper, to taste
- 2 heads romaine lettuce, chopped
- ¾ cup Caesar dressing
- ½ cup grated Parmesan cheese

Directions:
1. Insert the Grill Grate and close the hood. Select GRILL, set the temperature to MAX, and set the time to 5 minutes. Select START/STOP to begin preheating.
2. In a large bowl, toss the shrimp with the lemon juice, garlic, salt, and pepper. Let marinate while the grill is preheating.
3. When the unit beeps to signify it has preheated, carefully place the shrimp on the Grill Grate. Close the hood and GRILL for 5 minutes. (There is no need to flip the shrimp during grilling.)
4. While the shrimp grills, toss the romaine lettuce with the Caesar dressing, then divide evenly among four plates or bowls.
5. When cooking is complete, use tongs to remove the shrimp from the grill and place on top of each salad. Sprinkle with the Parmesan cheese and serve.

Crusted Pork Chops With Honey-maple Jalapeño Glaze

Servings: 6
Cooking Time: 15 Minutes
Ingredients:
- 2 large eggs
- 2 cups panko bread crumbs
- 1 teaspoon Italian seasoning
- 1 teaspoon garlic powder
- 6 (6-ounce) boneless pork chops
- ¼ cup honey
- ¼ cup maple syrup
- ¼ cup soy sauce
- 1 jalapeño, sliced (seeds optional)

Directions:
1. Insert the Grill Grate and close the hood. Select GRILL, set the temperature to MED, and set the time to 15 minutes. Select START/STOP to begin preheating.
2. While the unit is preheating, create an assembly line with 2 large bowls. In one bowl, whisk the eggs. In the other bowl, combine the panko bread crumbs, Italian seasoning, and garlic powder. One at a time, dip the pork chops in the egg and then in the panko mixture until fully coated and set aside.
3. In a small bowl, combine the honey, maple syrup, soy sauce, and jalapeño slices.
4. When the unit beeps to signify it has preheated, place the pork chops on the Grill Grate. Close the hood and grill for 7 minutes, 30 seconds.

5. After 7 minutes, 30 seconds, open the hood and flip the pork chops. Spoon half of the honey glaze over the chops. Close the hood and cook for 7 minutes, 30 seconds more.
6. When cooking is complete, remove the pork chops from the grill and drizzle with the remaining glaze. Let the pork chops rest for a few minutes before serving.

Lechon Kawali

Servings: 4
Cooking Time: 30 Minutes
Ingredients:
- 1 pound pork belly, cut into three thick chunks
- 6 garlic cloves
- 2 bay leaves
- 2 tablespoons soy sauce
- 1 teaspoon kosher salt
- 1 teaspoon ground black pepper
- 3 cups water
- Cooking spray

Directions:
1. Put all the ingredients in a pressure cooker, then put the lid on and cook on high for 15 minutes.
2. Natural release the pressure and release any remaining pressure, transfer the tender pork belly on a clean work surface. Allow to cool under room temperature until you can handle.
3. Generously spritz the Crisper Basket with cooking spray.
4. Insert the Crisper Basket and close the hood. Select AIR CRISP, set the temperature to 400ºF, and set the time to 15 minutes. Select START/STOP to begin preheating.
5. Cut each chunk into two slices, then put the pork slices in the basket.
6. Close the hood and AIR CRISP for 15 minutes or until the pork fat is crispy. Spritz the pork with more cooking spray, if necessary.
7. Serve immediately.

Baked Flounder Fillets

Servings: 2
Cooking Time: 12 Minutes
Ingredients:
- 2 flounder fillets, patted dry
- 1 egg
- ½ teaspoon Worcestershire sauce
- ¼ cup almond flour
- ¼ cup coconut flour
- ½ teaspoon coarse sea salt
- ½ teaspoon lemon pepper
- ¼ teaspoon chili powder
- Cooking spray

Directions:
1. Insert the Crisper Basket and close the hood. Select BAKE, set the temperature to 390ºF, and set the time to 12 minutes. Select START/STOP to begin preheating.
2. Spritz the Crisper Basket with cooking spray.
3. In a shallow bowl, beat together the egg with Worcestershire sauce until well incorporated.
4. In another bowl, thoroughly combine the almond flour, coconut flour, sea salt, lemon pepper, and chili powder.
5. Dredge the fillets in the egg mixture, shaking off any excess, then roll in the flour mixture to coat well.

6. Place the fillets in the Crisper Basket. Close the hood and BAKE for 7 minutes. Flip the fillets and spray with cooking spray. Continue cooking for 5 minutes, or until the fish is flaky.
7. Serve warm.

Southwest Shrimp And Cabbage Tacos

Servings: 4
Cooking Time: 10 Minutes
Ingredients:
- 4 corn tortillas
- Nonstick cooking spray
- 1 pound fresh jumbo shrimp
- Juice of ½ lemon
- 1 teaspoon chili powder
- 1 teaspoon ground cumin
- 1 teaspoon Southwestern seasoning
- ¼ teaspoon cayenne pepper
- 2 cups shredded green cabbage
- 1 avocado, peeled and sliced

Directions:
1. Insert the Grill Grate and close the hood. Select GRILL, set the temperature to MAX, and set the time to 10 minutes. Select START/STOP to begin preheating.
2. While the unit is preheating, spray both sides of the tortillas with cooking spray, and in a large bowl, toss the shrimp with the lemon juice, chili powder, cumin, Southwestern seasoning, and cayenne pepper, until evenly coated. Let marinate while grilling the tortillas in the next step.
3. When the unit beeps to signify it has preheated, place 1 tortilla on the Grill Grate. Close the hood and GRILL for 1 minute. After 1 minute, open the hood and remove the tortilla; set aside. Repeat with the remaining 3 tortillas.
4. After removing the final tortilla, carefully place the shrimp on the Grill Grate. Close the hood and GRILL for 5 minutes. (There is no need to flip the shrimp during grilling.)
5. Remove the shrimp from the grill, arrange on the grilled tortillas, and top with cabbage and avocado. Feel free to include other toppings, such as cotija cheese, cilantro, and lime wedges.

Crispy Pork Belly Bites

Servings: 6
Cooking Time: 20 Minutes
Ingredients:
- 1 tablespoon garlic powder
- 1 tablespoon sea salt
- 1 tablespoon paprika
- ¼ teaspoon freshly ground black pepper
- 2 pounds pork belly (3 to 4 slabs)

Directions:
1. Insert the Grill Grate and close the hood. Select GRILL, set the temperature to HI, and set the time to 20 minutes. Select START/STOP to begin preheating.
2. While the unit is preheating, in a large bowl, combine the garlic powder, salt, paprika, and pepper.
3. Pat the pork belly dry with a paper towel. Place it in the seasoning and toss to generously coat the pork belly on all sides.

4. When the unit beeps to signify it has preheated, place the pork belly on the Grill Grate, skin-side up. Close the hood and grill for 10 minutes.
5. After 10 minutes, open the hood and flip the pork. Close the hood and cook for 10 minutes more.
6. When cooking is complete, remove the pork belly from the grill and serve.

Herbed Scallops With Vegetables

Servings: 4
Cooking Time: 8 To 11 Minutes
Ingredients:
- 1 cup frozen peas
- 1 cup green beans
- 1 cup frozen chopped broccoli
- 2 teaspoons olive oil
- ½ teaspoon dried oregano
- ½ teaspoon dried basil
- 12 ounces sea scallops, rinsed and patted dry

Directions:
1. Insert the Crisper Basket and close the hood. Select AIR CRISP, set the temperature to 400ºF, and set the time to 6 minutes. Select START/STOP to begin preheating.
2. Put the peas, green beans, and broccoli in a large bowl. Drizzle with the olive oil and toss to coat well. Transfer the vegetables to the Crisper Basket. Close the hood and AIR CRISP for 4 to 6 minutes, or until they are fork-tender.
3. Remove the vegetables from the basket to a serving bowl. Scatter with the oregano and basil and set aside.
4. Place the scallops in the Crisper Basket. Close the hood and AIR CRISP for 4 to 5 minutes, or until the scallops are firm and just opaque in the center.
5. Transfer the cooked scallops to the bowl of vegetables and toss well. Serve warm.

Spicy Beef Lettuce Wraps

Servings: 4
Cooking Time: 10 Minutes
Ingredients:
- 1 pound ground beef
- 1 tablespoon sesame oil
- 1 tablespoon minced garlic
- 1 teaspoon peeled minced fresh ginger
- 3 tablespoons light brown sugar, packed
- ¼ cup soy sauce
- 1 teaspoon salt
- ½ teaspoon freshly ground black pepper
- 2 teaspoons sriracha
- 1 red chile, thinly sliced, or ¼ teaspoon red pepper flakes
- ½ cup sliced scallions, both white and green parts
- 12 butter lettuce leaves

Directions:
1. Insert the Cooking Pot and close the hood. Select GRILL, set the temperature to HI, and set the time to 10 minutes. Select START/STOP to begin preheating.
2. When the unit beeps to signify it has preheated, place the ground beef in the Cooking Pot. Carefully break the ground beef apart with a wooden spoon or spatula. Stir in the sesame oil, garlic, and ginger. Close the hood and cook for 5 minutes.

3. After 5 minutes, open the hood and stir the ground beef. Stir in the brown sugar, soy sauce, salt, pepper, and sriracha. Close the hood and cook for 5 minutes more.
4. When cooking is complete, open the hood and stir in the chile and scallions. Close the hood and let sit for about 3 minutes for the mixture to set.
5. Scoop the ground beef mixture into the lettuce leaves and serve.

Burnt Ends

Servings: 6
Cooking Time: 40 Minutes
Ingredients:
- 1 tablespoon garlic powder
- 1 tablespoon sea salt
- 1 tablespoon paprika
- ¼ teaspoon freshly ground black pepper
- 2 pounds pork butt, cut into 1-inch cubes
- ½ cup barbecue sauce
- ¼ cup light brown sugar, packed
- ¼ cup honey
- 4 tablespoons (½ stick) unsalted butter, sliced

Directions:
1. Insert the Cooking Pot and close the hood. Select ROAST, set the temperature to 300°F, and set the time to 20 minutes. Select START/STOP to begin preheating.
2. While the unit is preheating, in a large bowl, combine the garlic powder, salt, paprika, and pepper. Add the pork and toss until generously coated on all sides.
3. When the unit beeps to signify it has preheated, place the pork in the Cooking Pot in a single layer. Close the hood and roast for 10 minutes.
4. After 10 minutes, open the hood and flip the pork cubes. Close the hood and cook for 10 minutes more.
5. At this point, the pork should have a nice char. Place the pork cubes in the center of a large piece of aluminum foil. Add the barbecue sauce, brown sugar, and honey and massage them into the roasted pork. Add the butter, then seal the foil. Place the packet back in the Cooking Pot.
6. Select ROAST, set the temperature to 350°F, and set the time to 20 minutes. Select START/STOP and then press PREHEAT to skip preheating. Close the hood and cook for 20 minutes.
7. When cooking is complete, remove the foil packet. Be careful opening the foil, because the steam will be very hot. The pork should be nicely coated with sauce that has thickened. If you want more char and caramelization of the burnt ends, carefully place the open foil packet back in the Cooking Pot. Select GRILL, set the temperature to HI, and set the time to 10 minutes. Select START/STOP and then press PREHEAT to skip preheating. Close the hood and cook for 10 minutes or until charred to your liking.

Bacon-wrapped Scallops

Servings: 4
Cooking Time: 10 Minutes
Ingredients:
- 8 slices bacon, cut in half
- 16 sea scallops, patted dry
- Cooking spray
- Salt and freshly ground black pepper, to taste
- 16 toothpicks, soaked in water for at least 30 minutes

Directions:
1. Insert the Crisper Basket and close the hood. Select AIR CRISP, set the temperature to 370°F, and set the time to 10 minutes. Select START/STOP to begin preheating.
2. On a clean work surface, wrap half of a slice of bacon around each scallop and secure with a toothpick.
3. Lay the bacon-wrapped scallops in the Crisper Basket in a single layer. You may need to work in batches to avoid overcrowding.
4. Spritz the scallops with cooking spray and sprinkle the salt and pepper to season.
5. Close the hood and AIR CRISP for 10 minutes, flipping the scallops halfway through, or until the bacon is cooked through and the scallops are firm.
6. Remove the scallops from the basket to a plate and repeat with the remaining scallops. Serve warm.

Pork Sausage With Cauliflower Mash

Servings: 6
Cooking Time: 27 Minutes
Ingredients:
- 1 pound cauliflower, chopped
- 6 pork sausages, chopped
- ½ onion, sliced
- 3 eggs, beaten
- ⅓ cup Colby cheese
- 1 teaspoon cumin powder
- ½ teaspoon tarragon
- ½ teaspoon sea salt
- ½ teaspoon ground black pepper
- Cooking spray

Directions:
1. Select BAKE, set the temperature to 365°F, and set the time to 27 minutes. Select START/STOP to begin preheating.
2. Spritz a baking pan with cooking spray.
3. In a saucepan over medium heat, boil the cauliflower until tender. Place the boiled cauliflower in a food processor and pulse until puréed. Transfer to a large bowl and combine with remaining ingredients until well blended.
4. Pour the cauliflower and sausage mixture into the baking pan. Place the pan directly in the pot. Close the hood and BAKE for 27 minutes, or until lightly browned.
5. Divide the mixture among six serving dishes and serve warm.

Cajun-style Fish Tacos

Servings: 6
Cooking Time: 10 To 15 Minutes
Ingredients:
- 2 teaspoons avocado oil
- 1 tablespoon Cajun seasoning
- 4 tilapia fillets
- 1 package coleslaw mix
- 12 corn tortillas
- 2 limes, cut into wedges

Directions:
1. Insert the Crisper Basket and close the hood. Select AIR CRISP, set the temperature to 380°F, and set the time to 15 minutes. Select START/STOP to begin preheating.
2. Line the Crisper Basket with parchment paper.

3. In a medium, shallow bowl, mix the avocado oil and the Cajun seasoning to make a marinade. Add the tilapia fillets and coat evenly.
4. Place the fillets in the basket in a single layer, leaving room between each fillet. You may need to cook in batches.
5. Close the hood and AIR CRISP for 10 to 15 minutes until the fish is cooked and easily flakes with a fork.
6. Assemble the tacos by placing some of the coleslaw mix in each tortilla. Add ⅓ of a tilapia fillet to each tortilla. Squeeze some lime juice over the top of each taco and serve.

Asian-flavored Steak Kebabs

Servings: 4
Cooking Time: 12 Minutes
Ingredients:
- ¾ cup soy sauce
- 5 garlic cloves, minced
- 3 tablespoons sesame oil
- ½ cup canola oil
- ⅓ cup sugar
- ¼ teaspoon dried ground ginger
- 2 New York strip steaks, cut in 2-inch cubes
- 1 cup whole white mushrooms
- 1 red bell pepper, seeded, and cut into 2-inch cubes
- 1 red onion, cut into 2-inch wedges

Directions:
1. In a medium bowl, whisk together the soy sauce, garlic, sesame oil, canola oil, sugar, and ginger until well combined. Add the steak and toss to coat. Cover and refrigerate for at least 30 minutes.
2. Insert the Grill Grate and close the hood. Select GRILL, set the temperature to MEDIUM, and set the time to 12 minutes. Select START/STOP to begin preheating.
3. While the unit is preheating, assemble the skewers in the following order: steak, mushroom, bell pepper, onion. Ensure the ingredients are pushed almost completely down to the end of the wood skewers.
4. When the unit beeps to signify it has preheated, place the skewers on the Grill Grate. Close the hood and GRILL for 8 minutes without flipping.
5. After 8 minutes, check the steak for desired doneness, grilling up to 4 minutes more if desired.
6. When cooking is complete, serve immediately.

Green Curry Shrimp

Servings: 4
Cooking Time: 5 Minutes
Ingredients:
- 1 to 2 tablespoons Thai green curry paste
- 2 tablespoons coconut oil, melted
- 1 tablespoon half-and-half or coconut milk
- 1 teaspoon fish sauce
- 1 teaspoon soy sauce
- 1 teaspoon minced fresh ginger
- 1 clove garlic, minced
- 1 pound jumbo raw shrimp, peeled and deveined
- ¼ cup chopped fresh Thai basil or sweet basil
- ¼ cup chopped fresh cilantro

Directions:
1. In a baking pan, combine the curry paste, coconut oil, half-and-half, fish sauce, soy sauce, ginger, and garlic. Whisk until well combined.

2. Add the shrimp and toss until well coated. Marinate at room temperature for 15 to 30 minutes.
3. Insert the Crisper Basket and close the hood. Select AIR CRISP, set the temperature to 400°F, and set the time to 5 minutes. Select START/STOP to begin preheating.
4. Place the pan directly in the pot. Close the hood and AIR CRISP for 5 minutes, stirring halfway through the cooking time.
5. Transfer the shrimp to a serving bowl or platter. Garnish with the basil and cilantro. Serve immediately.

Lamb Kefta Kebabs

Servings: 4 To 6
Cooking Time: 10 Minutes
Ingredients:
- 1 small red onion, minced
- 4 garlic cloves, minced
- 2 teaspoons dried parsley
- 2 teaspoons dried oregano
- 2 teaspoons ground cumin
- 2 teaspoons salt
- 2 pounds ground lamb

Directions:
1. In a large bowl, combine the onion, garlic, parsley, oregano, cumin, and salt. Add the ground lamb in chunks and loosely mix. Form the mixture into 2-inch-long cylinders about 1 inch thick.
2. Insert the Grill Grate and close the hood. Select GRILL, set the temperature to MED, and set the time to 10 minutes. Select START/STOP to begin preheating.
3. While the unit is preheating, thread 2 or 3 lamb cylinders each onto skewers.
4. When the unit beeps to signify it has preheated, place the skewers on the Grill Grate. Close the hood and cook for 5 minutes.
5. After 5 minutes, open the hood and flip the skewers. Close the hood and cook for 5 minutes more.
6. When cooking is complete, remove the kebabs from the grill. Serve with store-bought or homemade tzatziki sauce (see here).

Honey-garlic Ribs

Servings: 6
Cooking Time: 1 Hour 10 Minutes
Ingredients:
- 2 (2- to 3-pound) racks baby back ribs
- Sea salt
- ½ cup soy sauce
- 1 cup honey
- 4 garlic cloves, minced
- 1 teaspoon paprika
- 3 tablespoons light brown sugar, packed

Directions:
1. Insert the Grill Grate and close the hood. Select BAKE, set the temperature to 300°F, and set the time to 1 hour. Select START/STOP to begin preheating.
2. While the unit is preheating, generously season each rack with salt, then wrap each in aluminum foil.
3. When the unit beeps to signify it has preheated, place the foil-wrapped ribs on the Grill Grate. Close the hood and cook for 1 hour.

4. While the ribs are cooking, in a small bowl, combine the soy sauce, honey, garlic, paprika, and brown sugar until the sugar is dissolved.

5. When cooking is complete, remove the ribs from the grill. Slowly open the foil (but don't remove it) and brush the sauce over the ribs. Pour the remaining sauce over both racks.

6. Place the slightly opened packets of racks back onto the Grill Grate. Select GRILL, set the temperature to HI, and set the time to 10 minutes. Select START/STOP and then press the PREHEAT button to skip preheating. Close the hood and cook for 5 minutes.

7. After 5 minutes, open the hood, flip the rib racks, and place them back in the foil. Close the hood and cook for 5 minutes more or until you achieve your desired level of char.

8. When cooking is complete, remove the racks from the grill and serve.

Grilled Swordfish Steaks

Servings: 4
Cooking Time: 8 Minutes
Ingredients:
- 1 tablespoon freshly squeezed lemon juice
- 1 tablespoon extra-virgin olive oil
- Sea salt, to taste
- Freshly ground black pepper, to taste
- 4 fresh swordfish steaks, about 1-inch thick
- 4 tablespoons unsalted butter
- 1 lemon, sliced crosswise into 8 slices
- 2 tablespoons capers, drained

Directions:
1. In a large shallow bowl, whisk together the lemon juice and oil. Season the swordfish steaks with salt and pepper on each side, and place them in the oil mixture. Turn to coat both sides. Refrigerate for 15 minutes.

2. Insert the Grill Grate and close the hood. Select GRILL, set the temperature to MAX, and set the time to 8 minutes. Select START/STOP to begin preheating.

3. When the unit beeps to signify it has preheated, place the swordfish on the Grill Grate. Close the hood and GRILL for 9 minutes. (There is no need to flip the swordfish during cooking.)

4. While the swordfish grills, melt the butter in a small saucepan over medium heat. Stir and GRILL for about 3 minutes, until the butter has slightly browned. Add the lemon slices and capers to the pan, and GRILL for 1 minute. Turn off the heat.

5. Remove the swordfish from the grill and transfer it to a cutting board. Slice the fish into thick strips, transfer to serving platter, pour the caper sauce over the top, and serve immediately.

Citrus Carnitas

Servings: 6
Cooking Time: 25 Minutes
Ingredients:
- 2½ pounds boneless country-style pork ribs, cut into 2-inch pieces
- 3 tablespoons olive brine
- 1 tablespoon minced fresh oregano leaves
- ⅓ cup orange juice
- 1 teaspoon ground cumin

- 1 tablespoon minced garlic
- 1 teaspoon salt
- 1 teaspoon ground black pepper
- Cooking spray

Directions:
1. Combine all the ingredients in a large bowl. Toss to coat the pork ribs well. Wrap the bowl in plastic and refrigerate for at least an hour to marinate.

2. Spritz the Crisper Basket with cooking spray.

3. Insert the Crisper Basket and close the hood. Select AIR CRISP, set the temperature to 400ºF, and set the time to 25 minutes. Select START/STOP to begin preheating.

4. Arrange the marinated pork ribs in a single layer in the basket and spritz with cooking spray.

5. Close the hood and AIR CRISP for 25 minutes or until well browned. Flip the ribs halfway through.

6. Serve immediately.

Spanish Garlic Shrimp

Servings: 4
Cooking Time: 10 To 15 Minutes
Ingredients:
- 2 teaspoons minced garlic
- 2 teaspoons lemon juice
- 2 teaspoons olive oil
- ½ to 1 teaspoon crushed red pepper
- 12 ounces medium shrimp, deveined, with tails on
- Cooking spray

Directions:
1. In a medium bowl, mix together the garlic, lemon juice, olive oil, and crushed red pepper to make a marinade.

2. Add the shrimp and toss to coat in the marinade. Cover with plastic wrap and place the bowl in the refrigerator for 30 minutes.

3. Spray the Crisper Basket lightly with cooking spray.

4. Insert the Crisper Basket and close the hood. Select AIR CRISP, set the temperature to 400ºF, and set the time to 15 minutes. Select START/STOP to begin preheating.

5. Place the shrimp in the Crisper Basket. Close the hood and AIR CRISP for 5 minutes. Shake the basket and AIR CRISP until the shrimp are cooked through and nicely browned, for an additional 5 to 10 minutes. Cool for 5 minutes before serving.

Garlic-lemon Tilapia

Servings: 4
Cooking Time: 10 To 15 Minutes
Ingredients:
- 1 tablespoon lemon juice
- 1 tablespoon olive oil
- 1 teaspoon minced garlic
- ½ teaspoon chili powder
- 4 tilapia fillets

Directions:
1. Insert the Crisper Basket and close the hood. Select AIR CRISP, set the temperature to 380ºF, and set the time to 15 minutes. Select START/STOP to begin preheating.

2. Line the Crisper Basket with parchment paper.

3. In a large, shallow bowl, mix together the lemon juice, olive oil, garlic, and chili powder to make a marinade. Place the tilapia fillets in the bowl and coat evenly.

4. Place the fillets in the basket in a single layer, leaving space between each fillet. You may need to cook in more than one batch.
5. Close the hood and AIR CRISP for 10 to 15 minutes until the fish is cooked and flakes easily with a fork.
6. Serve hot.

Crispy Cod Sandwich

Servings: 4
Cooking Time: 15 Minutes
Ingredients:
- 2 large eggs
- 10 ounces beer (an ale, IPA, or any type you have on hand will work)
- 1½ teaspoons hot sauce
- 1½ cups cornstarch
- 1½ cups all-purpose flour
- 1 teaspoon sea salt
- 1 teaspoon freshly ground black pepper
- 4 fresh cod fillets
- Nonstick cooking spray
- 4 soft rolls, sliced
- Tartar sauce
- Lettuce leaves
- Lemon wedges

Directions:
1. Insert the Crisper Basket and close the hood. Select AIR CRISP, set the temperature to 375ºF, and set the time to 15 minutes. Select START/STOP to begin preheating.
2. While the unit is preheating, whisk together the eggs, beer, and hot sauce in a large shallow bowl. In a separate large bowl, whisk together the cornstarch, flour, salt, and pepper.
3. One at a time, coat the cod fillets in the egg mixture, then dredge them in the flour mixture and coat on all sides. Repeat with the remaining cod fillets.
4. When the unit beeps to signify it has preheated, spray the Crisper Basket with the cooking spray. Place the fish fillets in the basket and coat them with the cooking spray. Close the hood and AIR CRISP for 15 minutes.
5. After 15 minutes, check the fish for desired crispiness. Remove from the basket.
6. Assemble the sandwiches by spreading tartar sauce on one half of each of the sliced rolls. Add one fish fillet and lettuce leaves, and serve with lemon wedges.

Golden Wasabi Spam

Servings: 3
Cooking Time: 12 Minutes
Ingredients:
- ⅔ cup all-purpose flour
- 2 large eggs
- 1½ tablespoons wasabi paste
- 2 cups panko breadcrumbs
- 6 ½-inch-thick spam slices
- Cooking spray

Directions:
1. Spritz the Crisper Basket with cooking spray.
2. Insert the Crisper Basket and close the hood. Select AIR CRISP, set the temperature to 400ºF, and set the time to 12 minutes. Select START/STOP to begin preheating.

3. Pour the flour in a shallow plate. Whisk the eggs with wasabi in a large bowl. Pour the panko in a separate shallow plate.
4. Dredge the spam slices in the flour first, then dunk in the egg mixture, and then roll the spam over the panko to coat well. Shake the excess off.
5. Arrange the spam slices in a single layer in the basket and spritz with cooking spray.
6. Close the hood and AIR CRISP for 12 minutes or until the spam slices are golden and crispy. Flip the spam slices halfway through.
7. Serve immediately.

Spaghetti Squash Lasagna

Servings: 6
Cooking Time: 1 Hour 15 Minutes
Ingredients:
- 2 large spaghetti squash, cooked
- 4 pounds ground beef
- 1 large jar Marinara sauce
- 25 slices Mozzarella cheese
- 30 ounces whole-milk ricotta cheese

Directions:
1. Select BAKE, set the temperature to 375ºF, and set the time to 45 minutes. Select START/STOP to begin preheating.
2. Slice the spaghetti squash and place it face down inside a baking pan. Fill with water until covered.
3. Place the pan directly in the pot. Close the hood and BAKE for 45 minutes until skin is soft.
4. Sear the ground beef in a skillet over medium-high heat for 5 minutes or until browned, then add the marinara sauce and heat until warm. Set aside.
5. Scrape the flesh off the cooked squash to resemble strands of spaghetti.
6. Layer the lasagna in a large greased pan in alternating layers of spaghetti squash, beef sauce, Mozzarella, ricotta. Repeat until all the ingredients have been used.
7. Place the pan directly in the pot. Close the hood and BAKE for 30 minutes.
8. Serve.

Balsamic London Broil

Servings: 8
Cooking Time: 25 Minutes
Ingredients:
- 2 pounds London broil
- 3 large garlic cloves, minced
- 3 tablespoons balsamic vinegar
- 3 tablespoons whole-grain mustard
- 2 tablespoons olive oil
- Sea salt and ground black pepper, to taste
- ½ teaspoons dried hot red pepper flakes

Directions:
1. Wash and dry the London broil. Score its sides with a knife.
2. Mix the remaining ingredients. Rub this mixture into the broil, coating it well. Allow to marinate for a minimum of 3 hours.
3. Insert the Crisper Basket and close the hood. Select AIR CRISP, set the temperature to 400ºF, and set the time to 25 minutes. Select START/STOP to begin preheating.

4. Place the meat in the basket. Close the hood and AIR CRISP for 15 minutes. Turn it over and AIR CRISP for an additional 10 minutes before serving.

Grilled Filet Mignon With Pineapple Salsa

Servings: 4
Cooking Time: 8 Minutes
Ingredients:
- 4 filet mignon steaks
- 1 tablespoon canola oil, divided
- Sea salt, to taste
- Freshly ground black pepper, to taste
- ½ medium pineapple, cored and diced
- 1 medium red onion, diced
- 1 jalapeño pepper, seeded, stemmed, and diced
- 1 tablespoon freshly squeezed lime juice
- ¼ cup chopped fresh cilantro leaves
- Chili powder
- Ground coriander

Directions:
1. Rub each filet on all sides with ½ tablespoon of the oil, then season with the salt and pepper.
2. Insert the Grill Grate and close the hood. Select GRILL, set temperature to HIGH, and set time to 8 minutes. Select START/STOP to begin preheating.
3. When the unit beeps to signify it has preheated, add the filets to the Grill Grate. Gently press the filets down to maximize grill marks, then close the hood.
4. After 4 minutes, open the hood and flip the filets. Close the hood and continue grilling for an additional 4 minutes, or until the filets' internal temperature reads 125ºF on a food thermometer. Remove the filets from the grill; they will continue to cook (called carry-over cooking) to a food-safe temperature even after you've removed them from the grill.
5. Let the filets rest for a total of 10 minutes; this allows the natural juices to redistribute into the steak.
6. While the filets rest, in a medium bowl, combine the pineapple, onion, and jalapeño. Stir in the lime juice and cilantro, then season to taste with the chili powder and coriander.
7. Plate the filets, and pile the salsa on top of each before serving.

Lamb Ribs With Fresh Mint

Servings: 4
Cooking Time: 18 Minutes
Ingredients:
- 2 tablespoons mustard
- 1 pound lamb ribs
- 1 teaspoon rosemary, chopped
- Salt and ground black pepper, to taste
- ¼ cup mint leaves, chopped
- 1 cup Greek yogurt

Directions:
1. Insert the Crisper Basket and close the hood. Select AIR CRISP, set the temperature to 350ºF, and set the time to 18 minutes. Select START/STOP to begin preheating.
2. Use a brush to apply the mustard to the lamb ribs, and season with rosemary, salt, and pepper. Transfer to the basket.
3. Close the hood and AIR CRISP for 18 minutes.

4. Meanwhile, combine the mint leaves and yogurt in a bowl.
5. Remove the lamb ribs from the grill when cooked and serve with the mint yogurt.

Simple Pork Meatballs With Red Chili

Servings: 4
Cooking Time: 15 Minutes
Ingredients:
- 1 pound ground pork
- 2 cloves garlic, finely minced
- 1 cup scallions, finely chopped
- 1½ tablespoons Worcestershire sauce
- ½ teaspoon freshly grated ginger root
- 1 teaspoon turmeric powder
- 1 tablespoon oyster sauce
- 1 small sliced red chili, for garnish
- Cooking spray

Directions:
1. Spritz the Crisper Basket with cooking spray.
2. Insert the Crisper Basket and close the hood. Select AIR CRISP, set the temperature to 350ºF, and set the time to 15 minutes. Select START/STOP to begin preheating.
3. Combine all the ingredients, except for the red chili in a large bowl. Toss to mix well.
4. Shape the mixture into equally sized balls, then arrange them in the basket and spritz with cooking spray.
5. Close the hood and AIR CRISP for 15 minutes or until the balls are lightly browned. Flip the balls halfway through.
6. Serve the pork meatballs with red chili on top.

Flank Steak Pinwheels

Servings: 4 To 6
Cooking Time: 10 Minutes
Ingredients:
- 2 pounds flank steak
- Salt
- Freshly ground black pepper
- 4 ounces cream cheese, at room temperature
- 2 tablespoons minced garlic
- ½ cup shredded mozzarella cheese
- 4 tablespoons grated Parmesan cheese
- 2 cups fresh spinach

Directions:
1. Insert the Grill Grate and close the hood. Select GRILL, set the temperature to HI, and set the time to 10 minutes. Select START/STOP to begin preheating.
2. While the unit is preheating, butterfly the steaks and season both sides with salt and pepper. Spread the cream cheese across the cut side of each steak and evenly distribute the garlic over the cream cheese. Layer the mozzarella, Parmesan cheese, and spinach on top. Starting from the bottom of each steak, roll the meat upward tightly over the filling. Use about 6 toothpicks, evenly spaced, to secure the seam. Then slice in between the toothpicks, creating 1½- to 2-inch-thick rolls.
3. When the unit beeps to signify it has preheated, place the pinwheels on the Grill Grate, cut-side down. Close the hood and grill for 5 minutes.
4. After 5 minutes, open the hood and flip the pinwheels. Close the hood and cook for 5 minutes more.

5. When cooking is complete, check the meat for doneness. If you prefer your beef more well done, continue cooking to your liking. Remove the pinwheels from the grill and serve.
6. Cut the steak almost in half from one side (parallel to the cutting board), stopping just before you reach the other side. When you open the steak up, it'll be thinner and have two matching wings like a butterfly.

Pork Chops In Bourbon

Servings: 4
Cooking Time: 35 Minutes
Ingredients:
- 2 cups ketchup
- ¾ cup bourbon
- ¼ cup apple cider vinegar
- ¼ cup soy sauce
- 1 cup packed brown sugar
- 3 tablespoons Worcestershire sauce
- ½ tablespoon dry mustard powder
- 4 boneless pork chops
- Sea salt, to taste
- Freshly ground black pepper, to taste

Directions:
1. In a medium saucepan over high heat, combine the ketchup, bourbon, vinegar, soy sauce, sugar, Worcestershire sauce, and mustard powder. Stir to combine and bring to a boil.
2. Reduce the heat to low and simmer, uncovered and stirring occasionally, for 20 minutes. The barbecue sauce will thicken while cooking. Once thickened, remove the pan from the heat and set aside.
3. While the barbecue sauce is cooking, insert the Grill Grate into the unit and close the hood. Select GRILL, set the temperature to MEDIUM, and set the time to 15 minutes. Select START/STOP to begin preheating.
4. When the unit beeps to signify it has preheated, place the pork chops on the Grill Grate. Close the hood, and GRILL for 8 minutes. After 8 minutes, flip the pork chops and baste the cooked side with the barbecue sauce. Close the hood, and GRILL for 5 minutes more.
5. Open the hood, and flip the pork chops again, basting both sides with the barbecue sauce. Close the hood, and GRILL for the final 2 minutes.
6. When cooking is complete, season with salt and pepper and serve immediately.

Simple Salmon Patty Bites

Servings: 4
Cooking Time: 10 To 15 Minutes
Ingredients:
- 4 cans pink salmon, skinless, boneless in water, drained
- 2 eggs, beaten
- 1 cup whole-wheat panko bread crumbs
- 4 tablespoons finely minced red bell pepper
- 2 tablespoons parsley flakes
- 2 teaspoons Old Bay seasoning
- Cooking spray

Directions:
1. Insert the Crisper Basket and close the hood. Select AIR CRISP, set the temperature to 360ºF, and set the time to 15 minutes. Select START/STOP to begin preheating.
2. Spray the Crisper Basket lightly with cooking spray.

3. In a medium bowl, mix the salmon, eggs, panko bread crumbs, red bell pepper, parsley flakes, and Old Bay seasoning.
4. Using a small cookie scoop, form the mixture into 20 balls.
5. Place the salmon bites in the Crisper Basket in a single layer and spray lightly with cooking spray. You may need to cook them in batches.
6. Close the hood and AIR CRISP for 10 to 15 minutes until crispy, shaking the basket a couple of times for even cooking.
7. Serve immediately.

Lime-chili Shrimp Bowl

Servings: 4
Cooking Time: 10 To 15 Minutes
Ingredients:
- 2 teaspoons lime juice
- 1 teaspoon olive oil
- 1 teaspoon honey
- 1 teaspoon minced garlic
- 1 teaspoon chili powder
- Salt, to taste
- 12 ounces medium shrimp, peeled and deveined
- 2 cups cooked brown rice
- 1 can seasoned black beans, warmed
- 1 large avocado, chopped
- 1 cup sliced cherry tomatoes
- Cooking spray

Directions:
1. Insert the Crisper Basket and close the hood. Select AIR CRISP, set the temperature to 400ºF, and set the time to 15 minutes. Select START/STOP to begin preheating.
2. Spray the Crisper Basket lightly with cooking spray.
3. In a medium bowl, mix together the lime juice, olive oil, honey, garlic, chili powder, and salt to make a marinade.
4. Add the shrimp and toss to coat evenly in the marinade.
5. Place the shrimp in the Crisper Basket. Close the hood and AIR CRISP for 5 minutes. Shake the basket and AIR CRISP until the shrimp are cooked through and starting to brown, an additional 5 to 10 minutes.
6. To assemble the bowls, spoon ¼ of the rice, black beans, avocado, and cherry tomatoes into each of four bowls. Top with the shrimp and serve.

Spicy Pork With Candy Onions

Servings: 4
Cooking Time: 52 Minutes
Ingredients:
- 2 teaspoons sesame oil
- 1 teaspoon dried sage, crushed
- 1 teaspoon cayenne pepper
- 1 rosemary sprig, chopped
- 1 thyme sprig, chopped
- Sea salt and ground black pepper, to taste
- 2 pounds pork leg roast, scored
- ½ pound candy onions, sliced
- 4 cloves garlic, finely chopped
- 2 chili peppers, minced

Directions:

1. Select AIR CRISP, set the temperature to 400ºF, and set the time to 52 minutes. Select START/STOP to begin preheating.
2. In a mixing bowl, combine the sesame oil, sage, cayenne pepper, rosemary, thyme, salt and black pepper until well mixed. In another bowl, place the pork leg and brush with the seasoning mixture.
3. Place the seasoned pork leg in a baking pan. Place the pan directly in the pot. Close the hood and AIR CRISP for 40 minutes, or until lightly browned, flipping halfway through. Add the candy onions, garlic and chili peppers to the pan and AIR CRISP for another 12 minutes.
4. Transfer the pork leg to a plate. Let cool for 5 minutes and slice. Spread the juices left in the pan over the pork and serve warm with the candy onions.

Lemongrass Beef Skewers

Servings: 4
Cooking Time: 8 Minutes
Ingredients:
* 3 tablespoons minced garlic
* 3 tablespoons light brown sugar, packed
* 3 tablespoons lemongrass paste
* 1 tablespoon soy sauce
* 1 tablespoon peeled minced fresh ginger
* 1 tablespoon avocado oil
* ½ small red onion, minced
* 2 pounds sirloin steak, cut into 1-inch cubes
* Chopped fresh cilantro, for garnish

Directions:
1. In a large bowl, combine the garlic, brown sugar, lemongrass paste, soy sauce, ginger, avocado oil, and onion until the sugar is dissolved. Add the steak cubes and massage them with the marinade. Place 5 or 6 cubes on each of 6 to 8 skewers, then place the skewers in a large rimmed baking sheet and coat with the remaining marinade. Set aside to marinate for at least 30 minutes. If marinating for longer, cover and refrigerate.
2. Insert the Grill Grate and close the hood. Select GRILL, set the temperature to HI, and set the time to 8 minutes. Select START/STOP to begin preheating.
3. When the unit beeps to signify it has preheated, place the skewers on the Grill Grate. Close the hood and grill for 4 minutes.
4. After 4 minutes, open the hood and flip the skewers. Close the hood and cook for 4 minutes more. If you prefer extra char, add 2 minutes to the cook time.
5. When cooking is complete, remove the skewers from the grill and serve, garnished with the cilantro.

Miso Marinated Steak

Servings: 4
Cooking Time: 12 Minutes
Ingredients:
* ¾ pound flank steak
* 1½ tablespoons sake
* 1 tablespoon brown miso paste
* 1 teaspoon honey
* 2 cloves garlic, pressed
* 1 tablespoon olive oil

Directions:

1. Put all the ingredients in a Ziploc bag. Shake to cover the steak well with the seasonings and refrigerate for at least 1 hour.
2. Insert the Crisper Basket and close the hood. Select AIR CRISP, set the temperature to 400ºF, and set the time to 12 minutes. Select START/STOP to begin preheating.
3. Coat all sides of the steak with cooking spray. Put the steak in the basket.
4. Close the hood and AIR CRISP for 12 minutes, turning the steak twice during the cooking time, then serve immediately.

Piri-piri King Prawn

Servings: 2
Cooking Time: 8 Minutes
Ingredients:
* 12 king prawns, rinsed
* 1 tablespoon coconut oil
* Salt and ground black pepper, to taste
* 1 teaspoon onion powder
* 1 teaspoon garlic paste
* 1 teaspoon curry powder
* ½ teaspoon piri piri powder
* ½ teaspoon cumin powder

Directions:
1. Insert the Crisper Basket and close the hood. Select AIR CRISP, set the temperature to 360ºF, and set the time to 8 minutes. Select START/STOP to begin preheating.
2. Combine all the ingredients in a large bowl and toss until the prawns are completely coated.
3. Place the prawns in the Crisper Basket. Close the hood and AIR CRISP for 8 minutes, shaking the basket halfway through, or until the prawns turn pink.
4. Serve hot.

Balsamic Honey Mustard Lamb Chops

Servings: 4 To 6
Cooking Time: 45 Minutes To 1 Hour
Ingredients:
* ¼ cup avocado oil
* ½ cup balsamic vinegar
* 2 garlic cloves, minced
* 1 teaspoon salt
* ½ teaspoon freshly ground black pepper
* 2 tablespoons honey
* 1 tablespoon yellow mustard
* 1 tablespoon fresh rosemary
* 1 (2- to 3-pound) rack of lamb

Directions:
1. In a large bowl, whisk together the avocado oil, vinegar, garlic, salt, pepper, honey, mustard, and rosemary. Add the lamb and massage and coat all sides of the meat with the marinade. Cover and refrigerate for at least 1 hour.
2. Plug the thermometer into the unit. Insert the Cooking Pot and close the hood. Select ROAST, set the temperature to 350°F, and select PRESET. Use the arrows to the right to select BEEF/ LAMB. The unit will default to WELL to cook lamb to a safe temperature. Insert the Smart Thermometer in the thickest part of the lamb without touching bone. Select START/STOP to begin preheating.

3. When the unit beeps to signify it has preheated, place the rack of lamb in the Cooking Pot. Close the hood to begin cooking.
4. When cooking is complete, the Smart Thermometer will indicate that the specified internal temperature has been reached. Remove the lamb from the pot and serve.

One-pot Chili

Servings: 4
Cooking Time: 25 Minutes
Ingredients:
- 1 small onion
- 1 pound ground beef
- 3 cloves garlic, minced
- 1 (14-ounce) can crushed tomatoes
- 1 (6-ounce) can tomato paste
- 1 cup beef broth
- 3 tablespoons chili powder
- 1 tablespoon ground cumin
- 1 teaspoon dried oregano
- 1 teaspoon paprika
- 1 (15-ounce) can beans (such as kidney, pinto, or black beans), drained and rinsed

Directions:
1. Insert the Cooking Pot and close the hood. Select GRILL, set the temperature to LO, and set the time to 25 minutes. Select START/STOP to begin preheating.
2. While the unit is preheating, dice the onion.
3. When the unit beeps to signify it has preheated, put the ground beef, onion, and garlic in the Cooking Pot. Break apart the ground beef with a wooden spoon or spatula. Close the hood and cook for 5 minutes.
4. After 5 minutes, open the hood, stir, then stir in the crushed tomatoes, tomato paste, and beef broth. Add the chili powder, cumin, oregano, paprika, and beans and stir. Close the hood and cook for 10 minutes. After 10 minutes, open the hood and stir. Close the hood and cook for 10 minutes more.
5. When cooking is complete, serve the chili garnished with your favorite toppings, such as sour cream, shredded cheese, sliced scallions, and bacon bits.

Spiced Crab Cakes

Servings: 4
Cooking Time: 10 Minutes
Ingredients:
- 1 egg
- ½ cup mayonnaise, plus 3 tablespoons
- Juice of ½ lemon
- 1 tablespoon minced scallions (green parts only)
- 1 teaspoon Old Bay seasoning
- 8 ounces lump crab meat
- ⅓ cup bread crumbs
- Nonstick cooking spray
- ½ teaspoon cayenne pepper
- ¼ teaspoon paprika
- ¼ teaspoon garlic powder
- ¼ teaspoon chili powder
- ¼ teaspoon onion powder
- ¼ teaspoon freshly ground black pepper
- ⅛ teaspoon ground nutmeg

Directions:
1. Insert the Crisper Basket and close the hood. Select AIR CRISP, set the temperature to 375ºF, and set the time to 10 minutes. Select START/STOP to begin preheating.
2. While the unit is preheating, in a medium bowl, whisk together the egg, 3 tablespoons of mayonnaise, lemon juice, scallions, and Old Bay seasoning. Gently stir in the crab meat, making sure not to break up the meat into small pieces. Add the bread crumbs, and gradually mix them in. Form the mixture into four patties.
3. When the unit beeps to signify it has preheated, place the crab cakes in the basket and coat them with the cooking spray. Close the hood and AIR CRISP for 10 minutes.
4. While the crab cakes are cooking, in a small bowl, mix the remaining ½ cup of mayonnaise, cayenne pepper, paprika, garlic powder, chili powder, onion powder, black pepper, and nutmeg until fully combined.
5. When cooking is complete, serve the crab cakes with the Cajun aioli spooned on top.

Brown-sugared Ham

Servings: 6 To 8
Cooking Time: 30 Minutes
Ingredients:
- 1 (3-pound) bone-in, fully cooked ham quarter
- 3 tablespoons Dijon mustard
- ¼ cup pineapple juice
- ¼ cup apple cider vinegar
- 1 cup light brown sugar, packed
- 1 teaspoon cinnamon
- ½ teaspoon ground ginger

Directions:
1. Plug the thermometer into the unit. Insert the Cooking Pot and close the hood. Select ROAST, set the temperature to 350°F, then select PRESET. Use the arrows to the right to select PORK. The unit will default to WELL to cook pork to a safe temperature. Insert the Smart Thermometer into the thickest part of the ham. Select START/STOP to begin preheating.
2. While the unit is preheating, score the ham using a sharp knife, creating a diamond pattern on top. Brush on the Dijon mustard.
3. In a small bowl, combine the pineapple juice, vinegar, brown sugar, cinnamon, and ginger.
4. When the unit beeps to signify it has preheated, place the ham in the Cooking Pot. Brush some of the glaze over the entire ham, then pour the rest on top so the glaze can seep into the scores. Close the hood to begin cooking.
5. When cooking is complete, the Smart Thermometer will indicate that the desired temperature has been reached. Remove the ham from the pot and let rest for at least 10 minutes before slicing. Serve.

Air-fried Scallops

Servings: 2
Cooking Time: 12 Minutes
Ingredients:
- ⅓ cup shallots, chopped
- 1½ tablespoons olive oil
- 1½ tablespoons coconut aminos
- 1 tablespoon Mediterranean seasoning mix
- ½ tablespoon balsamic vinegar
- ½ teaspoon ginger, grated
- 1 clove garlic, chopped
- 1 pound scallops, cleaned
- Cooking spray
- Belgian endive, for garnish

Directions:
1. Place all the ingredients except the scallops and Belgian endive in a small skillet over medium heat and stir to combine. Let this mixture simmer for about 2 minutes.
2. Remove the mixture from the skillet to a large bowl and set aside to cool.
3. Add the scallops, coating them all over, then transfer to the refrigerator to marinate for at least 2 hours.
4. Insert the Crisper Basket and close the hood. Select AIR CRISP, set the temperature to 345ºF, and set the time to 10 minutes. Select START/STOP to begin preheating.
5. Arrange the scallops in the Crisper Basket in a single layer and spray with cooking spray.
6. Close the hood and AIR CRISP for 10 minutes, flipping the scallops halfway through, or until the scallops are tender and opaque.
7. Serve garnished with the Belgian endive

Meatless

Cheese And Spinach Stuffed Portobellos

Servings: 4
Cooking Time: 8 Minutes
Ingredients:
- 4 large portobello mushrooms, rinsed, stemmed, and gills removed
- 4 ounces cream cheese, at room temperature
- ½ cup mayonnaise
- ½ cup sour cream
- 1 teaspoon onion powder
- ¼ teaspoon garlic powder
- ¼ cup grated Parmesan cheese
- ½ cup shredded mozzarella cheese
- 2 cups fresh spinach

Directions:
1. Insert the Grill Grate and close the hood. Select GRILL, set the temperature to HI, and set the time to 8 minutes. Select START/STOP to begin preheating.
2. When the unit beeps to signify it has preheated, place the mushrooms on the Grill Grate, cap-side up. Close the hood and cook for 4 minutes.
3. While the mushrooms are grilling, in a large bowl, combine the cream cheese, mayonnaise, sour cream, onion powder, garlic powder, Parmesan cheese, mozzarella cheese, and spinach. Mix well.
4. After 4 minutes, open the hood and flip the mushrooms. Evenly distribute the filling inside the caps. Close the hood and cook for 4 minutes more.
5. When cooking is complete, remove the stuffed mushrooms from the grill and serve.

Grilled Mozzarella Eggplant Stacks

Servings: 4
Cooking Time: 14 Minutes
Ingredients:
- 1 eggplant, sliced ¼-inch thick
- 2 tablespoons canola oil
- 2 beefsteak or heirloom tomatoes, sliced ¼-inch thick
- 12 large basil leaves
- ½ pound buffalo Mozzarella, sliced ¼-inch thick
- Sea salt, to taste

Directions:
1. Insert the Grill Grate and close the hood. Select GRILL, set the temperature to MAX, and set the time to 14 minutes. Select START/STOP to begin preheating.
2. Meanwhile, in a large bowl, toss the eggplant and oil until evenly coated.
3. When the unit beeps to signify it has preheated, place the eggplant on the Grill Grate. Close the hood and GRILL for 8 to 12 minutes, until charred on all sides.
4. After 8 to 12 minutes, top the eggplant with one slice each of tomato and Mozzarella. Close the hood and GRILL for 2 minutes, until the cheese melts.
5. When cooking is complete, remove the eggplant stacks from the grill. Place 2 or 3 basil leaves on top of half of the stacks. Place the remaining eggplant stacks on top of those with basil so that there are four stacks total. Season with salt, garnish with the remaining basil, and serve.

Vegetable And Cheese Stuffed Tomatoes

Servings: 4
Cooking Time: 16 To 20 Minutes
Ingredients:
- 4 medium beefsteak tomatoes, rinsed
- ½ cup grated carrot
- 1 medium onion, chopped
- 1 garlic clove, minced
- 2 teaspoons olive oil
- 2 cups fresh baby spinach
- ¼ cup crumbled low-sodium feta cheese
- ½ teaspoon dried basil

Directions:
1. Select BAKE, set the temperature to 350ºF, and set the time to 20 minutes. Select START/STOP to begin preheating.
2. On your cutting board, cut a thin slice off the top of each tomato. Scoop out a ¼- to ½-inch-thick tomato pulp and place the tomatoes upside down on paper towels to drain. Set aside.
3. Stir together the carrot, onion, garlic, and olive oil in a baking pan. Place the pan directly in the pot. Close the hood and BAKE for 4 to 6 minutes, or until the carrot is crisp-tender.
4. Remove the pan from the grill and stir in the spinach, feta cheese, and basil.
5. Spoon ¼ of the vegetable mixture into each tomato and transfer the stuffed tomatoes to the pan.
6. Place the pan directly in the pot. Close the hood and BAKE for 12 to 14 minutes, or until the filling is hot and the tomatoes are lightly caramelized.
7. Let the tomatoes cool for 5 minutes and serve.

Double "egg" Plant (eggplant Omelets)

Servings: 4
Cooking Time: 16 Minutes
Ingredients:
- 4 Chinese eggplants
- 2 large eggs
- Garlic powder
- Salt
- Freshly ground black pepper
- ¼ cup ketchup
- 1 tablespoon hot sauce (optional)

Directions:
1. Insert the Grill Grate. Select GRILL, set the temperature to HI, and set the time to 10 minutes. Select START/STOP to begin preheating.
2. When the unit beeps to signify it has preheated, place the whole eggplants on the Grill Grate. Close the hood and cook for 5 minutes.
3. After 5 minutes, open the hood and flip the eggplants. Close the hood and cook for 5 minutes more.
4. When cooking is complete, the eggplant skin will be charred and cracked and the flesh will be soft. Remove the eggplants from the grill and set aside to cool.
5. Once the eggplants have cooled down, peel the skin. Then, using a fork, flatten the eggplants with a brushing motion until they become pear shaped and about the thickness of a pancake.

6. Select GRILL, set the temperature to HI, and set the time to 6 minutes. Select START/STOP to begin preheating.
7. While the unit is preheating, in a large bowl, whisk the eggs. Dip each eggplant into the egg mixture to coat both sides, then season both sides with garlic powder, salt, and pepper.
8. When the grill beeps to signify it has preheated, place the coated eggplants on the Grill Grate. Close the hood and grill for 3 minutes.
9. After 3 minutes, open the hood and flip the eggplants. Close the hood and cook for 3 minutes more. Add more time if needed until you get your desired crispiness of the omelets.
10. When cooking is complete, remove the eggplant omelets from the grill. In a small bowl, combine the ketchup and hot sauce (if using), or just use ketchup if you do not like spice, and serve alongside the omelets for dipping.

Spicy Cauliflower Roast

Servings: 4
Cooking Time: 20 Minutes
Ingredients:
- Cauliflower:
- 5 cups cauliflower florets
- 3 tablespoons vegetable oil
- ½ teaspoon ground cumin
- ½ teaspoon ground coriander
- ½ teaspoon kosher salt
- Sauce:
- ½ cup Greek yogurt or sour cream
- ¼ cup chopped fresh cilantro
- 1 jalapeño, coarsely chopped
- 4 cloves garlic, peeled
- ½ teaspoon kosher salt
- 2 tablespoons water

Directions:
1. Insert the Crisper Basket and close the hood. Select ROAST, set the temperature to 400ºF, and set the time to 20 minutes. Select START/STOP to begin preheating.
2. In a large bowl, combine the cauliflower, oil, cumin, coriander, and salt. Toss to coat.
3. Put the cauliflower in the Crisper Basket. Close the hood and ROAST for 20 minutes, stirring halfway through the roasting time.
4. Meanwhile, in a blender, combine the yogurt, cilantro, jalapeño, garlic, and salt. Blend, adding the water as needed to keep the blades moving and to thin the sauce.
5. At the end of roasting time, transfer the cauliflower to a large serving bowl. Pour the sauce over and toss gently to coat. Serve immediately.

Cheesy Rice And Olives Stuffed Peppers

Servings: 4
Cooking Time: 16 To 17 Minutes
Ingredients:
- 4 red bell peppers, tops sliced off
- 2 cups cooked rice
- 1 cup crumbled feta cheese
- 1 onion, chopped
- ¼ cup sliced kalamata olives
- ¾ cup tomato sauce

- 1 tablespoon Greek seasoning
- Salt and black pepper, to taste
- 2 tablespoons chopped fresh dill, for serving

Directions:

1. Select BAKE, set the temperature to 360°F, and set the time to 15 minutes. Select START/STOP to begin preheating.
2. Microwave the red bell peppers for 1 to 2 minutes until tender.
3. When ready, transfer the red bell peppers to a plate to cool.
4. Mix together the cooked rice, feta cheese, onion, kalamata olives, tomato sauce, Greek seasoning, salt, and pepper in a medium bowl and stir until well combined.
5. Divide the rice mixture among the red bell peppers and transfer to a greased baking pan.
6. Place the pan directly in the pot. Close the hood and BAKE for 15 minutes, or until the rice is heated through and the vegetables are soft.
7. Remove from the basket and serve with the dill sprinkled on top.

Cheesy Broccoli Gratin

Servings: 2
Cooking Time: 12 To 14 Minutes
Ingredients:

- ⅓ cup fat-free milk
- 1 tablespoon all-purpose or gluten-free flour
- ½ tablespoon olive oil
- ½ teaspoon ground sage
- ¼ teaspoon kosher salt
- ⅛ teaspoon freshly ground black pepper
- 2 cups roughly chopped broccoli florets
- 6 tablespoons shredded Cheddar cheese
- 2 tablespoons panko bread crumbs
- 1 tablespoon grated Parmesan cheese
- Olive oil spray

Directions:

1. Select BAKE, set the temperature to 330°F, and set the time to 14 minutes. Select START/STOP to begin preheating.
2. Spritz a baking pan with olive oil spray.
3. Mix the milk, flour, olive oil, sage, salt, and pepper in a medium bowl and whisk to combine. Stir in the broccoli florets, Cheddar cheese, bread crumbs, and Parmesan cheese and toss to coat.
4. Pour the broccoli mixture into the prepared baking pan. Place the pan directly in the pot.
5. Close the hood and BAKE for 12 to 14 minutes until the top is golden brown and the broccoli is tender.
6. Serve immediately.

Sesame-thyme Whole Maitake Mushrooms

Servings: 2
Cooking Time: 15 Minutes
Ingredients:

- 1 tablespoon soy sauce
- 2 teaspoons toasted sesame oil
- 3 teaspoons vegetable oil, divided
- 1 garlic clove, minced
- 7 ounces maitake (hen of the woods) mushrooms
- ½ teaspoon flaky sea salt
- ½ teaspoon sesame seeds
- ½ teaspoon finely chopped fresh thyme leaves

Directions:

1. Insert the Crisper Basket and close the hood. Select ROAST, set the temperature to 300°F, and set the time to 15 minutes. Select START/STOP to begin preheating.
2. Whisk together the soy sauce, sesame oil, 1 teaspoon of vegetable oil, and garlic in a small bowl.
3. Arrange the mushrooms in the Crisper Basket in a single layer. Drizzle the soy sauce mixture over the mushrooms. Close the hood and ROAST for 10 minutes.
4. Flip the mushrooms and sprinkle the sea salt, sesame seeds, and thyme leaves on top. Drizzle the remaining 2 teaspoons of vegetable oil all over. Roast for an additional 5 minutes.
5. Remove the mushrooms from the basket to a plate and serve hot.

Creamy And Cheesy Spinach

Servings: 4
Cooking Time: 15 Minutes
Ingredients:

- Vegetable oil spray
- 1 package frozen spinach, thawed and squeezed dry
- ½ cup chopped onion
- 2 cloves garlic, minced
- 4 ounces cream cheese, diced
- ½ teaspoon ground nutmeg
- 1 teaspoon kosher salt
- 1 teaspoon black pepper
- ½ cup grated Parmesan cheese

Directions:

1. Select BAKE, set the temperature to 350°F, and set the time to 15 minutes. Select START/STOP to begin preheating.
2. Spray a heatproof pan with vegetable oil spray.
3. In a medium bowl, combine the spinach, onion, garlic, cream cheese, nutmeg, salt, and pepper. Transfer to the prepared pan.
4. Place the pan directly in the pot. Close the hood and BAKE for 10 minutes. Open and stir to thoroughly combine the cream cheese and spinach.
5. Sprinkle the Parmesan cheese on top. Bake for 5 minutes, or until the cheese has melted and browned.
6. Serve hot.

Balsamic Mushroom Sliders With Pesto

Servings: 4
Cooking Time: 8 Minutes
Ingredients:

- 8 small portobello mushrooms, trimmed with gills removed
- 2 tablespoons canola oil
- 2 tablespoons balsamic vinegar
- 8 slider buns
- 1 tomato, sliced
- ½ cup pesto
- ½ cup micro greens

Directions:

1. Insert the Grill Grate and close the hood. Select GRILL, set the temperature to HIGH, and set the time to 8 minutes. Select START/STOP to begin preheating.
2. While the unit is preheating, brush the mushrooms with the oil and balsamic vinegar.
3. When the unit beeps to signify it has preheated, place the mushrooms, gill-side down, on the Grill Grate. Close the hood and GRILL for 8 minutes until the mushrooms are tender.
4. When cooking is complete, remove the mushrooms from the grill, and layer on the buns with tomato, pesto, and micro greens.

Grilled Artichokes With Garlic Aioli

Servings: 4
Cooking Time: 33 Minutes
Ingredients:
- For the artichokes
- 4 artichokes
- 8 tablespoons avocado oil
- 8 tablespoons minced garlic
- Salt
- Freshly ground black pepper
- For the garlic aioli
- ½ cup mayonnaise
- 1 garlic clove, minced
- 1 tablespoon apple cider vinegar
- ⅛ teaspoon paprika

Directions:
1. Pull off the tough outer leaves near the stem of the artichoke and trim the bottom of the stem. Cut off the top third (½ to 1 inch) of the artichoke. Trim the tips of the leaves that surround the artichoke, as they can be sharp and thorny. Then cut the artichoke in half lengthwise. This exposes the artichoke heart. Use a spoon to remove the fuzzy choke, scraping to make sure it is cleaned away, then rinse the artichoke.
2. Insert the Grill Grate and close the hood. Select GRILL, set the temperature to LO, and set the time to 25 minutes. Select START/STOP to begin preheating.
3. While the unit is preheating, prepare 8 large pieces of aluminum foil for wrapping. Place an artichoke half, cut-side up, in the center of a foil piece. Drizzle 1 tablespoon of avocado oil into the center of the artichoke half and add 1 tablespoon of minced garlic. Season with salt and pepper. Seal the foil packet, making sure all sides are closed. Repeat for each artichoke half.
4. When the unit beeps to signify it has preheated, place the foil-wrapped artichokes on the Grill Grate. Close the hood and grill for 25 minutes.
5. When cooking is complete, the stem and heart will be soft, about the consistency of a cooked potato. Remove the artichokes from the foil.
6. Select GRILL, set the temperature to MAX, and set the time to 8 minutes. Place the artichokes on the Grill Grate, cut-side down. Select START/STOP and then press the PREHEAT button to skip preheating. Close the hood and cook for 4 minutes.
7. After 4 minutes, open the hood and flip the artichokes. Season with additional salt and pepper, if desired. Close the hood and cook for 4 minutes more.
8. When cooking is complete, remove the artichokes from the grill.

9. In a small bowl, combine the mayonnaise, garlic, vinegar, and paprika. Serve alongside the artichokes for dipping.

Cinnamon-spiced Acorn Squash

Servings: 2
Cooking Time: 15 Minutes
Ingredients:
- 1 medium acorn squash, halved crosswise and deseeded
- 1 teaspoon coconut oil
- 1 teaspoon light brown sugar
- Few dashes of ground cinnamon
- Few dashes of ground nutmeg

Directions:
1. Insert the Crisper Basket and close the hood. Select AIR CRISP, set the temperature to 325°F, and set the time to 15 minutes. Select START/STOP to begin preheating.
2. On a clean work surface, rub the cut sides of the acorn squash with coconut oil. Scatter with the brown sugar, cinnamon, and nutmeg.
3. Put the squash halves in the Crisper Basket, cut-side up. Close the hood and AIR CRISP for 15 minutes until just tender when pierced in the center with a paring knife.
4. Rest for 5 to 10 minutes and serve warm.

Fast And Easy Asparagus

Servings: 4
Cooking Time: 5 Minutes
Ingredients:
- 1 pound fresh asparagus spears, trimmed
- 1 tablespoon olive oil
- Salt and ground black pepper, to taste

Directions:
1. Insert the Crisper Basket and close the hood. Select AIR CRISP, set the temperature to 375°F, and set the time to 5 minutes. Select START/STOP to begin preheating.
2. Combine all the ingredients and transfer to the Crisper Basket.
3. Close the hood and AIR CRISP for 5 minutes or until soft.
4. Serve hot.

Honey-sriracha Brussels Sprouts

Servings: 8
Cooking Time: 20 Minutes
Ingredients:
- 2 pounds Brussels sprouts, halved lengthwise, ends trimmed
- 2 tablespoons avocado oil
- 4 tablespoons honey or coconut palm sugar
- 2 teaspoons sriracha
- Juice of 1 lemon

Directions:
1. Insert the Crisper Basket and close the hood. Select AIR CRISP, set the temperature to 390°F, and set the time to 20 minutes. Select START/STOP to begin preheating.
2. While the unit is preheating, in a large bowl, toss the Brussels sprouts with the avocado oil.
3. When the unit beeps to signify it has preheated, place the Brussels sprouts in the Crisper Basket. Close the hood and cook for 10 minutes.

4. After 10 minutes, open the hood and toss the Brussels sprouts. Close the hood and cook for 10 minutes more. If you choose, before the last 5 minutes, open the hood and toss the Brussels sprouts one more time.

5. When cooking is complete, open the hood and transfer the Brussels sprouts to a large bowl. Or if you like more crisping and browning of your sprouts, continue cooking to your liking.

6. In a small bowl, whisk together the honey, sriracha, and lemon juice. Drizzle this over the Brussels sprouts and toss to coat. Serve.

Cauliflower Steaks With Ranch Dressing

Servings: 2
Cooking Time: 15 Minutes
Ingredients:
- 1 head cauliflower, stemmed and leaves removed
- ¼ cup canola oil
- ½ teaspoon garlic powder
- ½ teaspoon paprika
- Sea salt, to taste
- Freshly ground black pepper, to taste
- 1 cup shredded Cheddar cheese
- Ranch dressing, for garnish
- 4 slices bacon, cooked and crumbled
- 2 tablespoons chopped fresh chives

Directions:
1. Cut the cauliflower from top to bottom into two 2-inch "steaks"; reserve the remaining cauliflower to cook separately.

2. Insert the Grill Grate and close the hood. Select GRILL, set the temperature to MAX, and set the time to 15 minutes. Select START/STOP to begin preheating.

3. Meanwhile, in a small bowl, whisk together the oil, garlic powder, and paprika. Season with salt and pepper. Brush each steak with the oil mixture on both sides.

4. When the unit beeps to signify it has preheated, place the steaks on the Grill Grate. Close the hood and GRILL for 10 minutes.

5. After 10 minutes, flip the steaks and top each with ½ cup of cheese. Close the hood and continue to GRILL until the cheese is melted, about 5 minutes.

6. When cooking is complete, place the cauliflower steaks on a plate and drizzle with the ranch dressing. Top with the bacon and chives.

Corn And Potato Chowder

Servings: 4
Cooking Time: 50 Minutes
Ingredients:
- 4 ears corn, shucked
- 2 tablespoons canola oil
- 1½ teaspoons sea salt, plus additional to season the corn
- ½ teaspoon freshly ground black pepper, plus additional to season the corn
- 3 tablespoons unsalted butter
- 1 small onion, finely chopped
- 2½ cups vegetable broth
- 1½ cups milk
- 4 cups diced potatoes

- 2 cups half-and-half
- 1½ teaspoons chopped fresh thyme

Directions:
1. Insert the Grill Grate and close the hood. Select GRILL, set the temperature to MAX, and set the time to 12 minutes. Select START/STOP to begin preheating.

2. While the unit is preheating, brush each ear of corn with ½ tablespoon of oil. Season the corn with salt and pepper to taste.

3. When the unit beeps to signify it has preheated, place the corn on the Grill Grate and close the hood. GRILL for 6 minutes.

4. After 6 minutes, flip the corn. Close the hood and continue cooking for the remaining 6 minutes.

5. When cooking is complete, remove the corn and let cool. Cut the kernels from the cobs.

6. In a food processor, purée 1 cup of corn kernels until smooth.

7. In a large pot over medium-high heat, melt the butter. Add the onion and sauté until soft, 5 to 7 minutes. Add the broth, milk, and potatoes. Bring to a simmer and cook until the potatoes are just tender, 10 to 12 minutes. Stir in the salt and pepper.

8. Stir in the puréed corn, remaining corn kernels, and half-and-half. Bring to a simmer and cook, stirring occasionally, until the potatoes are cooked through, for 15 to 20 minutes.

9. Using a potato masher or immersion blender, slightly mash some of the potatoes. Stir in the thyme, and additional salt and pepper to taste.

Creamy Corn Casserole

Servings: 4
Cooking Time: 15 Minutes
Ingredients:
- 2 cups frozen yellow corn
- 1 egg, beaten
- 3 tablespoons flour
- ½ cup grated Swiss or Havarti cheese
- ½ cup light cream
- ¼ cup milk
- Pinch salt
- Freshly ground black pepper, to taste
- 2 tablespoons butter, cut into cubes
- Nonstick cooking spray

Directions:
1. Select BAKE, set the temperature to 320°F, and set the time to 15 minutes. Select START/STOP to begin preheating.

2. Spritz a baking pan with nonstick cooking spray.

3. Stir together the remaining ingredients except the butter in a medium bowl until well incorporated.

4. Transfer the mixture to the prepared baking pan and scatter with the butter cubes.

5. Place the pan directly in the pot. Close the hood and BAKE for 15 minutes, or until the top is golden brown and a toothpick inserted in the center comes out clean.

6. Let the casserole cool for 5 minutes before slicing into wedges and serving.

Loaded Zucchini Boats

Servings: 4
Cooking Time: 10 Minutes
Ingredients:
- 4 medium zucchini
- 1 cup panko bread crumbs
- 2 garlic cloves, minced
- ½ small white onion, diced
- ½ cup grated Parmesan cheese
- 1 tablespoon Italian seasoning

Directions:
1. Insert the Grill Grate and close the hood. Select GRILL, set the temperature to HI, and set the time to 10 minutes. Select START/STOP to begin preheating.
2. While the unit is preheating, cut the zucchini in half lengthwise. Carefully scoop out the flesh and put it in a medium bowl. Set the boats aside.
3. Add the panko bread crumbs, garlic, onion, Parmesan cheese, and Italian seasoning to the bowl and mix well. Spoon the filling into each zucchini half.
4. When the unit beeps to signify it has preheated, place the zucchini boats on the Grill Grate, cut-side up. Close the hood and grill for 10 minutes.
5. When cooking is complete, the cheese will be melted and the tops will be crispy and golden brown. Remove the zucchini boats from the grill and serve.

Rosemary Roasted Potatoes

Servings: 4
Cooking Time: 20 To 22 Minutes
Ingredients:
- 1½ pounds small red potatoes, cut into 1-inch cubes
- 2 tablespoons olive oil
- 2 tablespoons minced fresh rosemary
- 1 tablespoon minced garlic
- 1 teaspoon salt, plus additional as needed
- ½ teaspoon freshly ground black pepper, plus additional as needed

Directions:
1. Insert the Crisper Basket and close the hood. Select ROAST, set the temperature to 400°F, and set the time to 22 minutes. Select START/STOP to begin preheating.
2. Toss the potato cubes with the olive oil, rosemary, garlic, salt, and pepper in a large bowl until thoroughly coated.
3. Arrange the potato cubes in the Crisper Basket in a single layer. Close the hood and ROAST for 20 to 22 minutes until the potatoes are tender. Shake the basket a few times during cooking for even cooking.
4. Remove from the basket to a plate. Taste and add additional salt and pepper as needed.

Parmesan Asparagus Fries

Servings: 4
Cooking Time: 5 To 7 Minutes
Ingredients:
- 2 egg whites
- ¼ cup water
- ¼ cup plus 2 tablespoons grated Parmesan cheese, divided
- ¾ cup panko bread crumbs
- ¼ teaspoon salt
- 12 ounces fresh asparagus spears, woody ends trimmed
- Cooking spray

Directions:
1. Insert the Crisper Basket and close the hood. Select AIR CRISP, set the temperature to 390°F, and set the time to 7 minutes. Select START/STOP to begin preheating.
2. In a shallow dish, whisk together the egg whites and water until slightly foamy. In a separate shallow dish, thoroughly combine ¼ cup of Parmesan cheese, bread crumbs, and salt.
3. Dip the asparagus in the egg white, then roll in the cheese mixture to coat well.
4. Place the asparagus in the Crisper Basket in a single layer, leaving space between each spear. You may need to work in batches to avoid overcrowding.
5. Spritz the asparagus with cooking spray. Close the hood and AIR CRISP for 5 to 7 minutes until golden brown and crisp.
6. Repeat with the remaining asparagus spears.
7. Sprinkle with the remaining 2 tablespoons of cheese and serve hot.

Veggie Taco Pie

Servings: 4
Cooking Time: 15 Minutes
Ingredients:
- 1 (15-ounce) can pinto beans, drained and rinsed
- 1 tablespoon chili powder
- 2 teaspoons ground cumin
- 2 teaspoons sea salt
- 1 teaspoon paprika
- ½ teaspoon garlic powder
- ½ teaspoon onion powder
- ½ teaspoon dried oregano
- 4 small flour tortillas
- 1 cup sour cream
- 1 (14-ounce) can diced tomatoes, drained
- 1 (15-ounce) can black beans, drained and rinsed
- 2 cups shredded cheddar cheese

Directions:
1. Insert the Cooking Pot and close the hood. Select BAKE, set the temperature to 350°F, and set the time to 15 minutes. Select START/STOP to begin preheating.
2. While the unit is preheating, in a large bowl, mash the pinto beans with a fork. Add the chili powder, cumin, salt, paprika, garlic powder, onion powder, and oregano and mix until well combined. Place a tortilla in the bottom of a 6-inch springform pan. Spread a quarter of the mashed pinto beans on the tortilla in an even layer, then layer on a quarter each of the sour cream, tomatoes, black beans, and cheddar cheese in that order. Repeat the layers three more times, ending with cheese.
3. When the unit beeps to signify it has preheated, place the pan in the Cooking Pot. Close the hood and cook for 15 minutes.
4. When cooking is complete, the cheese will be melted. Remove the pan from the grill and serve.

Summer Squash And Zucchini Salad

Servings: 4
Cooking Time: 20 Minutes
Ingredients:
- 1 zucchini, sliced lengthwise about ¼-inch thick
- 1 summer squash, sliced lengthwise about ¼-inch thick
- ½ red onion, sliced
- 4 tablespoons canola oil, divided
- 2 portobello mushroom caps, trimmed with gills removed
- 2 ears corn, shucked
- 2 teaspoons freshly squeezed lemon juice
- Sea salt, to taste
- Freshly ground black pepper, to taste

Directions:
1. Insert the Grill Grate and close the hood. Select GRILL, set the temperature to MAX, and set the time to 25 minutes. Select START/STOP to begin preheating.
2. Meanwhile, in a large bowl, toss the zucchini, squash, and onion with 2 tablespoons of oil until evenly coated.
3. When the unit beeps to signify it has preheated, arrange the zucchini, squash, and onions on the Grill Grate. Close the hood and GRILL for 6 minutes.
4. After 6 minutes, open the hood and flip the squash. Close the hood and GRILL for 6 to 9 minutes more.
5. Meanwhile, brush the mushrooms and corn with the remaining 2 tablespoons of oil.
6. When cooking is complete, remove the zucchini, squash, and onions and swap in the mushrooms and corn. Close the hood and GRILL for the remaining 10 minutes.
7. When cooking is complete, remove the mushrooms and corn, and let cool.
8. Cut the kernels from the cobs. Roughly chop all the vegetables into bite-size pieces.
9. Place the vegetables in a serving bowl and drizzle with lemon juice. Season with salt and pepper, and toss until evenly mixed.

Prosciutto Mini Mushroom Pizza

Servings: 3
Cooking Time: 5 Minutes
Ingredients:
- 3 portobello mushroom caps, cleaned and scooped
- 3 tablespoons olive oil
- Pinch of salt
- Pinch of dried Italian seasonings
- 3 tablespoons tomato sauce
- 3 tablespoons shredded Mozzarella cheese
- 12 slices prosciutto

Directions:
1. Insert the Crisper Basket and close the hood. Select AIR CRISP, set the temperature to 330ºF, and set the time to 5 minutes. Select START/STOP to begin preheating.
2. Season both sides of the portobello mushrooms with a drizzle of olive oil, then sprinkle salt and the Italian seasonings on the insides.
3. With a knife, spread the tomato sauce evenly over the mushroom, before adding the Mozzarella on top.
4. Put the portobello in the Crisper Basket. Close the hood and AIR CRISP for 1 minutes, before taking the Crisper Basket out of the grill and putting the prosciutto slices on top. AIR CRISP for another 4 minutes.

5. Serve warm.

Mozzarella Broccoli Calzones

Servings: 4
Cooking Time: 24 Minutes
Ingredients:
- 1 head broccoli, trimmed into florets
- 2 tablespoons extra-virgin olive oil
- 1 store-bought pizza dough
- 2 to 3 tablespoons all-purpose flour, plus more for dusting
- 1 egg, beaten
- 2 cups shredded Mozzarella cheese
- 1 cup ricotta cheese
- ½ cup grated Parmesan cheese
- 1 garlic clove, grated
- Grated zest of 1 lemon
- ½ teaspoon red pepper flakes
- Cooking oil spray

Directions:
1. Insert the Crisper Basket and close the hood. Select AIR CRISP, set the temperature to 390ºF, and set the time to 12 minutes. Select START/STOP to begin preheating.
2. Meanwhile, in a large bowl, toss the broccoli and olive oil until evenly coated.
3. When the unit beeps to signify it has preheated, add the broccoli to the basket. Close the hood and AIR CRISP for 6 minutes.
4. While the broccoli is cooking, divide the pizza dough into four equal pieces. Dust a clean work surface with the flour. Place the dough on the floured surface and roll each piece into an 8-inch round of even thickness. Dust your rolling pin and work surface with additional flour, as needed, to ensure the dough does not stick. Brush a thin coating of egg wash around the edges of each round.
5. After 6 minutes, shake the basket of broccoli. Place the basket back in the unit and close the hood to resume cooking.
6. Meanwhile, in a medium bowl, combine the Mozzarella, ricotta, Parmesan cheese, garlic, lemon zest, and red pepper flakes.
7. After cooking is complete, add the broccoli to the cheese mixture. Spoon one-quarter of the mixture onto one side of each dough. Fold the other half over the filling, and press firmly to seal the edges together. Brush each calzone all over with the remaining egg wash.
8. Select AIR CRISP, set the temperature to 390ºF, and set the time to 12 minutes. Select START/STOP to begin preheating.
9. When the unit beeps to signify it has preheated, coat the Crisper Basket with cooking spray and place the calzones in the basket. AIR CRISP for 10 to 12 minutes, until golden brown.

Zucchini And Onions Au Gratin

Servings: 4
Cooking Time: 15 Minutes
Ingredients:

- 1 cup panko bread crumbs
- 1 cup grated Parmesan cheese
- 1 large white onion, sliced
- 3 zucchini, cut into thin discs
- 1 teaspoon sea salt
- 1 teaspoon freshly ground black pepper
- 1 teaspoon onion powder
- 1 cup heavy (whipping) cream
- 1 tablespoon unsalted butter, at room temperature
- 1 teaspoon cornstarch

Directions:
1. Insert the Cooking Pot and close the hood. Select GRILL, set the temperature to MED, and set the time to 15 minutes. Select START/STOP to begin preheating.
2. While the unit is preheating, in a large bowl, combine the panko bread crumbs and Parmesan cheese.
3. When the unit beeps to signify it has preheated, add the onion to the Cooking Pot. Close the hood and cook for 2 minutes.
4. After 2 minutes, open the hood and add the zucchini, salt, pepper, and onion powder. Stir to mix. Close the hood and cook for 2 minutes.
5. After 2 minutes, open the hood and stir in the heavy cream, butter, and cornstarch. Close the hood and cook for 3 minutes.
6. After 3 minutes, the vegetable mixture should be creamy and thick. Evenly spread the bread crumb mixture over the top. Close the hood and cook for 8 minutes more.
7. When cooking is complete, the top will be golden brown and crunchy. Remove from the grill and serve.

Charred Green Beans With Sesame Seeds

Servings: 4
Cooking Time: 8 Minutes
Ingredients:

- 1 tablespoon reduced-sodium soy sauce or tamari
- ½ tablespoon Sriracha sauce
- 4 teaspoons toasted sesame oil, divided
- 12 ounces trimmed green beans
- ½ tablespoon toasted sesame seeds

Directions:
1. Insert the Crisper Basket and close the hood. Select AIR CRISP, set the temperature to 375ºF, and set the time to 8 minutes. Select START/STOP to begin preheating.
2. Whisk together the soy sauce, Sriracha sauce, and 1 teaspoon of sesame oil in a small bowl until smooth.
3. Toss the green beans with the remaining sesame oil in a large bowl until evenly coated.
4. Place the green beans in the Crisper Basket in a single layer. You may need to work in batches to avoid overcrowding.
5. Close the hood and AIR CRISP for 8 minutes until the green beans are lightly charred and tender. Shake the basket halfway through the cooking time.
6. Remove from the basket to a platter. Repeat with the remaining green beans.

7. Pour the prepared sauce over the top of green beans and toss well. Serve sprinkled with the toasted sesame seeds.

Sweet Pepper Poppers

Servings: 4
Cooking Time: 7 Minutes
Ingredients:

- 10 mini sweet peppers
- ½ cup mayonnaise
- 1 cup shredded sharp cheddar cheese
- ½ teaspoon onion powder
- ⅛ teaspoon cayenne powder (optional)

Directions:
1. Insert the Grill Grate and close the hood. Select GRILL, set the temperature to HI, and set the time to 7 minutes. Select START/STOP to begin preheating.
2. While the unit is preheating, cut the peppers in half lengthwise and scoop out the seeds and membranes. In a small bowl, combine the mayonnaise, cheddar cheese, onion powder, and cayenne powder (if using). Spoon the cheese mixture into each sweet pepper half.
3. When the unit beeps to signify it has preheated, place the sweet peppers on the Grill Grate, cut-side up. Close the hood and grill for 7 minutes.
4. When cooking is complete, remove the peppers from the grill and serve. Or if you prefer your peppers more charred, continue cooking to your liking.

Simple Pesto Gnocchi

Servings: 4
Cooking Time: 15 Minutes
Ingredients:

- 1 package gnocchi
- 1 medium onion, chopped
- 3 cloves garlic, minced
- 1 tablespoon extra-virgin olive oil
- 1 jar pesto
- ⅓ cup grated Parmesan cheese

Directions:
1. Insert the Crisper Basket and close the hood. Select AIR CRISP, set the temperature to 340ºF, and set the time to 15 minutes. Select START/STOP to begin preheating.
2. In a large bowl combine the onion, garlic, and gnocchi, and drizzle with the olive oil. Mix thoroughly.
3. Transfer the mixture to the basket. Close the hood and AIR CRISP for 15 minutes, stirring occasionally, making sure the gnocchi become light brown and crispy.
4. Add the pesto and Parmesan cheese, and give everything a good stir before serving.

Stuffed Squash With Tomatoes And Poblano

Servings: 4
Cooking Time: 30 Minutes
Ingredients:

- 1 pound butternut squash, ends trimmed
- 2 teaspoons olive oil, divided
- 6 grape tomatoes, halved
- 1 poblano pepper, cut into strips
- Salt and black pepper, to taste
- ¼ cup grated Mozzarella cheese

Directions:

1. Insert the Crisper Basket and close the hood. Select ROAST, set the temperature to 350ºF, and set the time to 30 minutes. Select START/STOP to begin preheating.
2. Using a large knife, cut the squash in half lengthwise on a flat work surface. This recipe just needs half of the squash. Scoop out the flesh to make room for the stuffing. Coat the squash half with 1 teaspoon of olive oil.
3. Put the squash half in the Crisper Basket. Close the hood and ROAST for 15 minutes.
4. Meanwhile, thoroughly combine the tomatoes, poblano pepper, remaining 1 teaspoon of olive oil, salt, and pepper in a bowl.
5. Remove the basket and spoon the tomato mixture into the squash. Return to the grill and roast for 12 minutes until the tomatoes are soft.
6. Scatter the Mozzarella cheese on top and continue roasting for about 3 minutes, or until the cheese is melted.
7. Cool for 5 minutes before serving.

Crispy Noodle Vegetable Stir-fry

Servings: 4
Cooking Time: 20 Minutes
Ingredients:
- 4 cups water
- 3 (5-ounce) packages instant ramen noodles (flavor packets removed) or 1 (12-ounce) package chow mein noodles
- Extra-virgin olive oil, for drizzling, plus 3 tablespoons
- 3 garlic cloves, minced
- 3 teaspoons peeled minced fresh ginger
- 1 red bell pepper, cut into thin strips
- 4 ounces white mushrooms, sliced
- 1 (8-ounce) can sweet baby corn, drained
- 2 cups snap peas
- 2 cups broccoli florets
- 1 small carrot, diagonally sliced
- 1 cup vegetable broth
- 1 cup soy sauce
- ¼ cup rice vinegar
- 1 tablespoon sesame oil
- 3 tablespoons sugar
- 1 tablespoon cornstarch
Directions:
1. Insert the Cooking Pot and close the hood. Select GRILL, set the temperature to HI, and set the time to 20 minutes. Select START/STOP to begin preheating.
2. When the unit beeps to signify it has preheated, pour the water into the Cooking Pot and add the ramen noodles. Close the hood and cook for 5 minutes.
3. After 5 minutes, open the hood and remove the Cooking Pot. Drain the noodles and set aside. Insert the Grill Grate (along with the Cooking Pot). Make a large bed of noodles on the Grill Grate and drizzle olive oil over them. Close the hood and cook for 5 minutes. (If using chow mein noodles, flip them halfway through.)
4. After 5 minutes, the ramen noodles should be crispy and golden brown. Transfer the crispy noodles to a large serving plate.
5. Use grill mitts to remove the Grill Grate. To the Cooking Pot, add the remaining 3 tablespoons of olive oil and the garlic and ginger. Close the hood and cook for 2 minutes.

6. After 2 minutes, open the hood and add the red bell pepper, mushrooms, baby corn, snap peas, broccoli, and carrot. Close the hood and cook for 5 minutes.
7. While the vegetables are cooking, in a small bowl, combine the vegetable broth, soy sauce, vinegar, sesame oil, sugar, and cornstarch and mix until the sugar and cornstarch are dissolved.
8. After 5 minutes, open the hood, stir the vegetables, and add the broth mixture. Close the hood and cook for 3 minutes more.
9. When cooking is complete, open the hood and stir once more. Close the hood and let the vegetables sit in the pot for 3 minutes. Then, pour the vegetables and sauce on top of the crispy noodle bed and serve.

Kidney Beans Oatmeal In Peppers

Servings: 2 To 4
Cooking Time: 6 Minutes
Ingredients:
- 2 large bell peppers, halved lengthwise, deseeded
- 2 tablespoons cooked kidney beans
- 2 tablespoons cooked chick peas
- 2 cups cooked oatmeal
- 1 teaspoon ground cumin
- ½ teaspoon paprika
- ½ teaspoon salt or to taste
- ¼ teaspoon black pepper powder
- ¼ cup yogurt
Directions:
1. Insert the Crisper Basket and close the hood. Select AIR CRISP, set the temperature to 355ºF, and set the time to 6 minutes. Select START/STOP to begin preheating.
2. Put the bell peppers, cut-side down, in the Crisper Basket. Close the hood and AIR CRISP for 2 minutes.
3. Take the peppers out of the grill and let cool.
4. In a bowl, combine the rest of the ingredients.
5. Divide the mixture evenly and use each portion to stuff a pepper.
6. Return the stuffed peppers to the basket. Close the hood and AIR CRISP for 4 minutes.
7. Serve hot.

Potatoes With Zucchinis

Servings: 4
Cooking Time: 45 Minutes
Ingredients:
- 2 potatoes, peeled and cubed
- 4 carrots, cut into chunks
- 1 head broccoli, cut into florets
- 4 zucchinis, sliced thickly
- Salt and ground black pepper, to taste
- ¼ cup olive oil
- 1 tablespoon dry onion powder
Directions:
1. Select BAKE, set the temperature to 400ºF, and set the time to 45 minutes. Select START/STOP to begin preheating.
2. In a baking pan, add all the ingredients and combine well.
3. Place the pan directly in the pot. Close the hood and BAKE for 45 minutes, ensuring the vegetables are soft and the sides have browned before serving.

Chermoula Beet Roast

Servings: 4
Cooking Time: 25 Minutes
Ingredients:
- Chermoula:
- 1 cup packed fresh cilantro leaves
- ½ cup packed fresh parsley leaves
- 6 cloves garlic, peeled
- 2 teaspoons smoked paprika
- 2 teaspoons ground cumin
- 1 teaspoon ground coriander
- ½ to 1 teaspoon cayenne pepper
- Pinch of crushed saffron (optional)
- ½ cup extra-virgin olive oil
- Kosher salt, to taste
- Beets:
- 3 medium beets, trimmed, peeled, and cut into 1-inch chunks
- 2 tablespoons chopped fresh cilantro
- 2 tablespoons chopped fresh parsley

Directions:
1. In a food processor, combine the cilantro, parsley, garlic, paprika, cumin, coriander, and cayenne. Pulse until coarsely chopped. Add the saffron, if using, and process until combined. With the food processor running, slowly add the olive oil in a steady stream; process until the sauce is uniform. Season with salt.
2. Insert the Crisper Basket and close the hood. Select ROAST, set the temperature to 375°F, and set the time to 25 minutes. Select START/STOP to begin preheating.
3. In a large bowl, drizzle the beets with ½ cup of the chermoula to coat. Arrange the beets in the Crisper Basket. Close the hood and ROAST for 25 minutes, or until the beets are tender.
4. Transfer the beets to a serving platter. Sprinkle with the chopped cilantro and parsley and serve.

Cheesy Macaroni Balls

Servings: 2
Cooking Time: 10 Minutes
Ingredients:
- 2 cups leftover macaroni
- 1 cup shredded Cheddar cheese
- ½ cup flour
- 1 cup bread crumbs
- 3 large eggs
- 1 cup milk
- ½ teaspoon salt
- ¼ teaspoon black pepper

Directions:
1. Insert the Crisper Basket and close the hood. Select AIR CRISP, set the temperature to 365°F, and set the time to 10 minutes. Select START/STOP to begin preheating.
2. In a bowl, combine the leftover macaroni and shredded cheese.
3. Pour the flour in a separate bowl. Put the bread crumbs in a third bowl. Finally, in a fourth bowl, mix the eggs and milk with a whisk.
4. With an ice-cream scoop, create balls from the macaroni mixture. Coat them the flour, then in the egg mixture, and lastly in the bread crumbs.

5. Arrange the balls in the basket. Close the hood and AIR CRISP for 10 minutes, giving them an occasional stir. Ensure they crisp up nicely.
6. Serve hot.

Rosemary Roasted Squash With Cheese

Servings: 2
Cooking Time: 20 Minutes
Ingredients:
- 1 pound butternut squash, cut into wedges
- 2 tablespoons olive oil
- 1 tablespoon dried rosemary
- Salt, to salt
- 1 cup crumbled goat cheese
- 1 tablespoon maple syrup

Directions:
1. Insert the Crisper Basket and close the hood. Select ROAST, set the temperature to 350°F, and set the time to 20 minutes. Select START/STOP to begin preheating.
2. Toss the squash wedges with the olive oil, rosemary, and salt in a large bowl until well coated.
3. Transfer the squash wedges to the Crisper Basket, spreading them out in as even a layer as possible.
4. Close the hood and ROAST for 10 minutes. Flip the squash and roast for another 10 minutes until golden brown.
5. Sprinkle the goat cheese on top and serve drizzled with the maple syrup.

Black-pepper Garlic Tofu

Servings: 4
Cooking Time: 9 Minutes
Ingredients:
- 1 (14-ounce) package firm tofu, cut into 1-inch cubes
- 1½ teaspoons cornstarch, divided
- 2 tablespoons avocado oil
- 1 medium white onion, diced
- 1 red bell pepper, cut into thin strips
- 1 teaspoon peeled minced fresh ginger
- 2 garlic cloves, minced
- 2 tablespoons black peppercorns, crushed
- 2 tablespoons soy sauce
- 1 tablespoon light brown sugar, packed
- ¼ cup ketchup
- 1 tablespoon unsalted butter, melted

Directions:
1. Insert the Cooking Pot and close the hood. Select GRILL, set the temperature to MED, and set the time to 9 minutes. Select START/STOP to begin preheating.
2. While the unit is preheating, on a large plate, coat the tofu cubes with 1 teaspoon of cornstarch.
3. When the unit beeps to signify it has preheated, add the avocado oil to the Cooking Pot. Then add the tofu and stir with a wooden spoon. Close the hood and cook for 3 minutes.
4. After 3 minutes, open the hood and flip and mix the tofu around. Add the onion, red bell pepper, ginger, and garlic. Stir to mix well. Close the hood and cook for 3 minutes.
5. While the tofu is cooking, in a small bowl, mix together the black peppercorns, soy sauce, brown sugar, ketchup, butter, and remaining ½ teaspoon of cornstarch until the sugar and cornstarch are dissolved.

6. After 3 minutes, open the hood. Pour in the sauce and stir. Close the hood and cook for 3 minutes more.
7. When cooking is complete, open the hood and stir the mixture one more time. Serve.

Arugula And Broccoli Salad

Servings: 4
Cooking Time: 12 Minutes
Ingredients:
- 2 heads broccoli, trimmed into florets
- ½ red onion, sliced
- 1 tablespoon canola oil
- 2 tablespoons extra-virgin olive oil
- 1 tablespoon freshly squeezed lemon juice
- 1 teaspoon honey
- 1 teaspoon Dijon mustard
- 1 garlic clove, minced
- Pinch red pepper flakes
- ¼ teaspoon fine sea salt
- Freshly ground black pepper, to taste
- 4 cups arugula, torn
- 2 tablespoons grated Parmesan cheese

Directions:
1. Insert the Grill Grate and close the hood. Select GRILL, set the temperature to MAX, and set the time to 12 minutes. Select START/STOP to begin preheating.
2. While the unit is preheating, in a large bowl, combine the broccoli, sliced onions, and canola oil and toss until coated.
3. When the unit beeps to signify it has preheated, place the vegetables on the Grill Grate. Close the hood and GRILL for 8 to 12 minutes, until charred on all sides.
4. Meanwhile, in a medium bowl, whisk together the olive oil, lemon juice, honey, mustard, garlic, red pepper flakes, salt, and pepper.
5. When cooking is complete, combine the roasted vegetables and arugula in a large serving bowl. Drizzle with the vinaigrette, and sprinkle with the Parmesan cheese.

Simple Ratatouille

Servings: 2
Cooking Time: 16 Minutes
Ingredients:
- 2 Roma tomatoes, thinly sliced
- 1 zucchini, thinly sliced
- 2 yellow bell peppers, sliced
- 2 garlic cloves, minced
- 2 tablespoons olive oil
- 2 tablespoons herbes de Provence
- 1 tablespoon vinegar
- Salt and black pepper, to taste

Directions:
1. Select ROAST, set the temperature to 390ºF, and set the time to 16 minutes. Select START/STOP to begin preheating.
2. Place the tomatoes, zucchini, bell peppers, garlic, olive oil, herbes de Provence, and vinegar in a large bowl and toss until the vegetables are evenly coated. Sprinkle with salt and pepper and toss again. Pour the vegetable mixture into the pot.
3. Close the hood and ROAST for 8 minutes. Stir and continue roasting for 8 minutes until tender.

4. Let the vegetable mixture stand for 5 minutes in the basket before removing and serving.

Grilled Vegetable Pizza

Servings: 2
Cooking Time: 10 Minutes
Ingredients:
- 2 tablespoons all-purpose flour, plus more as needed
- ½ store-bought pizza dough
- 1 tablespoon canola oil, divided
- ½ cup pizza sauce
- 1 cup shredded Mozzarella cheese
- ½ zucchini, thinly sliced
- ½ red onion, sliced
- ½ red bell pepper, seeded and thinly sliced

Directions:
1. Insert the Grill Grate and close the hood. Select GRILL, set the temperature to MAX, and set the time to 7 minutes. Select START/STOP to begin preheating.
2. While the unit is preheating, dust a clean work surface with the flour.
3. Place the dough on the floured surface and roll it into a 9-inch round of even thickness. Dust your rolling pin and work surface with additional flour, as needed, to ensure the dough does not stick.
4. Evenly brush the surface of the rolled-out dough with ½ tablespoon of oil. Flip the dough over and brush the other side with the remaining ½ tablespoon of oil. Poke the dough with a fork 5 or 6 times across its surface to prevent air pockets from forming while it cooks.
5. When the unit beeps to signify it has preheated, place the dough on the Grill Grate. Close the hood and GRILL for 4 minutes.
6. After 4 minutes, flip the dough, then spread the pizza sauce evenly over it. Sprinkle with the cheese, and top with the zucchini, onion, and pepper.
7. Close the hood and continue cooking for the remaining 2 to 3 minutes until the cheese is melted and the veggie slices begin to crisp.
8. When cooking is complete, let cool slightly before slicing.

Eggplant Parmigiana

Servings: 4
Cooking Time: 12 Minutes
Ingredients:
- 2 large eggs
- ½ cup grated Parmesan cheese, plus more for garnish
- 1 tablespoon Italian seasoning
- 1 teaspoon garlic powder
- 2 Italian eggplants, cut into ¾-inch-thick discs
- ½ cup ricotta cheese
- 1 cup prepared marinara sauce
- ½ cup shredded mozzarella cheese
- Fresh basil, for garnish

Directions:
1. Insert the Grill Grate and close the hood. Select GRILL, set the temperature to HI, and set the time to 12 minutes. Select START/STOP to begin preheating.
2. While the unit is preheating, create an assembly line with 2 large bowls. In one bowl, whisk the eggs. In the other bowl, combine the Parmesan cheese, Italian seasoning, and

garlic powder. Dip the eggplant discs in the egg wash and then into the Parmesan crumbs until fully coated.

3. When the unit beeps to signify it has preheated, place the eggplant on the Grill Grate in a single layer. Close the hood and grill for 4 minutes.

4. After 4 minutes, open the hood and flip the eggplant. Close the hood and cook for 4 minutes.

5. After 4 minutes, open the hood and use grill mitts to remove the Grill Grate and eggplant.

6. Place an eggplant disc in the Cooking Pot. Spoon about 1 teaspoon of ricotta cheese across the disc and then top with another eggplant disc, forming a sandwich. Add a teaspoon of marinara sauce on top, followed by shredded mozzarella cheese. Repeat with the remaining eggplant discs, ricotta cheese, marinara sauce, and mozzarella cheese. Close the hood and cook for 4 minutes more.

7. When cooking is complete, remove the eggplant. Garnish with fresh basil leaves and top with more grated Parmesan, and serve.

Green Beans With Sun-dried Tomatoes And Feta

Servings: 8
Cooking Time: 8 Minutes
Ingredients:
*   2 pounds green beans, ends trimmed
*   2 tablespoons extra-virgin olive oil
*   1 teaspoon salt
*   ½ teaspoon freshly ground black pepper
*   1 cup sun-dried tomatoes packed in oil, undrained, sliced
*   6 ounces feta cheese, crumbled
Directions:
1. Insert the Grill Grate and close the hood. Select GRILL, set the temperature to HI, and set the time to 8 minutes. Select START/STOP to begin preheating.

2. While the unit is preheating, in a large bowl, toss the green beans with the olive oil, salt, and pepper.

3. When the unit beeps to signify it has preheated, place the green beans on the Grill Grate. Close the hood and grill for 4 minutes.

4. After 4 minutes, open the hood and flip the green beans. Close the hood and cook for 4 minutes more.

5. When cooking is complete, transfer the green beans to a large bowl. Add the sun-dried tomatoes and mix together. Top with the feta cheese and serve.

Honey-glazed Baby Carrots

Servings: 4
Cooking Time: 12 Minutes
Ingredients:
*   1 pound baby carrots
*   2 tablespoons olive oil
*   1 tablespoon honey
*   1 teaspoon dried dill
*   Salt and black pepper, to taste
Directions:
1. Insert the Crisper Basket and close the hood. Select ROAST, set the temperature to 350°F, and set the time to 12 minutes. Select START/STOP to begin preheating.

2. Place the carrots in a large bowl. Add the olive oil, honey, dill, salt, and pepper and toss to coat well.

3. Arrange the carrots in the Crisper Basket. Close the hood and ROAST for 12 minutes, until crisp-tender. Shake the basket once during cooking.

4. Serve warm.

Flatbread Pizza

Servings: 4
Cooking Time: 10 Minutes
Ingredients:
*   1 (14-ounce) package refrigerated pizza dough
*   2 tablespoons extra-virgin olive oil
*   ½ cup prepared Alfredo sauce
*   1 medium zucchini, cut into ⅛-inch-thick discs
*   ½ cup fresh spinach
*   ½ red onion, sliced
*   4 cherry tomatoes, sliced
Directions:
1. Insert the Grill Grate and close the hood. Select GRILL, set the temperature to MED, and set the time to 10 minutes. Select START/STOP to begin preheating.

2. While the unit is preheating, roll out the dough into a rectangle slightly smaller than the Grill Grate (8 by 11 inches). Brush the olive oil on both sides of the dough.

3. When the unit beeps to signify it has preheated, place the dough on the Grill Grate. Close the hood and grill for 5 minutes.

4. After 5 minutes, open the hood and flip the dough. (Or skip flipping, if you'd rather.) Spread the Alfredo sauce across the dough, leaving a 1-inch border. Layer the zucchini, spinach, red onion, and cherry tomatoes across the dough. Close the hood and cook for 5 minutes more.

5. When cooking is complete, remove the pizza from the grill. Slice and serve.

Grilled Mozzarella And Tomatoes

Servings: 4
Cooking Time: 5 Minutes
Ingredients:
*   4 large, round, firm tomatoes
*   ½ cup Italian dressing
*   1 cup shredded mozzarella
*   ½ cup chopped fresh basil, for garnish
Directions:
1. Insert the Grill Grate and close the hood. Select GRILL, set the temperature to HI, and set the time to 5 minutes. Select START/STOP to begin preheating.

2. While the unit is preheating, cut the tomatoes in half crosswise. Pour about 1 tablespoon of Italian dressing on each tomato half.

3. When the unit beeps to signify it has preheated, place the tomatoes on the Grill Grate, cut-side up. If the tomatoes won't stand upright, slice a small piece from the bottom to level them out. Close the hood and grill for 2 minutes.

4. After 2 minutes, open the hood and evenly distribute the mozzarella cheese on top of the tomatoes. Close the hood and cook for 3 minutes more, or until the cheese is melted.

5. When cooking is complete, remove the tomatoes from the grill. Garnish with the basil and serve.

Hearty Roasted Veggie Salad

Servings: 2
Cooking Time: 20 Minutes
Ingredients:
- 1 potato, chopped
- 1 carrot, sliced diagonally
- 1 cup cherry tomatoes
- ½ small beetroot, sliced
- ¼ onion, sliced
- ½ teaspoon turmeric
- ½ teaspoon cumin
- ¼ teaspoon sea salt
- 2 tablespoons olive oil, divided
- A handful of arugula
- A handful of baby spinach
- Juice of 1 lemon
- 3 tablespoons canned chickpeas, for serving
- Parmesan shavings, for serving

Directions:
1. Insert the Crisper Basket and close the hood. Select ROAST, set the temperature to 370ºF, and set the time to 20 minutes. Select START/STOP to begin preheating.
2. Combine the potato, carrot, cherry tomatoes, beetroot, onion, turmeric, cumin, salt, and 1 tablespoon of olive oil in a large bowl and toss until well coated.
3. Arrange the veggies in the Crisper Basket. Close the hood and ROAST for 20 minutes, shaking the basket halfway through.
4. Let the veggies cool for 5 to 10 minutes in the basket.
5. Put the arugula, baby spinach, lemon juice, and remaining 1 tablespoon of olive oil in a salad bowl and stir to combine. Mix in the roasted veggies and toss well.
6. Scatter the chickpeas and Parmesan shavings on top and serve immediately.

Sweet And Spicy Corn On The Cob

Servings: 6
Cooking Time: 12 Minutes
Ingredients:
- 6 ears corn, shucked
- Avocado oil, for drizzling
- Salt
- Freshly ground black pepper
- ½ cup sweet chili sauce
- ¼ cup sour cream
- ¼ cup mayonnaise
- 2 tablespoons sriracha
- Juice of 1 lime
- ¼ cup chopped cilantro, for garnish

Directions:
1. Insert the Grill Grate and close the hood. Select GRILL, set the temperature to MAX, and set the time to 12 minutes. Select START/STOP to begin preheating.
2. While the unit is preheating, drizzle the corn with avocado oil, rubbing it in to coat. Season with salt and pepper all over.
3. When the unit beeps to signify it has preheated, place the corn on the Grill Grate. Close the hood and grill for 6 minutes.
4. After 6 minutes, open the hood and flip the corn. Close the hood and cook 6 minutes more.

5. While the corn is cooking, in a small bowl, combine the sweet chili sauce, sour cream, mayonnaise, sriracha, and lime juice.
6. When cooking is complete, remove the corn from the grill. Coat the ears with the sweet chili sauce mixture. Garnish with the cilantro and serve.

Sriracha Golden Cauliflower

Servings: 4
Cooking Time: 17 Minutes
Ingredients:
- ¼ cup vegan butter, melted
- ¼ cup sriracha sauce
- 4 cups cauliflower florets
- 1 cup bread crumbs
- 1 teaspoon salt

Directions:
1. Insert the Crisper Basket and close the hood. Select AIR CRISP, set the temperature to 375ºF, and set the time to 17 minutes. Select START/STOP to begin preheating.
2. Mix the sriracha and vegan butter in a bowl and pour this mixture over the cauliflower, taking care to cover each floret entirely.
3. In a separate bowl, combine the bread crumbs and salt.
4. Dip the cauliflower florets in the bread crumbs, coating each one well. Transfer to the basket. Close the hood and AIR CRISP for 17 minutes.
5. Serve hot.

Perfect Grilled Asparagus

Servings: 4
Cooking Time: 6 Minutes
Ingredients:
- 24 asparagus spears, woody ends trimmed
- Extra-virgin olive oil, for drizzling
- Sea salt
- Freshly ground black pepper

Directions:
1. Insert the Grill Grate and close the hood. Select GRILL, set the temperature to HI, and set the time to 6 minutes. Select START/STOP to begin preheating.
2. While the unit is preheating, place the asparagus in a large bowl and drizzle with the olive oil. Toss to coat, then season with salt and pepper.
3. When the unit beeps to signify it has preheated, place the spears evenly spread out on the Grill Grate. Close the hood and grill for 3 minutes.
4. After 3 minutes, open the hood and flip and move the spears around. Close the hood and cook for 3 minutes more.
5. When cooking is complete, remove the asparagus from the grill and serve.

Buttered Broccoli With Parmesan

Servings: 4
Cooking Time: 4 Minutes
Ingredients:
- 1 pound broccoli florets
- 1 medium shallot, minced
- 2 tablespoons olive oil
- 2 tablespoons unsalted butter, melted
- 2 teaspoons minced garlic
- ¼ cup grated Parmesan cheese

Directions:
1. Insert the Crisper Basket and close the hood. Select ROAST, set the temperature to 360ºF, and set the time to 4 minutes. Select START/STOP to begin preheating.
2. Combine the broccoli florets with the shallot, olive oil, butter, garlic, and Parmesan cheese in a medium bowl and toss until the broccoli florets are thoroughly coated.
3. Arrange the broccoli florets in the Crisper Basket in a single layer. Close the hood and ROAST for 4 minutes until crisp-tender.
4. Serve warm.

Italian Baked Tofu

Servings: 2
Cooking Time: 10 Minutes
Ingredients:
- 1 tablespoon soy sauce
- 1 tablespoon water
- ⅓ teaspoon garlic powder
- ⅓ teaspoon onion powder
- ⅓ teaspoon dried oregano
- ⅓ teaspoon dried basil
- Black pepper, to taste
- 6 ounces extra firm tofu, pressed and cubed

Directions:
1. In a large mixing bowl, whisk together the soy sauce, water, garlic powder, onion powder, oregano, basil, and black pepper. Add the tofu cubes, stirring to coat, and let them marinate for 10 minutes.
2. Select BAKE, set the temperature to 390ºF, and set the time to 10 minutes. Select START/STOP to begin preheating.
3. Arrange the tofu in the baking pan. Place the pan directly in the pot. Close the hood and BAKE for 10 minutes until crisp. Flip the tofu halfway through the cooking time.
4. Remove from the basket to a plate and serve.

Cheesy Asparagus And Potato Platter

Servings: 5
Cooking Time: 26 To 30 Minutes
Ingredients:
- 4 medium potatoes, cut into wedges
- Cooking spray
- 1 bunch asparagus, trimmed
- 2 tablespoons olive oil
- Salt and pepper, to taste
- Cheese Sauce:
- ¼ cup crumbled cottage cheese
- ¼ cup buttermilk
- 1 tablespoon whole-grain mustard
- Salt and black pepper, to taste

Directions:
1. Insert the Crisper Basket and close the hood. Select ROAST, set the temperature to 400ºF, and set the time to 30 minutes. Select START/STOP to begin preheating.
2. Spritz the Crisper Basket with cooking spray.
3. Put the potatoes in the Crisper Basket. Close the hood and ROAST for 20 to 22 minutes, until golden brown. Shake the basket halfway through the cooking time.
4. When ready, remove the potatoes from the basket to a platter. Cover the potatoes with foil to keep warm. Set aside.

5. Place the asparagus in the Crisper Basket and drizzle with the olive oil. Sprinkle with salt and pepper.
6. Close the hood and ROAST for 6 to 8 minutes, shaking the basket once or twice during cooking, or until the asparagus is cooked to your desired crispiness.
7. Meanwhile, make the cheese sauce by stirring together the cottage cheese, buttermilk, and mustard in a small bowl. Season with salt and pepper.
8. Transfer the asparagus to the platter of potatoes and drizzle with the cheese sauce. Serve immediately.

Roasted Butternut Squash

Servings: 6 To 8
Cooking Time: 40 Minutes
Ingredients:
- 2 butternut squash
- Avocado oil, for drizzling
- Salt
- Freshly ground black pepper

Directions:
1. Cut off the stem end of each squash, then cut the squash in half lengthwise. To do this, carefully rock the knife back and forth to cut through the tough skin and flesh. Use a spoon to scrape out the seeds from each half.
2. Insert the Cooking Pot and close the hood. Select ROAST, set the temperature to 400°F, and set the time to 40 minutes. Select START/STOP to begin preheating.
3. While the unit is preheating, drizzle the avocado oil over the butternut squash flesh. I also like to rub it in with my hands. Season with salt and pepper.
4. When the unit beeps to signify it has preheated, place the butternut squash in the Cooking Pot, cut-side down. Close the hood and cook for 40 minutes.
5. When cooking is complete, the flesh will be soft and easy to scoop out with a spoon. Remove from the grill and serve.

Mascarpone Mushrooms

Servings: 4
Cooking Time: 15 Minutes
Ingredients:
- Vegetable oil spray
- 4 cups sliced mushrooms
- 1 medium yellow onion, chopped
- 2 cloves garlic, minced
- ¼ cup heavy whipping cream or half-and-half
- 8 ounces mascarpone cheese
- 1 teaspoon dried thyme
- 1 teaspoon kosher salt
- 1 teaspoon black pepper
- ½ teaspoon red pepper flakes
- 4 cups cooked konjac noodles, for serving
- ½ cup grated Parmesan cheese

Directions:
1. Select BAKE, set the temperature to 350ºF, and set the time to 15 minutes. Select START/STOP to begin preheating.
2. Spray a heatproof pan with vegetable oil spray.
3. In a medium bowl, combine the mushrooms, onion, garlic, cream, mascarpone, thyme, salt, black pepper, and red pepper flakes. Stir to combine. Transfer the mixture to the prepared pan.

4. Place the pan directly in the pot. Close the hood and BAKE for 15 minutes, stirring halfway through the baking time.
5. Divide the pasta among four shallow bowls. Spoon the mushroom mixture evenly over the pasta. Sprinkle with Parmesan cheese and serve.

Bean And Corn Stuffed Peppers

Servings: 6
Cooking Time: 32 Minutes
Ingredients:
- 6 red or green bell peppers, seeded, ribs removed, and top ½-inch cut off and reserved
- 4 garlic cloves, minced
- 1 small white onion, diced
- 2 bags instant rice, cooked in microwave
- 1 can red or green enchilada sauce
- ½ teaspoon chili powder
- ¼ teaspoon ground cumin
- ½ cup canned black beans, rinsed and drained
- ½ cup frozen corn
- ½ cup vegetable stock
- 1 bag shredded Colby Jack cheese, divided

Directions:
1. Chop the ½-inch portions of reserved bell pepper and place in a large mixing bowl. Add the garlic, onion, cooked instant rice, enchilada sauce, chili powder, cumin, black beans, corn, vegetable stock, and half the cheese. Mix to combine.
2. Use the cooking pot without the Grill Grate or Crisper Basket installed. Close the hood. Select ROAST, set the temperature to 350ºF, and set the time to 32 minutes. Select START/STOP to begin preheating.
3. While the unit is preheating, spoon the mixture into the peppers, filling them up as full as possible. If necessary, lightly press the mixture down into the peppers to fit more in.
4. When the unit beeps to signify it has preheated, place the peppers, upright, in the pot. Close the hood and ROAST for 30 minutes.
5. After 30 minutes, sprinkle the remaining cheese over the top of the peppers. Close the hood and ROAST for the remaining 2 minutes.
6. When cooking is complete, serve immediately.

Black Bean And Tomato Chili

Servings: 6
Cooking Time: 23 Minutes
Ingredients:
- 1 tablespoon olive oil
- 1 medium onion, diced
- 3 garlic cloves, minced
- 1 cup vegetable broth
- 3 cans black beans, drained and rinsed
- 2 cans diced tomatoes
- 2 chipotle peppers, chopped
- 2 teaspoons cumin
- 2 teaspoons chili powder
- 1 teaspoon dried oregano
- ½ teaspoon salt

Directions:

1. Over a medium heat, fry the garlic and onions in the olive oil for 3 minutes.
2. Add the remaining ingredients, stirring constantly and scraping the bottom to prevent sticking.
3. Select BAKE, set the temperature to 400ºF, and set the time to 20 minutes. Select START/STOP to begin preheating.
4. Take a baking pan and place the mixture inside. Put a sheet of aluminum foil on top.
5. Place the pan directly in the pot. Close the hood and BAKE for 20 minutes.
6. When ready, plate up and serve immediately.

Beef Stuffed Bell Peppers

Servings: 4
Cooking Time: 30 Minutes
Ingredients:
- 1 pound ground beef
- 1 tablespoon taco seasoning mix
- 1 can diced tomatoes and green chilis
- 4 green bell peppers
- 1 cup shredded Monterey jack cheese, divided

Directions:
1. Insert the Crisper Basket and close the hood. Select AIR CRISP, set the temperature to 350ºF, and set the time to 15 minutes. Select START/STOP to begin preheating.
2. Set a skillet over a high heat and cook the ground beef for 8 minutes. Make sure it is cooked through and browned all over. Drain the fat.
3. Stir in the taco seasoning mix, and the diced tomatoes and green chilis. Allow the mixture to cook for a further 4 minutes.
4. In the meantime, slice the tops off the green peppers and remove the seeds and membranes.
5. When the meat mixture is fully cooked, spoon equal amounts of it into the peppers and top with the Monterey jack cheese. Then place the peppers into the basket. Close the hood and AIR CRISP for 15 minutes.
6. The peppers are ready when they are soft, and the cheese is bubbling and brown. Serve warm.

Buffalo Cauliflower Bites

Servings: 4
Cooking Time: 15 Minutes
Ingredients:
- 2 heads cauliflower, cut into florets
- Extra-virgin olive oil
- ⅛ teaspoon garlic powder
- 1 teaspoon salt
- Freshly ground black pepper
- 4 tablespoons (½ stick) unsalted butter, sliced
- 1 cup hot sauce

Directions:
1. Insert the Grill Grate and close the hood. Select GRILL, set the temperature to LO, and set the time to 15 minutes. Select START/STOP to begin preheating.
2. While the unit is preheating, put the cauliflower in a large bowl and drizzle with olive oil. Toss to coat, then season with the garlic powder, salt, and pepper. Toss to mix.
3. When the unit beeps to signify it has preheated, place the florets on the Grill Grate. Close the hood and cook for 7 minutes.

4. After 7 minutes, open the hood and flip and mix the florets. Close the hood and cook for 5 minutes.
5. After 5 minutes, open the hood and use grill mitts to remove the Grill Grate and cauliflower. Add the butter and hot sauce to the Cooking Pot. If you want the cauliflower a little more grilled, place the Grill Grate back in the unit. Either way, close the hood and cook for 3 minutes more.
6. When cooking is complete, transfer the cauliflower to a large bowl. Pour the Buffalo sauce over the florets and toss. Serve alone or with ranch dressing, carrots, and celery sticks.

Garlic Roasted Asparagus

Servings: 4
Cooking Time: 10 Minutes
Ingredients:
- 1 pound asparagus, woody ends trimmed
- 2 tablespoons olive oil
- 1 tablespoon balsamic vinegar
- 2 teaspoons minced garlic
- Salt and freshly ground black pepper, to taste

Directions:
1. Insert the Crisper Basket and close the hood. Select ROAST, set the temperature to 400°F, and set the time to 10 minutes. Select START/STOP to begin preheating.
2. In a large shallow bowl, toss the asparagus with the olive oil, balsamic vinegar, garlic, salt, and pepper until thoroughly coated.
3. Arrange the asparagus in the Crisper Basket. Close the hood and ROAST for 10 minutes until crispy. Flip the asparagus with tongs halfway through the cooking time.
4. Serve warm.

Roasted Lemony Broccoli

Servings: 6
Cooking Time: 15 Minutes
Ingredients:
- 2 heads broccoli, cut into florets
- 2 teaspoons extra-virgin olive oil, plus more for coating
- 1 teaspoon salt
- ½ teaspoon black pepper
- 1 clove garlic, minced
- ½ teaspoon lemon juice

Directions:
1. Cover the Crisper Basket with aluminum foil and coat with a light brushing of oil.
2. Insert the Crisper Basket and close the hood. Select ROAST, set the temperature to 375°F, and set the time to 15 minutes. Select START/STOP to begin preheating.
3. In a bowl, combine all ingredients, save for the lemon juice, and transfer to the Crisper Basket. Close the hood and ROAST for 15 minutes.
4. Serve with the lemon juice.

Cashew Stuffed Mushrooms

Servings: 6
Cooking Time: 15 Minutes
Ingredients:
- 1 cup basil
- ½ cup cashew, soaked overnight
- ½ cup nutritional yeast
- 1 tablespoon lemon juice
- 2 cloves garlic

- 1 tablespoon olive oil
- Salt, to taste
- 1 pound baby bella mushroom, stems removed

Directions:
1. Insert the Crisper Basket and close the hood. Select AIR CRISP, set the temperature to 400°F, and set the time to 15 minutes. Select START/STOP to begin preheating.
2. Prepare the pesto. In a food processor, blend the basil, cashew nuts, nutritional yeast, lemon juice, garlic and olive oil to combine well. Sprinkle with salt, as desired.
3. Turn the mushrooms cap-side down and spread the pesto on the underside of each cap.
4. Transfer to the basket. Close the hood and AIR CRISP for 15 minutes.
5. Serve warm.

Honey-glazed Roasted Veggies

Servings: 3
Cooking Time: 20 Minutes
Ingredients:
- Glaze:
- 2 tablespoons raw honey
- 2 teaspoons minced garlic
- ¼ teaspoon dried marjoram
- ¼ teaspoon dried basil
- ¼ teaspoon dried oregano
- ⅛ teaspoon dried sage
- ⅛ teaspoon dried rosemary
- ⅛ teaspoon dried thyme
- ½ teaspoon salt
- ¼ teaspoon ground black pepper
- Veggies:
- 3 to 4 medium red potatoes, cut into 1- to 2-inch pieces
- 1 small zucchini, cut into 1- to 2-inch pieces
- 1 small carrot, sliced into ¼-inch rounds
- 1 package cherry tomatoes, halved
- 1 cup sliced mushrooms
- 3 tablespoons olive oil

Directions:
1. Insert the Crisper Basket and close the hood. Select ROAST, set the temperature to 380°F, and set the time to 15 minutes. Select START/STOP to begin preheating.
2. Combine the honey, garlic, marjoram, basil, oregano, sage, rosemary, thyme, salt, and pepper in a small bowl and stir to mix well. Set aside.
3. Place the red potatoes, zucchini, carrot, cherry tomatoes, and mushroom in a large bowl. Drizzle with the olive oil and toss to coat.
4. Pour the veggies into the Crisper Basket. Close the hood and ROAST for 15 minutes, shaking the basket halfway through.
5. When ready, transfer the roasted veggies to the large bowl. Pour the honey mixture over the veggies, tossing to coat.
6. Spread out the veggies in a baking pan and place in the grill.
7. Increase the temperature to 390°F and ROAST for an additional 5 minutes, or until the veggies are tender and glazed. Serve warm.

Broccoli And Tofu Teriyaki

Servings: 4
Cooking Time: 8 Minutes
Ingredients:
- 1 (14-ounce) package firm tofu, cut into ½-inch cubes
- 1 medium head broccoli, chopped into florets (3 to 4 cups)
- Extra-virgin olive oil
- 1 cup water
- ⅓ cup soy sauce
- 3 tablespoons light brown sugar, packed
- 1 tablespoon peeled minced fresh ginger
- ¼ teaspoon garlic powder
- 1 teaspoon cornstarch

Directions:
1. Insert the Grill Grate and close the hood. Select GRILL, set the temperature to HI, and set the time to 8 minutes. Select START/STOP to begin preheating.
2. While the unit is preheating, on a large plate, lightly coat the tofu and broccoli florets with extra-virgin olive oil.
3. When the unit beeps to signify it has preheated, place the broccoli and tofu pieces on the Grill Grate. Close the hood and grill for 4 minutes.
4. While the tofu and broccoli are cooking, in a small bowl, mix together the water, soy sauce, brown sugar, ginger, garlic powder, and cornstarch until the sugar and cornstarch are dissolved.
5. After 4 minutes, open the hood and use grill mitts to remove the Grill Grate and the broccoli and tofu. Carefully pour the soy sauce mix into the Cooking Pot and add the broccoli and tofu. Close the hood and cook for 4 minutes more.
6. When cooking is complete, open the hood and stir. Serve.

Baked Potatoes With Yogurt And Chives

Servings: 4
Cooking Time: 35 Minutes
Ingredients:
- 4 russet potatoes, rinsed
- Olive oil spray
- ½ teaspoon kosher salt, divided
- ½ cup 2% plain Greek yogurt
- ¼ cup minced fresh chives
- Freshly ground black pepper, to taste

Directions:
1. Insert the Crisper Basket and close the hood. Select BAKE, set the temperature to 400ºF, and set the time to 35 minutes. Select START/STOP to begin preheating.
2. Pat the potatoes dry and pierce them all over with a fork. Spritz the potatoes with olive oil spray. Sprinkle with ¼ teaspoon of the salt.
3. Put the potatoes in the Crisper Basket. Close the hood and BAKE for 35 minutes, or until a knife can be inserted into the center of the potatoes easily.
4. Remove from the basket and split open the potatoes. Top with the yogurt, chives, the remaining ¼ teaspoon of salt, and finish with the black pepper. Serve immediately.

Crusted Brussels Sprouts With Sage

Servings: 4
Cooking Time: 15 Minutes
Ingredients:
- 1 pound Brussels sprouts, halved
- 1 cup bread crumbs
- 2 tablespoons grated Grana Padano cheese
- 1 tablespoon paprika
- 2 tablespoons canola oil
- 1 tablespoon chopped sage

Directions:
1. Line the Crisper Basket with parchment paper.
2. Insert the Crisper Basket and close the hood. Select ROAST, set the temperature to 400ºF, and set the time to 15 minutes. Select START/STOP to begin preheating.
3. In a small bowl, thoroughly mix the bread crumbs, cheese, and paprika. In a large bowl, place the Brussels sprouts and drizzle the canola oil over the top. Sprinkle with the bread crumb mixture and toss to coat.
4. Place the Brussels sprouts in the Crisper Basket. Close the hood and ROAST for 15 minutes, or until the Brussels sprouts are lightly browned and crisp. Shake the basket a few times during cooking to ensure even cooking.
5. Transfer the Brussels sprouts to a plate and sprinkle the sage on top before serving.

Asian-inspired Broccoli

Servings: 2
Cooking Time: 10 Minutes
Ingredients:
- 12 ounces broccoli florets
- 2 tablespoons Asian hot chili oil
- 1 teaspoon ground Sichuan peppercorns (or black pepper)
- 2 garlic cloves, finely chopped
- 1 piece fresh ginger, peeled and finely chopped
- Kosher salt and freshly ground black pepper

Directions:
1. Insert the Crisper Basket and close the hood. Select ROAST, set the temperature to 375ºF, and set the time to 10 minutes. Select START/STOP to begin preheating.
2. Toss the broccoli florets with the chili oil, Sichuan peppercorns, garlic, ginger, salt, and pepper in a mixing bowl until thoroughly coated.
3. Transfer the broccoli florets to the Crisper Basket. Close the hood and ROAST for 10 minutes, shaking the basket halfway through, or until the broccoli florets are lightly browned and tender.
4. Remove the broccoli from the basket and serve on a plate.

Corn Pakodas

Servings: 5
Cooking Time: 8 Minutes
Ingredients:
- 1 cup flour
- ¼ teaspoon baking soda
- ¼ teaspoon salt
- ½ teaspoon curry powder
- ½ teaspoon red chili powder
- ¼ teaspoon turmeric powder
- ¼ cup water
- 10 cobs baby corn, blanched
- Cooking spray

Directions:
1. Insert the Crisper Basket and close the hood. Select AIR CRISP, set the temperature to 425°F, and set the time to 8 minutes. Select START/STOP to begin preheating.
2. Cover the Crisper Basket with aluminum foil and spritz with the cooking spray.
3. In a bowl, combine all the ingredients, save for the corn. Stir with a whisk until well combined.
4. Coat the corn in the batter and put inside the basket.
5. Close the hood and AIR CRISP for 8 minutes until a golden brown color is achieved.
6. Serve hot.

Vegetarian Meatballs

Servings: 3
Cooking Time: 18 Minutes
Ingredients:
- ½ cup grated carrots
- ½ cup sweet onions
- 2 tablespoons olive oil
- 1 cup rolled oats
- ½ cup roasted cashews
- 2 cups cooked chickpeas
- Juice of 1 lemon
- 2 tablespoons soy sauce
- 1 tablespoon flax meal
- 1 teaspoon garlic powder
- 1 teaspoon cumin
- ½ teaspoon turmeric

Directions:
1. Select ROAST, set the temperature to 350°F, and set the time to 6 minutes. Select START/STOP to begin preheating.
2. Mix together the carrots, onions, and olive oil in the pot and stir to combine.
3. Close the hood and ROAST for 6 minutes.
4. Meanwhile, put the oats and cashews in a food processor or blender and pulse until coarsely ground. Transfer the mixture to a large bowl. Add the chickpeas, lemon juice, and soy sauce to the food processor and pulse until smooth. Transfer the chickpea mixture to the bowl of oat and cashew mixture.
5. Remove the carrots and onions from the pot to the bowl of chickpea mixture. Add the flax meal, garlic powder, cumin, and turmeric and stir to incorporate.
6. Scoop tablespoon-sized portions of the veggie mixture and roll them into balls with your hands. Transfer the balls to the Crisper Basket in a single layer.

7. Increase the temperature to 370°F and BAKE for 12 minutes until golden through. Flip the balls halfway through the cooking time.
8. Serve warm.

Spicy Cabbage

Servings: 4
Cooking Time: 7 Minutes
Ingredients:
- 1 head cabbage, sliced into 1-inch-thick ribbons
- 1 tablespoon olive oil
- 1 teaspoon garlic powder
- 1 teaspoon red pepper flakes
- 1 teaspoon salt
- 1 teaspoon freshly ground black pepper

Directions:
1. Insert the Crisper Basket and close the hood. Select ROAST, set the temperature to 350°F, and set the time to 7 minutes. Select START/STOP to begin preheating.
2. Toss the cabbage with the olive oil, garlic powder, red pepper flakes, salt, and pepper in a large mixing bowl until well coated.
3. Arrange the cabbage in the Crisper Basket. Close the hood and ROAST for 7 minutes until crisp. Flip the cabbage with tongs halfway through the cooking time.
4. Remove from the basket to a plate and serve warm.

Grilled Vegetable Quesadillas

Servings: 4
Cooking Time: 8 Minutes
Ingredients:
- 1 medium onion, chopped
- 1 medium summer squash, halved lengthwise and thinly sliced into half-moons
- 1 medium zucchini, halved lengthwise and thinly sliced into half-moons
- Extra-virgin olive oil
- 4 (10-inch) flour tortillas
- 1 cup shredded mozzarella cheese
- ¼ cup chopped fresh cilantro (optional)

Directions:
1. Insert the Grill Grate and close the hood. Select GRILL, set the temperature to HI, and set the time to 8 minutes. Select START/STOP to begin preheating.
2. In a large bowl, combine the onion, summer squash, and zucchini and lightly coat with olive oil.
3. When the unit beeps to signify it has preheated, place the vegetables on the Grill Grate in a single layer. Close the hood and cook for 4 minutes.
4. While the vegetables are grilling, place the tortillas on a large tray and cover half of each with about ¼ cup of mozzarella.
5. After 4 minutes, open the hood and transfer the vegetables to the tortillas, evenly spreading on top of the cheese. Top the vegetables with the cilantro (if using). Fold the other half of each tortilla over to close. Place the quesadillas on the Grill Grate. Close the hood and cook for 2 minutes.
6. After 2 minutes, open the hood and flip the quesadillas. Close the hood and cook for 2 minutes more.

7. When cooking is complete, the cheese will be melted and the tortillas will be crispy. Remove the quesadillas from the grill and serve.

Tofu, Carrot And Cauliflower Rice

Servings: 4
Cooking Time: 22 Minutes
Ingredients:
- ½ block tofu, crumbled
- 1 cup diced carrot
- ½ cup diced onions
- 2 tablespoons soy sauce
- 1 teaspoon turmeric
- Cauliflower:
- 3 cups cauliflower rice
- ½ cup chopped broccoli
- ½ cup frozen peas
- 2 tablespoons soy sauce
- 1 tablespoon minced ginger
- 2 garlic cloves, minced
- 1 tablespoon rice vinegar
- 1½ teaspoons toasted sesame oil

Directions:
1. Select ROAST, set the temperature to 370ºF, and set the time to 22 minutes. Select START/STOP to begin preheating.
2. Mix together the tofu, carrot, onions, soy sauce, and turmeric in the pot and stir until well incorporated.
3. Place the pot in the grill. Close the hood and ROAST for 10 minutes.
4. Meanwhile, in a large bowl, combine all the ingredients for the cauliflower and toss well.
5. Remove the pot and add the cauliflower mixture to the tofu and stir to combine.
6. Return the pot to the grill and continue roasting for 12 minutes, or until the vegetables are cooked to your preference.
7. Cool for 5 minutes before serving

Poultry

Roasted Cajun Turkey

Servings: 4
Cooking Time: 30 Minutes
Ingredients:
- 2 pounds turkey thighs, skinless and boneless
- 1 red onion, sliced
- 2 bell peppers, sliced
- 1 habanero pepper, minced
- 1 carrot, sliced
- 1 tablespoon Cajun seasoning mix
- 1 tablespoon fish sauce
- 2 cups chicken broth
- Nonstick cooking spray

Directions:
1. Select ROAST, set the temperature to 360ºF, and set the time to 30 minutes. Select START/STOP to begin preheating.
2. Spritz the bottom and sides of the pot with nonstick cooking spray.
3. Arrange the turkey thighs in the pot. Add the onion, peppers, and carrot. Sprinkle with Cajun seasoning. Add the fish sauce and chicken broth.
4. Close the hood and ROAST for 30 minutes until cooked through. Serve warm.

Blackened Chicken

Servings: 4

Cooking Time: 10 Minutes
Ingredients:
- 1 tablespoon paprika
- 1 tablespoon garlic powder
- 1 tablespoon onion powder
- 1 tablespoon freshly ground black pepper
- 1 teaspoon Italian seasoning
- 1 teaspoon salt
- ½ teaspoon ground cumin
- ½ teaspoon cayenne pepper
- 4 tablespoons (½ stick) unsalted butter, melted
- ¼ cup avocado oil
- 4 boneless, skinless chicken breasts (about 2 pounds), halved crosswise

Directions:
1. Insert the Grill Grate and close the hood. Select GRILL, set the temperature to III, and set the time to 10 minutes. Select START/STOP to begin preheating.
2. In a small bowl, combine the paprika, garlic powder, onion powder, black pepper, Italian seasoning, salt, cumin, and cayenne pepper.
3. In a separate small bowl, whisk together the butter and avocado oil. Lightly coat the chicken breasts on both sides with the butter-and-oil mixture, and then season both sides with the spice mix to get a nice coating.
4. When the unit beeps to signify it has preheated, open the hood and place the seasoned chicken on the Grill Grate. Close the hood and grill for 5 minutes.

After 5 minutes, open the hood and flip the chicken. Close the hood and cook for 5 minutes more.
. When cooking is complete, remove the chicken from the grill and serve.

Deep Fried Duck Leg Quarters

Servings: 4
Cooking Time: 45 Minutes
Ingredients:
- 4 skin-on duck leg quarters
- 2 medium garlic cloves, minced
- ½ teaspoon salt
- ½ teaspoon ground black pepper
Directions:
1. Spritz the Crisper Basket with cooking spray.
2. Insert the Crisper Basket and close the hood. Select AIR CRISP, set the temperature to 300ºF, and set the time to 45 minutes. Select START/STOP to begin preheating.
3. On a clean work surface, rub the duck leg quarters with garlic, salt, and black pepper.
4. Arrange the leg quarters in the basket and spritz with cooking spray.
5. Close the hood and AIR CRISP for 30 minutes, then flip the leg quarters and increase the temperature to 375ºF. AIR CRISP for 15 more minutes or until well browned and crispy.
6. Remove the duck leg quarters from the grill and allow to cool for 10 minutes before serving.

Lemon-pepper Chicken Wings

Servings: 4
Cooking Time: 40 Minutes
Ingredients:
- 20 to 24 frozen chicken wings
- 4 tablespoons extra-virgin olive oil
- 4 tablespoons (½ stick) unsalted butter, melted
- 3 tablespoons lemon-pepper seasoning
Directions:
1. Place the frozen wings in a large bowl. Drizzle with the olive oil and toss so the wings are well coated.
2. Insert the Grill Grate and close the hood. Select GRILL, set the temperature to MED, and set the time to 40 minutes. Select START/STOP to begin preheating.
3. When the unit beeps to signify it has preheated, place the chicken wings on the Grill Grate. Close the hood and cook for 30 minutes.
4. After 30 minutes, open the hood and flip the chicken. Close the hood and cook for 10 minutes more.
5. When cooking is complete, remove the wings from the grill and place in a large bowl.
6. In a small bowl, combine the butter and lemon-pepper seasoning. Pour this over the wings and toss to coat. Serve with celery and carrot sticks along with your favorite ranch or blue cheese dressing.

Teriyaki Chicken And Bell Pepper Kebabs

Servings: 4
Cooking Time: 14 Minutes
Ingredients:
- 1 pound boneless, skinless chicken breasts, cut into 2-inch cubes
- 1 cup teriyaki sauce, divided
- 2 green bell peppers, seeded and cut into 1-inch cubes
- 2 cups fresh pineapple, cut into 1-inch cubes
Directions:
1. Place the chicken and ½ cup of teriyaki sauce in a large resealable plastic bag or container. Toss to coat evenly. Refrigerate for at least 30 minutes.
2. Insert the Grill Grate and close the hood. Select GRILL, set the temperature to MEDIUM, and set the time to 14 minutes. Select START/STOP to begin preheating.
3. While the unit is preheating, assemble the kebabs by threading the chicken onto the wood skewers, alternating with the peppers and pineapple. Ensure the ingredients are pushed almost completely down to the end of the skewers.
4. When the unit beeps to signify it has preheated, place the skewers on the Grill Grate. Close the hood and GRILL for 10 to 14 minutes, occasionally basting the kebabs with the remaining ½ cup of teriyaki sauce while cooking.
5. Cooking is complete when the internal temperature of the chicken reaches 165ºF on a food thermometer.

Orange And Honey Glazed Duck With Apples

Servings: 2 To 3
Cooking Time: 15 Minutes
Ingredients:
- 1 pound duck breasts
- Kosher salt and pepper, to taste
- Juice and zest of 1 orange
- ¼ cup honey
- 2 sprigs thyme, plus more for garnish
- 2 firm tart apples, such as Fuji
Directions:
1. Insert the Crisper Basket and close the hood. Select ROAST, set the temperature to 400ºF, and set the time to 13 minutes. Select START/STOP to begin preheating.
2. Pat the duck breasts dry and, using a sharp knife, make 3 to 4 shallow, diagonal slashes in the skin. Turn the breasts and score the skin on the diagonal in the opposite direction to create a cross-hatch pattern. Season well with salt and pepper.
3. Place the duck breasts skin-side up in the Crisper Basket. Close the hood and ROAST for 8 minutes. Flip and roast for 4 more minutes on the second side.
4. While the duck is roasting, prepare the sauce. Combine the orange juice and zest, honey, and thyme in a small saucepan. Bring to a boil, stirring to dissolve the honey, then reduce the heat and simmer until thickened. Core the apples and cut into quarters. Cut each quarter into 3 or 4 slices depending on the size.
5. After the duck has cooked on both sides, turn it and brush the skin with the orange-honey glaze. Roast for 1 more minute. Remove the duck breasts to a cutting board and allow to rest.
6. Toss the apple slices with the remaining orange-honey sauce in a medium bowl. Arrange the apples in a single layer in the Crisper Basket. AIR CRISP for 10 minutes while the duck breast rests. Slice the duck breasts on the bias and divide them and the apples among 2 or 3 plates.
7. Serve warm, garnished with additional thyme.

Roasted Chicken Tenders With Veggies

Servings: 4
Cooking Time: 18 To 20 Minutes
Ingredients:
- 1 pound chicken tenders
- 1 tablespoon honey
- Pinch salt
- Freshly ground black pepper, to taste
- ½ cup soft fresh bread crumbs
- ½ teaspoon dried thyme
- 1 tablespoon olive oil
- 2 carrots, sliced
- 12 small red potatoes

Directions:
1. Insert the Crisper Basket and close the hood. Select ROAST, set the temperature to 380ºF, and set the time to 20 minutes. Select START/STOP to begin preheating.
2. In a medium bowl, toss the chicken tenders with the honey, salt, and pepper.
3. In a shallow bowl, combine the bread crumbs, thyme, and olive oil, and mix.
4. Coat the tenders in the bread crumbs, pressing firmly onto the meat.
5. Place the carrots and potatoes in the Crisper Basket and top with the chicken tenders.
6. Close the hood and ROAST for 18 to 20 minutes, or until the chicken is cooked to 165ºF and the vegetables are tender, shaking the basket halfway during the cooking time.
7. Serve warm.

Lime Chicken With Cilantro

Servings: 4
Cooking Time: 20 Minutes
Ingredients:
- 4 boneless, skinless chicken breasts
- ½ cup chopped fresh cilantro
- Juice of 1 lime
- Chicken seasoning or rub, to taste
- Salt and ground black pepper, to taste
- Cooking spray

Directions:
1. Put the chicken breasts in the large bowl, then add the cilantro, lime juice, chicken seasoning, salt, and black pepper. Toss to coat well.
2. Wrap the bowl in plastic and refrigerate to marinate for at least 30 minutes.
3. Spritz the Crisper Basket with cooking spray.
4. Insert the Crisper Basket and close the hood. Select AIR CRISP, set the temperature to 400ºF, and set the time to 10 minutes. Select START/STOP to begin preheating.
5. Remove the marinated chicken breasts from the bowl and place in the preheated grill. Spritz with cooking spray. You may need to work in batches to avoid overcrowding.
6. Close the hood and AIR CRISP for 10 minutes or until the internal temperature of the chicken reaches at least 165ºF. Flip the breasts halfway through.
7. Serve immediately.

Lemony Chicken And Veggie Kebabs

Servings: 4
Cooking Time: 14 Minutes
Ingredients:

- 2 tablespoons plain Greek yogurt
- ¼ cup extra-virgin olive oil
- Juice of 4 lemons
- Grated zest of 1 lemon
- 4 garlic cloves, minced
- 2 tablespoons dried oregano
- 1 teaspoon sea salt
- ½ teaspoon freshly ground black pepper
- 1 pound boneless, skinless chicken breasts, cut into 2-inch cubes
- 1 red onion, quartered
- 1 zucchini, sliced

Directions:
1. In a large bowl, whisk together the Greek yogurt, oil, lemon juice, zest, garlic, oregano, salt, and pepper until well combined.
2. Place the chicken and half of the marinade into a large resealable plastic bag or container. Move the chicken around to coat evenly. Refrigerate for at least 30 minutes.
3. Insert the Grill Grate and close the hood. Select GRILL, set the temperature to MEDIUM, and set the time to 14 minutes. Select START/STOP to begin preheating.
4. While the unit is preheating, assemble the kebabs by threading the chicken on the wood skewers, alternating with the red onion and zucchini. Ensure the ingredients are pushed almost completely down to the end of the skewers.
5. When the unit beeps to signify it has preheated, place the skewers on the Grill Grate. Close hood and GRILL for 10 to 14 minutes, occasionally basting the kebabs with the remaining marinade while cooking.
6. Cooking is complete when the internal temperature of the chicken reaches 165ºF on a food thermometer.

Garlic Brown-butter Chicken With Tomatoes

Servings: 4
Cooking Time: 15 Minutes
Ingredients:
- 4 boneless, skinless chicken breasts
- Extra-virgin olive oil
- ½ teaspoon paprika
- ½ teaspoon sea salt
- 12 tablespoons (1½ sticks) unsalted butter
- 4 garlic cloves, minced
- 2 tablespoons light brown sugar, packed
- ½ teaspoon garlic powder
- 6 ounces cherry tomatoes

Directions:
1. Insert the Cooking Pot and close the hood. Select GRILL, set the temperature to MED, and set the time to 15 minutes. Select START/STOP to begin preheating.
2. While the unit is preheating, drizzle the chicken breasts with olive oil, then lightly sprinkle both sides with the paprika and salt.
3. When the unit beeps to signify it has preheated, place the butter and garlic in the Cooking Pot. Insert the Grill Grate on top and place the chicken breasts on the Grill Grate. Close the hood and grill for 8 minutes.
4. After 8 minutes, open the hood and use grill mitts to remove the Grill Grate and chicken. Add the brown sugar, garlic powder, and tomatoes to the butter and garlic and stir.

5. Transfer the chicken to the Cooking Pot, making sure you flip the breasts. Coat the chicken with the brown butter sauce. Close the hood and cook for 7 minutes more.
6. When cooking is complete, remove the chicken and place on a plate. Spoon the sauce over and serve.

Sweet-and-sour Drumsticks

Servings: 4
Cooking Time: 23 To 25 Minutes
Ingredients:
- 6 chicken drumsticks
- 3 tablespoons lemon juice, divided
- 3 tablespoons low-sodium soy sauce, divided
- 1 tablespoon peanut oil
- 3 tablespoons honey
- 3 tablespoons brown sugar
- 2 tablespoons ketchup
- ¼ cup pineapple juice

Directions:
1. Insert the Crisper Basket and close the hood. Select BAKE, set the temperature to 350ºF, and set the time to 18 minutes. Select START/STOP to begin preheating.
2. Sprinkle the drumsticks with 1 tablespoon of lemon juice and 1 tablespoon of soy sauce. Place in the Crisper Basket and drizzle with the peanut oil. Toss to coat. Close the hood and BAKE for 18 minutes, or until the chicken is almost done.
3. Meanwhile, in a metal bowl, combine the remaining 2 tablespoons of lemon juice, the remaining 2 tablespoons of soy sauce, honey, brown sugar, ketchup, and pineapple juice.
4. Add the cooked chicken to the bowl and stir to coat the chicken well with the sauce.
5. Place the metal bowl in the basket. Bake for 5 to 7 minutes or until the chicken is glazed and registers 165ºF on a meat thermometer. Serve warm.

Sweet Chili Turkey Kebabs

Servings: 4
Cooking Time: 12 Minutes
Ingredients:
- 2 pounds turkey breast, cut into 1-inch cubes
- ¼ cup honey
- 1 tablespoon extra-virgin olive oil
- 2 tablespoons apple cider vinegar
- 2 tablespoons soy sauce
- Juice of 1 lime
- 1 teaspoon red pepper flakes

Directions:
1. Place 5 or 6 turkey cubes on each of 8 to 10 skewers. In a zip-top bag, combine the honey, olive oil, vinegar, soy sauce, lime juice, and red pepper flakes. Shake to mix well. Place the turkey skewers in the marinade and massage to coat the meat. Seal the bag and let marinate at room temperature for 30 minutes or in the refrigerator overnight.
2. Insert the Grill Grate and close the hood. Select GRILL, set the temperature to MED, and set the time to 12 minutes. Select START/STOP to begin preheating.
3. When the unit beeps to signify it has preheated, place half of the skewers on the Grill Grate. Brush extra glaze on the skewers. Close the hood and grill for 3 minutes.
4. After 3 minutes, open the hood and flip the skewers. Close the hood and cook for 3 minutes more.

5. After 3 minutes, remove the skewers from the grill. Repeat steps 3 and 4 for the remaining skewers.
6. When cooking is complete, remove the kebabs from the grill and serve.

Lime-garlic Grilled Chicken

Servings: 4
Cooking Time: 18 Minutes
Ingredients:
- 1½ tablespoons extra-virgin olive oil
- 3 garlic cloves, minced
- ¼ teaspoon ground cumin
- Sea salt, to taste
- Freshly ground black pepper, to taste
- Grated zest of 1 lime
- Juice of 1 lime
- 4 boneless, skinless chicken breasts

Directions:
1. In a large shallow bowl, stir together the oil, garlic, cumin, salt, pepper, zest, and lime juice. Add the chicken breasts and coat well. Cover and marinate in the refrigerator for 30 minutes.
2. Insert the Grill Grate and close the hood. Select GRILL, set the temperature to MEDIUM, and set the time to 18 minutes. Select START/STOP to begin preheating.
3. When the unit has beeped to signify it has preheated, place the chicken breasts on the Grill Grate. Close the hood and GRILL for 7 minutes. After 7 minutes, flip the chicken, close the hood, and GRILL for an additional 7 minutes.
4. Check the chicken for doneness. If needed, GRILL up to 4 minutes more. Cooking is complete when the internal temperature of the chicken reaches at least 165ºF on a food thermometer.
5. Remove from the grill, and place on a cutting board or platter to rest for 5inutes. Serve.

Lemon And Rosemary Chicken

Servings: 4
Cooking Time: 15 Minutes
Ingredients:
- 3 pounds bone-in, skin-on chicken thighs
- 4 tablespoons avocado oil
- 2 tablespoons lemon-pepper seasoning
- 1 tablespoon chopped fresh rosemary
- 1 lemon, thinly sliced

Directions:
1. Insert the Grill Grate and close the hood. Select GRILL, set the temperature to LO, and set the time to 15 minutes. Select START/STOP to begin preheating.
2. Coat the chicken thighs with the avocado oil and rub the lemon-pepper seasoning and rosemary evenly over the chicken.
3. When the unit beeps to signify it has preheated, place the chicken thighs on the Grill Grate, skin-side up. Place the lemon slices on top of the chicken. Close the hood and grill for 8 minutes.
4. After 8 minutes, open the hood and remove the lemon slices. Flip the chicken and place the lemon slices back on top. Close the hood and cook for 7 minutes more.
5. When cooking is complete, remove the chicken from the grill and serve.

Spiced Turkey Tenderloin

Servings: 4
Cooking Time: 30 Minutes
Ingredients:
- ½ teaspoon paprika
- ½ teaspoon garlic powder
- ½ teaspoon salt
- ½ teaspoon freshly ground black pepper
- Pinch cayenne pepper
- 1½ pounds turkey breast tenderloin
- Olive oil spray

Directions:
1. Spray the Crisper Basket lightly with olive oil spray.
2. Insert the Crisper Basket and close the hood. Select AIR CRISP, set the temperature to 370ºF, and set the time to 30 minutes. Select START/STOP to begin preheating.
3. In a small bowl, combine the paprika, garlic powder, salt, black pepper, and cayenne pepper. Rub the mixture all over the turkey.
4. Place the turkey in the Crisper Basket and lightly spray with olive oil spray.
5. Close the hood and AIR CRISP for 15 minutes. Flip the turkey over and lightly spray with olive oil spray. AIR CRISP until the internal temperature reaches at least 170ºF for an additional 10 to 15 minutes.
6. Let the turkey rest for 10 minutes before slicing and serving.

Honey Rosemary Chicken

Servings: 4
Cooking Time: 20 Minutes
Ingredients:
- ¼ cup balsamic vinegar
- ¼ cup honey
- 2 tablespoons olive oil
- 1 tablespoon dried rosemary leaves
- 1 teaspoon salt
- ½ teaspoon freshly ground black pepper
- 2 whole boneless, skinless chicken breasts, halved
- Cooking spray

Directions:
1. In a large resealable bag, combine the vinegar, honey, olive oil, rosemary, salt, and pepper. Add the chicken pieces, seal the bag, and refrigerate to marinate for at least 2 hours.
2. Insert the Crisper Basket and close the hood. Select BAKE, set the temperature to 325ºF, and set the time to 20 minutes. Select START/STOP to begin preheating.
3. Line the Crisper Basket with parchment paper.
4. Remove the chicken from the marinade and place it on the parchment. Spritz with cooking spray.
5. Close the hood and BAKE for 10 minutes. Flip the chicken, spritz it with cooking spray, and bake for 10 minutes more until the internal temperature reaches 165ºF and the chicken is no longer pink inside. Let sit for 5 minutes before serving.

Fried Chicken Piccata

Servings: 2
Cooking Time: 22 Minutes
Ingredients:
- 2 large eggs
- ½ cup all-purpose flour

- ½ teaspoon freshly ground black pepper
- 2 boneless, skinless chicken breasts
- 4 tablespoons unsalted butter
- Juice of 1 lemon
- 1 tablespoon capers, drained

Directions:
1. Insert the Crisper Basket and close the hood. Select AIR CRISP, set the temperature to 375ºF, and set the time to 22 minutes. Select START/STOP to begin preheating.
2. Meanwhile, in a medium shallow bowl, whisk the eggs until they are fully beaten.
3. In a separate medium shallow bowl, combine the flour and black pepper, using a fork to distribute the pepper evenly throughout.
4. Dredge the chicken in the flour to coat it completely, then dip it into the egg, then back in the flour.
5. When the unit beeps to signify it has preheated, place the chicken in the basket. Close the hood and AIR CRISP for 18 minutes.
6. While the chicken is cooking, melt the butter in a skillet over medium heat. Add the lemon juice and capers, and bring to a simmer. Reduce the heat to low, and simmer for 4 minutes.
7. After 18 minutes, check the chicken. Cooking is complete when the internal temperature of the meat reaches at least 165ºF on a food thermometer. If necessary, close the hood and continue cooking for up to 3 minutes more.
8. Plate the chicken, and drizzle the butter sauce over each serving.

Sweet And Spicy Turkey Meatballs

Servings: 6
Cooking Time: 15 Minutes
Ingredients:
- 1 pound lean ground turkey
- ½ cup whole-wheat panko bread crumbs
- 1 egg, beaten
- 1 tablespoon soy sauce
- ¼ cup plus 1 tablespoon hoisin sauce, divided
- 2 teaspoons minced garlic
- ⅛ teaspoon salt
- ⅛ teaspoon freshly ground black pepper
- 1 teaspoon sriracha
- Olive oil spray

Directions:
1. Spray the Crisper Basket lightly with olive oil spray.
2. Insert the Crisper Basket and close the hood. Select AIR CRISP, set the temperature to 350ºF, and set the time to 15 minutes. Select START/STOP to begin preheating.
3. In a large bowl, mix together the turkey, panko bread crumbs, egg, soy sauce, 1 tablespoon of hoisin sauce, garlic, salt, and black pepper.
4. Using a tablespoon, form the mixture into 24 meatballs.
5. In a small bowl, combine the remaining ¼ cup of hoisin sauce and sriracha to make a glaze and set aside.
6. Place the meatballs in the Crisper Basket in a single layer. You may need to cook them in batches.
7. Close the hood and AIR CRISP for 8 minutes. Brush the meatballs generously with the glaze and AIR CRISP until cooked through, an additional 4 to 7 minutes.
8. Serve warm.

Glazed Duck With Cherry Sauce

Servings: 12
Cooking Time: 32 Minutes
Ingredients:
- 1 whole duck, split in half, back and rib bones removed, fat trimmed
- 1 teaspoon olive oil
- Salt and freshly ground black pepper, to taste
- Cherry Sauce:
- 1 tablespoon butter
- 1 shallot, minced
- ½ cup sherry
- 1 cup chicken stock
- 1 teaspoon white wine vinegar
- ¾ cup cherry preserves
- 1 teaspoon fresh thyme leaves
- Salt and freshly ground black pepper, to taste

Directions:
1. Insert the Crisper Basket and close the hood. Select AIR CRISP, set the temperature to 400ºF, and set the time to 25 minutes. Select START/STOP to begin preheating.
2. On a clean work surface, rub the duck with olive oil, then sprinkle with salt and ground black pepper to season.
3. Place the duck in the basket, breast side up. Close the hood and AIR CRISP for 25 minutes or until well browned. Flip the duck during the last 10 minutes.
4. Meanwhile, make the cherry sauce: Heat the butter in a nonstick skillet over medium-high heat or until melted.
5. Add the shallot and sauté for 5 minutes or until lightly browned.
6. Add the sherry and simmer for 6 minutes or until it reduces in half.
7. Add the chicken stick, white wine vinegar, and cherry preserves. Stir to combine well. Simmer for 6 more minutes or until thickened.
8. Fold in the thyme leaves and sprinkle with salt and ground black pepper. Stir to mix well.
9. When cooking of the duck is complete, glaze the duck with a quarter of the cherry sauce, then AIR CRISP for another 4 minutes.
10. Flip the duck and glaze with another quarter of the cherry sauce. AIR CRISP for an additional 3 minutes.
11. Transfer the duck on a large plate and serve with remaining cherry sauce.

Mini Turkey Meatloaves With Carrot

Servings: 4
Cooking Time: 20 To 24 Minutes
Ingredients:
- ⅓ cup minced onion
- ¼ cup grated carrot
- 2 garlic cloves, minced
- 2 tablespoons ground almonds
- 2 teaspoons olive oil
- 1 teaspoon dried marjoram
- 1 egg white
- ¾ pound ground turkey breast

Directions:
1. Select BAKE, set the temperature to 400ºF, and set the time to 24 minutes. Select START/STOP to begin preheating.
2. In a medium bowl, stir together the onion, carrot, garlic, almonds, olive oil, marjoram, and egg white.
3. Add the ground turkey. With your hands, gently but thoroughly mix until combined.
4. Double 16 foil muffin cup liners to make 8 cups. Divide the turkey mixture evenly among the liners. Transfer to the pot.
5. Close the hood and BAKE for 20 to 24 minutes, or until the meatloaves reach an internal temperature of 165ºF on a meat thermometer. Serve immediately.

Crispy Chicken Strips

Servings: 4
Cooking Time: 20 Minutes
Ingredients:
- 1 tablespoon olive oil
- 1 pound boneless, skinless chicken tenderloins
- 1 teaspoon salt
- ½ teaspoon freshly ground black pepper
- ½ teaspoon paprika
- ½ teaspoon garlic powder
- ½ cup whole-wheat seasoned bread crumbs
- 1 teaspoon dried parsley
- Cooking spray

Directions:
1. Spray the Crisper Basket lightly with cooking spray.
2. Insert the Crisper Basket and close the hood. Select AIR CRISP, set the temperature to 370ºF, and set the time to 20 minutes. Select START/STOP to begin preheating.
3. In a medium bowl, toss the chicken with the salt, pepper, paprika, and garlic powder until evenly coated.
4. Add the olive oil and toss to coat the chicken evenly.
5. In a separate, shallow bowl, mix together the bread crumbs and parsley.
6. Coat each piece of chicken evenly in the bread crumb mixture.
7. Place the chicken in the Crisper Basket in a single layer and spray it lightly with cooking spray. You may need to cook them in batches.
8. Close the hood and AIR CRISP for 10 minutes. Flip the chicken over, lightly spray it with cooking spray, and AIR CRISP for an additional 8 to 10 minutes, until golden brown. Serve.

Rosemary Turkey Breast

Servings: 6
Cooking Time: 30 Minutes
Ingredients:
- ½ teaspoon dried rosemary
- 2 minced garlic cloves
- 2 teaspoons salt
- 1 teaspoon ground black pepper
- ¼ cup olive oil
- 2½ pounds turkey breast
- ¼ cup pure maple syrup
- 1 tablespoon stone-ground brown mustard
- 1 tablespoon melted vegan butter

Directions:
1. Combine the rosemary, garlic, salt, ground black pepper, and olive oil in a large bowl. Stir to mix well.
2. Dunk the turkey breast in the mixture and wrap the bowl in plastic. Refrigerate for 2 hours to marinate.

3. Remove the bowl from the refrigerator and let sit for half an hour before cooking.
4. Spritz the Crisper Basket with cooking spray.
5. Insert the Crisper Basket and close the hood. Select AIR CRISP, set the temperature to 400ºF, and set the time to 30 minutes. Select START/STOP to begin preheating.
6. Remove the turkey from the marinade and place in the basket. Close the hood and AIR CRISP for 20 minutes or until well browned. Flip the breast halfway through.
7. Meanwhile, combine the remaining ingredients in a small bowl. Stir to mix well.
8. Pour half of the butter mixture over the turkey breast in the basket. Close the hood and AIR CRISP for 10 more minutes. Flip the breast and pour the remaining half of butter mixture over halfway through.
9. Transfer the turkey on a plate and slice to serve.

Chicken Cordon Bleu Roll-ups

Servings: 4
Cooking Time: 15 Minutes
Ingredients:
- 1 tablespoon garlic powder
- 1 tablespoon onion powder
- 1½ pounds boneless, skinless chicken breasts (about 3 breasts)
- 6 ounces thin-sliced deli ham
- 6 ounces Swiss cheese, sliced
- 2 large eggs
- 1 cup plain bread crumbs
- ¼ cup sour cream
- 3 tablespoons Dijon mustard
- ¼ teaspoon granulated sugar or honey

Directions:
1. Insert the Grill Grate and close the hood. Select GRILL, set the temperature to MED, and set the time to 15 minutes. Select START/STOP to begin preheating.
2. In a small bowl, combine the garlic powder and onion powder.
3. Cut each chicken breast in half from the side (parallel to the cutting board) to create 6 thinner, flatter chicken breasts. Lightly coat the chicken all over with the garlic-and-onion mixture.
4. Layer 3 or 4 slices of ham on top of each piece of chicken, and top with about 1 ounce of cheese. Starting at the short end, roll the chicken breasts to wrap the ham and cheese inside. Secure the chicken roll-ups with toothpicks.
5. In a large bowl, whisk the eggs. Put the bread crumbs in a separate large bowl. Dip the chicken roll-ups in the egg and then into the bread crumbs until fully coated.
6. When the unit beeps to signify it has preheated, place the roll-ups on the Grill Grate. Close the hood and grill for 7 minutes, 30 seconds.
7. After 7 minutes, 30 seconds, open the hood and flip the roll-ups. Close the hood and continue cooking for 7 minutes, 30 seconds more.
8. While the roll-ups are cooking, in a small bowl, combine the sour cream, Dijon mustard, and sugar and stir until the sugar is dissolved.
9. When cooking is complete, remove the roll-ups from the grill and serve with the sauce, for dipping.

Turkey Jerky

Servings: 2

Cooking Time: 3 To 5 Hours
Ingredients:
- 1 pound turkey breast, very thinly sliced
- 1 cup soy sauce
- 2 tablespoons light brown sugar, packed
- 2 tablespoons Worcestershire sauce
- ½ teaspoon garlic powder
- ½ teaspoon onion powder
- ½ teaspoon red pepper flakes

Directions:
1. In a resealable bag, combine the turkey, soy sauce, brown sugar, Worcestershire sauce, garlic powder, onion powder, and red pepper flakes. Massage the turkey slices so all are fully coated in the marinade. Seal the bag and refrigerate overnight.
2. An hour before you plan to put the turkey in the dehydrator, remove the turkey slices from the marinade and place them between two paper towels to dry out and come to room temperature.
3. Once dried, lay the turkey slices flat in the Crisper Basket in a single layer. Insert the Crisper Basket in the Cooking Pot and close the hood. Select DEHYDRATE, set the temperature to 150°F, and set the time to 5 hours. Select START/STOP.
4. After 3 hours, check for desired doneness. Continue dehydrating for up to 2 more hours, if desired.
5. When cooking is complete, the jerky should have a dry texture. Remove from the basket and serve, or store in a resealable bag in the refrigerator for up to 2 weeks.

Soy-garlic Crispy Chicken

Servings: 4
Cooking Time: 20 Minutes
Ingredients:
- 20 to 24 chicken wings
- 2 tablespoons cornstarch
- ¼ cup soy sauce
- ½ cup water
- 1 tablespoon sesame oil
- 1 teaspoon peeled minced fresh ginger
- 1 teaspoon garlic powder
- 1 teaspoon onion powder
- 1 tablespoon oyster sauce
- 2 tablespoons honey
- 1 tablespoon rice vinegar
- 1 tablespoon light brown sugar, packed

Directions:
1. Insert the Grill Grate and close the hood. Select GRILL, set the temperature to MED, and set the time to 20 minutes. Select START/STOP to begin preheating.
2. While the unit is preheating, pat the chicken wings dry with a paper towel and place them in a large bowl. Sprinkle the wings with the cornstarch and toss to coat.
3. In a separate large bowl, whisk together the soy sauce, water, sesame oil, ginger, garlic powder, onion powder, oyster sauce, honey, rice vinegar, and brown sugar until the sugar is dissolved. Place half the sauce in a small bowl and set aside.
4. When the unit beeps to signify it has preheated, place the chicken wings on the Grill Grate. Close the hood and cook for 10 minutes.

5. After 10 minutes, open the hood and flip the wings. Using a basting brush, brush the soy-garlic sauce from the small bowl on the chicken wings. Close the hood and cook for 10 minutes more.
6. When cooking is complete, remove the wings from the grill and place in the large bowl with the remaining soy-garlic sauce. Toss and coat the wings with the sauce, then serve.

Duck Breasts With Marmalade Balsamic Glaze

Servings: 4
Cooking Time: 13 Minutes
Ingredients:
- 4 skin-on duck breasts
- 1 teaspoon salt
- ¼ cup orange marmalade
- 1 tablespoon white balsamic vinegar
- ¾ teaspoon ground black pepper

Directions:
1. Insert the Crisper Basket and close the hood. Select AIR CRISP, set the temperature to 400ºF, and set the time to 10 minutes. Select START/STOP to begin preheating.
2. Cut 10 slits into the skin of the duck breasts, then sprinkle with salt on both sides.
3. Place the breasts in the basket, skin side up. Close the hood and AIR CRISP for 10 minutes.
4. Meanwhile, combine the remaining ingredients in a small bowl. Stir to mix well.
5. When the frying is complete, brush the duck skin with the marmalade mixture. Flip the breast and AIR CRISP for 3 more minutes or until the skin is crispy and the breast is well browned.
6. Serve immediately.

Blackened Chicken Breasts

Servings: 4
Cooking Time: 20 Minutes
Ingredients:
- 1 large egg, beaten
- ¾ cup Blackened seasoning
- 2 whole boneless, skinless chicken breasts, halved
- Cooking spray

Directions:
1. Line the Crisper Basket with parchment paper.
2. Insert the Crisper Basket and close the hood. Select AIR CRISP, set the temperature to 360ºF, and set the time to 20 minutes. Select START/STOP to begin preheating.
3. Place the beaten egg in one shallow bowl and the Blackened seasoning in another shallow bowl.
4. One at a time, dip the chicken pieces in the beaten egg and the Blackened seasoning, coating thoroughly.
5. Place the chicken pieces on the parchment and spritz with cooking spray.
6. Close the hood and AIR CRISP for 10 minutes. Flip the chicken, spritz it with cooking spray, and AIR CRISP for 10 minutes more until the internal temperature reaches 165ºF and the chicken is no longer pink inside.
7. Let sit for 5 minutes before serving.

Turkey Hoisin Burgers

Servings: 4

Cooking Time: 20 Minutes
Ingredients:
- 1 pound lean ground turkey
- ¼ cup whole-wheat bread crumbs
- ¼ cup hoisin sauce
- 2 tablespoons soy sauce
- 4 whole-wheat buns
- Olive oil spray

Directions:
1. In a large bowl, mix together the turkey, bread crumbs, hoisin sauce, and soy sauce.
2. Form the mixture into 4 equal patties. Cover with plastic wrap and refrigerate the patties for 30 minutes.
3. Spray the Crisper Basket lightly with olive oil spray.
4. Insert the Crisper Basket and close the hood. Select AIR CRISP, set the temperature to 370ºF, and set the time to 20 minutes. Select START/STOP to begin preheating.
5. Place the patties in the Crisper Basket in a single layer. Spray the patties lightly with olive oil spray.
6. Close the hood and AIR CRISP for 10 minutes. Flip the patties over, lightly spray with olive oil spray, and AIR CRISP for an additional 5 to 10 minutes, until golden brown.
7. Place the patties on buns and top with your choice of low-calorie burger toppings like sliced tomatoes, onions, and cabbage slaw. Serve immediately.

Teriyaki Chicken

Servings: 4
Cooking Time: 20 Minutes
Ingredients:
- ½ cup soy sauce
- ¾ cup light brown sugar, packed
- 1 cup water
- 1 teaspoon garlic powder
- 1 teaspoon peeled minced fresh ginger
- ¼ teaspoon cornstarch (optional)
- 6 boneless, skinless chicken thighs (about 2 pounds)

Directions:
1. Insert the Grill Grate and close the hood. Select GRILL, set the temperature to HI, and set the time to 10 minutes. Select START/STOP to begin preheating.
2. While the unit is preheating, in a large bowl, combine the soy sauce, brown sugar, water, garlic powder, ginger, and cornstarch (if using). Transfer about one-quarter of the sauce to a small bowl and set aside. Place the chicken thighs in the large bowl and coat with the teriyaki marinade. Set aside for about 5 minutes, or until the grill has been preheated.
3. When the unit beeps to signify it has preheated, place the chicken thighs on the Grill Grate. Close the hood and cook for 5 minutes.
4. After 5 minutes, open the hood and flip the chicken. Using a basting brush, glaze the chicken with the reserved teriyaki marinade, and carefully pour any remaining marinade over the chicken. Close the hood and cook for 5 minutes more.
5. When cooking is complete, remove the chicken from the grill and serve with your favorite veggies and a side of rice.

Maple-teriyaki Chicken Wings

Servings: 4
Cooking Time: 14 Minutes
Ingredients:
- 1 cup maple syrup
- ⅓ cup soy sauce
- ¼ cup teriyaki sauce
- 3 garlic cloves, minced
- 2 teaspoons garlic powder
- 2 teaspoons onion powder
- 1 teaspoon freshly ground black pepper
- 2 pounds bone-in chicken wings (drumettes and flats)

Directions:
1. Insert the Grill Grate and close the hood. Select GRILL, set the temperature to MEDIUM, and set the time to 14 minutes. Select START/STOP to begin preheating.
2. Meanwhile, in a large bowl, whisk together the maple syrup, soy sauce, teriyaki sauce, garlic, garlic powder, onion powder, and black pepper. Add the wings, and use tongs to toss and coat.
3. When the unit has beeped to signify it has preheated, place the chicken wings on the Grill Grate. Close the hood and GRILL for 5 minutes. After 5 minutes, flip the wings, close the hood, and GRILL for an additional 5 minutes.
4. Check the wings for doneness. Cooking is complete when the internal temperature of the meat reaches at least 165ºF on a food thermometer. If needed, GRILL for up to 4 minutes more.
5. Remove from the grill and serve.

Lemon Parmesan Chicken

Servings: 4
Cooking Time: 20 Minutes
Ingredients:
- 1 egg
- 2 tablespoons lemon juice
- 2 teaspoons minced garlic
- ½ teaspoon salt
- ½ teaspoon freshly ground black pepper
- 4 boneless, skinless chicken breasts, thin cut
- Olive oil spray
- ½ cup whole-wheat bread crumbs
- ¼ cup grated Parmesan cheese

Directions:
1. In a medium bowl, whisk together the egg, lemon juice, garlic, salt, and pepper. Add the chicken breasts, cover, and refrigerate for up to 1 hour.
2. In a shallow bowl, combine the bread crumbs and Parmesan cheese.
3. Spray the Crisper Basket lightly with olive oil spray.
4. Insert the Crisper Basket and close the hood. Select AIR CRISP, set the temperature to 360ºF, and set the time to 20 minutes. Select START/STOP to begin preheating.
5. Remove the chicken breasts from the egg mixture, then dredge them in the bread crumb mixture, and place in the Crisper Basket in a single layer. Lightly spray the chicken breasts with olive oil spray. You may need to cook the chicken in batches.
6. Close the hood and AIR CRISP for 8 minutes. Flip the chicken over, lightly spray with olive oil spray, and AIR

CRISP for an additional 7 to 12 minutes, until the chicken reaches an internal temperature of 165ºF.
7. Serve warm.

Rosemary Turkey Scotch Eggs

Servings: 4
Cooking Time: 12 Minutes
Ingredients:
- 1 egg
- 1 cup panko breadcrumbs
- ½ teaspoon rosemary
- 1 pound ground turkey
- 4 hard-boiled eggs, peeled
- Salt and ground black pepper, to taste
- Cooking spray

Directions:
1. Spritz the Crisper Basket with cooking spray.
2. Insert the Crisper Basket and close the hood. Select AIR CRISP, set the temperature to 400ºF, and set the time to 12 minutes. Select START/STOP to begin preheating.
3. Whisk the egg with salt in a bowl. Combine the breadcrumbs with rosemary in a shallow dish.
4. Stir the ground turkey with salt and ground black pepper in a separate large bowl, then divide the ground turkey into four portions.
5. Wrap each hard-boiled egg with a portion of ground turkey. Dredge in the whisked egg, then roll over the breadcrumb mixture.
6. Place the wrapped eggs in the basket and spritz with cooking spray. Close the hood and AIR CRISP for 12 minutes or until golden brown and crunchy. Flip the eggs halfway through.
7. Serve immediately.

Easy Asian Turkey Meatballs

Servings: 4
Cooking Time: 11 To 14 Minutes
Ingredients:
- 2 tablespoons peanut oil, divided
- 1 small onion, minced
- ¼ cup water chestnuts, finely chopped
- ½ teaspoon ground ginger
- 2 tablespoons low-sodium soy sauce
- ¼ cup panko bread crumbs
- 1 egg, beaten
- 1 pound ground turkey

Directions:
1. Select AIR CRISP, set the temperature to 400ºF, and set the time to 2 minutes. Select START/STOP to begin preheating.
2. In a round metal pan, combine 1 tablespoon of peanut oil and onion. Place the pan directly in the pot. Close the hood and AIR CRISP for 1 to 2 minutes or until crisp and tender. Transfer the onion to a medium bowl.
3. Add the water chestnuts, ground ginger, soy sauce, and bread crumbs to the onion and mix well. Add egg and stir well. Mix in the ground turkey until combined.
4. Form the mixture into 1-inch meatballs. Drizzle the remaining 1 tablespoon of oil over the meatballs. Arrange the meatballs in the pan.

5. Place the pan directly in the pot. Close the hood and BAKE for 10 to 12 minutes, or until they are 165°F on a meat thermometer. Rest for 5 minutes before serving.

Stuffed Spinach Chicken Breast

Servings: 6
Cooking Time: 12 Minutes
Ingredients:
- 6 ounces cream cheese, at room temperature
- 1 teaspoon salt
- ½ teaspoon freshly ground black pepper
- ¼ cup mayonnaise
- 2 teaspoons garlic powder
- ½ cup grated Parmesan cheese
- 3 cups loosely packed spinach
- 1 teaspoon red pepper flakes (optional)
- 6 (6- to 8-ounce) boneless, skinless chicken breasts, butterflied (see here)
- Avocado oil

Directions:
1. Insert the Grill Grate and close the hood. Select GRILL, set the temperature to HI, and set the time to 12 minutes. Select START/STOP to begin preheating.
2. While the unit is preheating, in a large bowl, combine the cream cheese, salt, pepper, mayonnaise, garlic powder, Parmesan cheese, spinach, and red pepper flakes (if using). Spread the mixture inside the chicken breasts evenly. Close the breasts (like a book), enclosing the stuffing. Drizzle both sides of the chicken breasts with avocado oil for a nice coating.
3. When the unit beeps to signify it has preheated, place the chicken breasts on the Grill Grate. Close the hood and grill for 6 minutes.
4. After 6 minutes, open the hood and flip the chicken. Close the hood and cook for 6 minutes more.
5. When cooking is complete, open the hood and remove the chicken breasts from the grill. Serve.

Salsa Verde Chicken Enchiladas

Servings: 4
Cooking Time: 20 Minutes
Ingredients:
- 1 tablespoon chili powder
- 1 teaspoon onion powder
- 1 teaspoon garlic powder
- 1 teaspoon ground cumin
- 2 teaspoons salt
- 3 boneless, skinless chicken breasts (about 1½ pounds)
- Extra-virgin olive oil
- 1 (16-ounce) jar salsa verde
- 2 cups shredded Mexican-style cheese blend
- 6 (8-inch) flour tortillas
- Diced tomatoes, for topping
- Sour cream, for topping

Directions:
1. Insert the Grill Grate and close the hood. Select GRILL, set the temperature to MED, and set the time to 12 minutes. Select START/STOP to begin preheating.
2. While the unit is preheating, in a small bowl, combine the chili powder, onion powder, garlic powder, ground cumin, and salt. Drizzle the chicken breasts with the olive oil and season the meat on both sides with the seasoning mixture.
3. When the unit beeps to signify it has preheated, place the chicken breasts on the Grill Grate. Close the hood and cook for 6 minutes.
4. After 6 minutes, open the hood and flip the chicken. Close the hood and cook for 6 minutes more.
5. When cooking is complete, open the hood and use grill mitts to remove the Grill Grate and chicken breasts. Let the chicken breasts cool for about 5 minutes. Use two forks to shred the chicken, or cut it into small chunks.
6. To assemble the enchiladas, place a generous amount of chicken on a tortilla. Lift one end of the tortilla and roll it over and around the chicken. Do not fold in the sides of the tortilla as you roll. Place the enchilada, seam-side down, in the Cooking Pot. Repeat with the remaining 5 tortillas and the rest of the chicken. Pour the salsa verde over the enchiladas, completely covering them. Top the salsa with the shredded cheese.
7. Select BAKE, set the temperature to 350°F, and set the time to 8 minutes. Select START/STOP and then press the PREHEAT button to skip preheating. Close the hood and cook for 8 minutes.
8. When cooking is complete, remove the enchiladas from the pot and serve topped with the diced tomatoes and sour cream.

Nutty Chicken Tenders

Servings: 4
Cooking Time: 12 Minutes
Ingredients:
- 1 pound chicken tenders
- 1 teaspoon kosher salt
- 1 teaspoon black pepper
- ½ teaspoon smoked paprika
- ¼ cup coarse mustard
- 2 tablespoons honey
- 1 cup finely crushed pecans

Directions:
1. Insert the Crisper Basket and close the hood. Select BAKE, set the temperature to 350°F, and set the time to 12 minutes. Select START/STOP to begin preheating.
2. Place the chicken in a large bowl. Sprinkle with the salt, pepper, and paprika. Toss until the chicken is coated with the spices. Add the mustard and honey and toss until the chicken is coated.
3. Place the pecans on a plate. Working with one piece of chicken at a time, roll the chicken in the pecans until both sides are coated. Lightly brush off any loose pecans. Place the chicken in the Crisper Basket.
4. Close the hood and BAKE for 12 minutes, or until the chicken is cooked through and the pecans are golden brown.
5. Serve warm.

Yellow Coconut Chicken Curry

Servings: 4
Cooking Time: 15 Minutes
Ingredients:
- ½ small yellow onion
- 1 large tomato
- 2 pounds boneless, skinless chicken thighs
- 2 tablespoons minced garlic
- 1 tablespoon chicken bouillon powder (1 cube)

105

- 1 tablespoon light brown sugar, packed
- 2 tablespoons yellow curry powder
- 1 teaspoon salt
- ½ teaspoon freshly ground black pepper
- 2 tablespoons fish sauce (optional)
- 1 (13-ounce) can full-fat unsweetened coconut milk
- Chopped fresh basil or cilantro, for garnish

Directions:
1. Insert the Cooking Pot and close the hood. Select GRILL, set the temperature to MED, and set the time to 15 minutes. Select START/STOP to begin preheating.
2. While the unit is preheating, dice the onion and tomato and set both aside separately. Cut the chicken thighs into 1-inch cubes.
3. When the unit beeps to signify it has preheated, put the onion and garlic in the Cooking Pot. Add the chicken and stir with a wooden spoon. Close the hood and cook for 5 minutes.
4. After 5 minutes, open the hood and add the chicken bouillon, brown sugar, curry powder, tomato, salt, pepper, and fish sauce (if using). Close the hood and cook for 5 minutes.
5. After 5 minutes, open the hood and pour in the coconut milk. Stir to combine. Close the hood and cook 5 minutes more.
6. When cooking is complete, open the hood and stir one more time. Close the hood and let the coconut curry sit for 5 minutes before removing from the Cooking Pot.
7. Serve over basmati rice or with flatbread or naan. Garnish with the basil or cilantro.

Spiced Breaded Chicken Cutlets

Servings: 2
Cooking Time: 11 Minutes
Ingredients:
- ½ pound boneless, skinless chicken breasts, horizontally sliced in half, into cutlets
- ½ tablespoon extra-virgin olive oil
- ⅛ cup bread crumbs
- ¼ teaspoon sea salt
- ¼ teaspoon freshly ground black pepper
- ¼ teaspoon paprika
- ¼ teaspoon garlic powder
- ⅛ teaspoon onion powder

Directions:
1. Insert the Crisper Basket and close the hood. Select AIR CRISP, set the temperature to 375ºF, and set the time to 11 minutes. Select START/STOP to begin preheating.
2. Brush each side of the chicken cutlets with the oil.
3. Combine the bread crumbs, salt, pepper, paprika, garlic powder, and onion powder in a medium shallow bowl. Dredge the chicken cutlets in the bread crumb mixture, turning several times, to ensure the chicken is fully coated.
4. When the unit beeps to signify it has preheated, place the chicken in the basket. Close the hood and AIR CRISP for 9 minutes. Cooking is complete when the internal temperature of the meat reaches at least 165ºF on a food thermometer. If needed, AIR CRISP for up to 2 minutes more.
5. Remove the chicken cutlets and serve immediately.

Strawberry-glazed Turkey

Servings: 2
Cooking Time: 37 Minutes
Ingredients:
- 2 pounds turkey breast
- 1 tablespoon olive oil
- Salt and ground black pepper, to taste
- 1 cup fresh strawberries

Directions:
1. Insert the Crisper Basket and close the hood. Select AIR CRISP, set the temperature to 375ºF, and set the time to 37 minutes. Select START/STOP to begin preheating.
2. Rub the turkey bread with olive oil on a clean work surface, then sprinkle with salt and ground black pepper.
3. Transfer the turkey in the basket. Close the hood and AIR CRISP for 30 minutes or until the internal temperature of the turkey reaches at least 165ºF. flip the turkey breast halfway through.
4. Meanwhile, put the strawberries in a food processor and pulse until smooth.
5. When the cooking of the turkey is complete, spread the puréed strawberries over the turkey. Close the hood and AIR CRISP for 7 more minutes.
6. Serve immediately.

Grilled Turkey Pesto Sandwiches

Servings: 4
Cooking Time: 6 Minutes
Ingredients:
- 4 tablespoons (½ stick) unsalted butter, at room temperature
- 8 slices sourdough bread
- 4 tablespoons jarred pesto
- 1 (16-ounce) package deli turkey meat (4 slices per sandwich)
- 4 slices Monterey Jack cheese

Directions:
1. Insert the Grill Grate and close the hood. Select GRILL, set the temperature to LO, and set the time to 6 minutes. Select START/STOP to begin preheating.
2. While the unit is preheating, spread about ½ tablespoon of butter on the outside of each bread slice. Flip the slices over so the buttered sides are down. Spread about ½ tablespoon of pesto on the unbuttered side of each slice. Place 4 slices of turkey and 1 slice of cheese on top of the pesto on half of the bread slices. Close each sandwich with the other 4 slices, butter-side up.
3. When the unit beeps to signify it has preheated, place the sandwiches on the Grill Grate. Close the hood and cook for 3 minutes.
4. After 3 minutes, open the hood and flip the sandwiches. Close the hood and cook for 3 minutes more.
5. When cooking is complete, the bread will be lightly browned and toasted and the cheese will be melted. Remove from the grill and serve.

Hearty Turkey Burger

Servings: 4
Cooking Time: 13 Minutes
Ingredients:
- 1 pound ground turkey
- ½ red onion, minced
- 1 jalapeño pepper, seeded, stemmed, and minced
- 3 tablespoons bread crumbs
- 1½ teaspoons ground cumin
- 1 teaspoon paprika
- ½ teaspoon cayenne pepper
- ½ teaspoon sea salt
- ½ teaspoon freshly ground black pepper
- 4 burger buns, for serving
- Lettuce, tomato, and cheese, if desired, for serving
- Ketchup and mustard, if desired, for serving

Directions:
1. Insert the Grill Grate and close the hood. Select GRILL, set the temperature to HIGH, and set the time to 13 minutes. Select START/STOP to begin preheating.
2. Meanwhile, in a large bowl, use your hands to combine the ground turkey, red onion, jalapeño pepper, bread crumbs, cumin, paprika, cayenne pepper, salt, and black pepper. Mix until just combined; be careful not to overwork the burger mixture.
3. Dampen your hands with cool water and form the turkey mixture into four patties.
4. When the unit beeps to signify it has preheated, place the burgers on the Grill Grate. Close the hood and GRILL for 11 minutes.
5. After 11 minutes, check the burgers for doneness. Cooking is complete when the internal temperature reaches at least 165°F on a food thermometer. If necessary, close the hood and continue grilling for up to 2 minutes more.
6. Once the burgers are done cooking, place each patty on a bun. Top with your preferred fixings, such as lettuce, tomato, cheese, ketchup, and/or mustard.

Creamy Tuscan Chicken

Servings: 4
Cooking Time: 15 Minutes
Ingredients:
- 2 tablespoons garlic powder
- 1 tablespoon paprika
- 2 teaspoons salt
- 1 teaspoon freshly ground black pepper
- 2 pounds boneless, skinless chicken thighs
- Avocado oil
- 1 cup heavy (whipping) cream
- ¼ cup grated Parmesan cheese
- 1 cup chicken broth
- 2 teaspoons minced garlic
- ¼ cup sun-dried tomatoes, drained
- 2 cups fresh spinach
- Fresh chopped basil or cilantro, for garnish (optional)

Directions:
1. Insert the Cooking Pot and close the hood. Select GRILL, set the temperature to MED, and set the time to 15 minutes. Select START/STOP to begin preheating.
2. While the unit is preheating, in a small bowl, combine the garlic powder, paprika, salt, and pepper. Lightly coat both sides of the chicken thighs with the seasoning and lightly drizzle with the avocado oil.
3. When the unit beeps to signify it has preheated, place the chicken in the Cooking Pot. Close the hood and cook for 2 minutes.
4. After 2 minutes, open the hood and flip the chicken. Close the hood and cook for 3 minutes more.
5. While the chicken is cooking, in a medium bowl, combine the heavy cream, Parmesan cheese, chicken broth, garlic, and sun-dried tomatoes.
6. After 3 minutes, open the hood and pour in the cream sauce. Close the hood and cook for 5 minutes more. After 5 minutes, open the hood and stir in the spinach. Close the hood and continue cooking for 5 minutes more.
7. When cooking is complete, open the hood and stir one more time. Close the hood and let the cream sauce sit for 5 minutes before removing the Cooking Pot.
8. Serve over basmati rice or with flatbread or naan. Garnish with fresh basil leaves or fresh cilantro, if desired.

China Spicy Turkey Thighs

Servings: 6
Cooking Time: 25 Minutes
Ingredients:
- 2 pounds turkey thighs
- 1 teaspoon Chinese five-spice powder
- ¼ teaspoon Sichuan pepper
- 1 teaspoon pink Himalayan salt
- 1 tablespoon Chinese rice vinegar
- 1 tablespoon mustard
- 1 tablespoon chili sauce
- 2 tablespoons soy sauce
- Cooking spray

Directions:
1. Spritz the Crisper Basket with cooking spray.
2. Insert the Crisper Basket and close the hood. Select AIR CRISP, set the temperature to 360°F, and set the time to 22 minutes. Select START/STOP to begin preheating.
3. Rub the turkey thighs with five-spice powder, Sichuan pepper, and salt on a clean work surface.
4. Put the turkey thighs in the basket and spritz with cooking spray. You may need to work in batches to avoid overcrowding.
5. Close the hood and AIR CRISP for 22 minutes or until well browned. Flip the thighs at least three times during the cooking.
6. Meanwhile, heat the remaining ingredients in a saucepan over medium-high heat. Cook for 3 minutes or until the sauce is thickened and reduces to two thirds.
7. Transfer the thighs onto a plate and baste with sauce before serving.

Ginger Chicken Thighs

Servings: 4
Cooking Time: 10 Minutes
Ingredients:
- ¼ cup julienned peeled fresh ginger
- 2 tablespoons vegetable oil
- 1 tablespoon honey
- 1 tablespoon soy sauce
- 1 tablespoon ketchup
- 1 teaspoon garam masala

- 1 teaspoon ground turmeric
- ¼ teaspoon kosher salt
- ½ teaspoon cayenne pepper
- Vegetable oil spray
- 1 pound boneless, skinless chicken thighs, cut crosswise into thirds
- ¼ cup chopped fresh cilantro, for garnish

Directions:
1. In a small bowl, combine the ginger, oil, honey, soy sauce, ketchup, garam masala, turmeric, salt, and cayenne. Whisk until well combined. Place the chicken in a resealable plastic bag and pour the marinade over. Seal the bag and massage to cover all of the chicken with the marinade. Marinate at room temperature for 30 minutes or in the refrigerator for up to 24 hours.
2. Insert the Crisper Basket and close the hood. Select BAKE, set the temperature to 350ºF, and set the time to 10 minutes. Select START/STOP to begin preheating.
3. Spray the Crisper Basket with vegetable oil spray and add the chicken and as much of the marinade and julienned ginger as possible.
4. Close the hood and BAKE for 10 minutes. Use a meat thermometer to ensure the chicken has reached an internal temperature of 165ºF.
5. To serve, garnish with cilantro.

Fried Buffalo Chicken Taquitos

Servings: 6
Cooking Time: 5 To 10 Minutes
Ingredients:
- 8 ounces fat-free cream cheese, softened
- ⅛ cup Buffalo sauce
- 2 cups shredded cooked chicken
- 12 low-carb flour tortillas
- Olive oil spray

Directions:
1. Spray the Crisper Basket lightly with olive oil spray.
2. Insert the Crisper Basket and close the hood. Select AIR CRISP, set the temperature to 360ºF, and set the time to 10 minutes. Select START/STOP to begin preheating.
3. In a large bowl, mix together the cream cheese and Buffalo sauce until well combined. Add the chicken and stir until combined.
4. Place the tortillas on a clean workspace. Spoon 2 to 3 tablespoons of the chicken mixture in a thin line down the center of each tortilla. Roll up the tortillas.
5. Place the tortillas in the Crisper Basket, seam-side down. Spray each tortilla lightly with olive oil spray. You may need to cook the taquitos in batches.
6. Close the hood and AIR CRISP for 5 to 10 minutes until golden brown.
7. Serve hot.

Lettuce Chicken Tacos With Peanut Sauce

Servings: 4
Cooking Time: 6 Minutes
Ingredients:
- 1 pound ground chicken
- 2 cloves garlic, minced
- ¼ cup diced onions
- ¼ teaspoon sea salt

- Cooking spray
- Peanut Sauce:
- ¼ cup creamy peanut butter, at room temperature
- 2 tablespoons tamari
- 1½ teaspoons hot sauce
- 2 tablespoons lime juice
- 2 tablespoons grated fresh ginger
- 2 tablespoons chicken broth
- 2 teaspoons sugar
- For Serving:
- 2 small heads butter lettuce, leaves separated
- Lime slices (optional)

Directions:
1. Select BAKE, set the temperature to 350ºF, and set the time to 5 minutes. Select START/STOP to begin preheating.
2. Spritz a baking pan with cooking spray.
3. Combine the ground chicken, garlic, and onions in the baking pan, then sprinkle with salt. Use a fork to break the ground chicken and combine them well.
4. Place the pan directly in the pot. Close the hood and BAKE for 5 minutes, or until the chicken is lightly browned. Stir them halfway through the cooking time.
5. Meanwhile, combine the ingredients for the sauce in a small bowl. Stir to mix well.
6. Pour the sauce in the pan of chicken, then cook for 1 more minute or until heated through.
7. Unfold the lettuce leaves on a large serving plate, then divide the chicken mixture on the lettuce leaves. Drizzle with lime juice and serve immediately.

Adobo Chicken

Servings: 4
Cooking Time: 15 Minutes
Ingredients:
- 2 tablespoons soy sauce
- 2 tablespoons rice vinegar
- 1 tablespoon balsamic vinegar
- ¼ teaspoon freshly ground black pepper
- 4 garlic cloves, minced
- ½ teaspoon peeled minced fresh ginger
- Juice of ½ lemon
- ¼ teaspoon granulated sugar
- 3 bay leaves
- Pinch Italian seasoning (optional)
- Pinch ground cumin (optional)
- 3 pounds chicken drumsticks

Directions:
1. In a large bowl, whisk together the soy sauce, rice vinegar, balsamic vinegar, pepper, garlic, ginger, lemon juice, sugar, bay leaves, Italian seasoning (if using), and cumin (if using). Add the drumsticks to the marinade, making sure the meat is coated. Cover and refrigerate for at least 1 hour. If you have the time, marinate the chicken overnight to let all the flavors settle in.
2. Insert the Grill Grate and close the hood. Select GRILL, set the temperature to MED, and set the time to 15 minutes. Select START/STOP to begin preheating.
3. When the unit beeps to signify it has preheated, place the chicken drumsticks on the Grill Grate. Brush any leftover marinade onto the drumsticks. Close the hood and grill for 8 minutes.

. After 8 minutes, open the hood and flip the drumsticks. Close the hood and continue cooking for 7 minutes more.
. When cooking is complete, remove the drumsticks from the grill and serve.

Spicy Bbq Chicken Drumsticks

Servings: 4
Cooking Time: 20 Minutes
Ingredients:

2 cups barbecue sauce
Juice of 1 lime
2 tablespoons honey
1 tablespoon hot sauce
Sea salt, to taste
Freshly ground black pepper, to taste
1 pound chicken drumsticks

Directions:
. In a large bowl, combine the barbecue sauce, lime juice, honey, and hot sauce. Season with salt and pepper. Set aside ½ cup of the sauce. Add the drumsticks to the bowl, and toss until evenly coated.
. Insert the Grill Grate and close the hood. Select GRILL, set the temperature to MEDIUM, and set the time to 20 minutes. Select START/STOP to begin preheating.
. When the unit beeps to signify it has preheated, place the drumsticks on the Grill Grate. Close the hood and GRILL for 18 minutes, basting often during cooking.
. Cooking is complete when the internal temperature of the meat reaches at least 165°F on a food thermometer. If necessary, close the hood and continue grilling for 2 minutes more.

Mayonnaise-mustard Chicken

Servings: 4
Cooking Time: 15 Minutes
Ingredients:

- 6 tablespoons mayonnaise
- 2 tablespoons coarse-ground mustard
- 2 teaspoons honey (optional)
- 2 teaspoons curry powder
- 1 teaspoon kosher salt
- 1 teaspoon cayenne pepper
- 1 pound chicken tenders

Directions:
. Insert the Crisper Basket and close the hood. Select BAKE, set the temperature to 350°F, and set the time to 15 minutes. Select START/STOP to begin preheating.
. In a large bowl, whisk together the mayonnaise, mustard, honey (if using), curry powder, salt, and cayenne. Transfer half of the mixture to a serving bowl to serve as a dipping sauce. Add the chicken tenders to the large bowl and toss until well coated.
. Place the tenders in the Crisper Basket. Close the hood and BAKE for 15 minutes. Use a meat thermometer to ensure the chicken has reached an internal temperature of 165°F.
. Serve the chicken with the dipping sauce.

Spicy Chicken Kebabs

Servings: 4
Cooking Time: 14 Minutes
Ingredients:

- 1 tablespoon ground cumin
- 1 tablespoon garlic powder
- 1 tablespoon chili powder
- 2 teaspoons paprika
- ¼ teaspoon sea salt
- ¼ teaspoon freshly ground black pepper
- 1 pound boneless, skinless chicken breasts, cut in 2-inch cubes
- 2 tablespoons extra-virgin olive oil, divided
- 2 red bell peppers, seeded and cut into 1-inch cubes
- 1 red onion, quartered
- Juice of 1 lime

Directions:
1. In a small mixing bowl, combine the cumin, garlic powder, chili powder, paprika, salt, and pepper, and mix well.
2. Place the chicken, 1 tablespoon oil, and half of the spice mixture into a large resealable plastic bag or container. Toss to coat evenly.
3. Place the bell pepper, onion, remaining 1 tablespoon of oil, and remaining spice mixture into a large resealable plastic bag or container. Toss to coat evenly. Refrigerate the chicken and vegetables for at least 30 minutes.
4. Insert the Grill Grate and close the hood. Select GRILL, set the temperature to HIGH, and set the time to 14 minutes. Select START/STOP to begin preheating.
5. While the unit is preheating, assemble the kebabs by threading the chicken onto the wood skewers, alternating with the peppers and onion. Ensure the ingredients are pushed almost completely down to the end of the skewers.
6. When the unit beeps to signify it has preheated, place the skewers on the Grill Grate. Close the hood and GRILL for 10 to 14 minutes.
7. Cooking is complete when the internal temperature of the chicken reaches 165°F. When cooking is complete, remove from the heat, and drizzle with lime juice.

Grilled Cornish Hens

Servings: 4
Cooking Time: 20 Minutes
Ingredients:
- ½ cup avocado oil
- 1 teaspoon dried oregano
- ½ teaspoon freshly ground black pepper
- 1 teaspoon garlic salt
- 2 tablespoons minced garlic
- 1 teaspoon chopped fresh thyme
- 1 teaspoon chopped fresh parsley
- 1 teaspoon chopped fresh rosemary
- 2 (1-pound) Cornish hens
- 1 large yellow onion, halved
- 4 garlic cloves, peeled

Directions:
1. Plug the thermometer into the unit. Insert the Grill Grate and close the hood. Select GRILL, set the temperature to LO, then select PRESET. Use the arrows to the right to select CHICKEN. The unit will default to WELL to cook poultry to a safe temperature. Select START/STOP to begin preheating.
2. While the unit is preheating, place the Smart Thermometer into the thickest part of the breast of one of the

hens. In a small bowl, whisk together the avocado oil, oregano, pepper, garlic salt, minced garlic, thyme, parsley, and rosemary. Cut a few small slits in the skin of each Cornish hen. Rub the seasoning oil all over the skin and between the skin and meat where you made the slits. Place an onion half and 2 garlic cloves inside the cavity of each hen.

3. When the unit beeps to signify it has preheated, place the hens on the Grill Grate. Close the hood and cook.

4. When the Foodi™ Grill tells you, open the hood and flip the hens. Close the hood and continue to cook.

5. When cooking is complete, remove the hens from the grill and let sit for 5 minutes. Serve.

Herbed Grilled Chicken Thighs

Servings: 4
Cooking Time: 13 Minutes
Ingredients:
- Grated zest of 2 lemons
- Juice of 2 lemons
- 3 sprigs fresh rosemary, leaves finely chopped
- 3 sprigs fresh sage, leaves finely chopped
- 2 garlic cloves, minced
- ¼ teaspoon red pepper flakes
- ¼ cup canola oil
- Sea salt
- 4 boneless chicken thighs

Directions:
1. In a small bowl, whisk together the lemon zest and juice, rosemary, sage, garlic, red pepper flakes, and oil. Season with salt.

2. Place the chicken and lemon-herb mixture in a large resealable plastic bag or container. Toss to coat evenly. Refrigerate the chicken for at least 30 minutes.

3. Insert the Grill Grate and close the hood. Select GRILL, set the temperature to HIGH, and set the time to 13 minutes. Select START/STOP to begin preheating.

4. When the unit beeps to signify it has preheated, place the chicken on the Grill Grate. Close the hood and GRILL for 10 to 13 minutes.

5. Cooking is complete when the internal temperature of the chicken reaches at least 165°F on a food thermometer.

Turkey Stuffed Bell Peppers

Servings: 4
Cooking Time: 15 Minutes
Ingredients:
- ½ pound lean ground turkey
- 4 medium bell peppers
- 1 can black beans, drained and rinsed
- 1 cup shredded reduced-fat Cheddar cheese
- 1 cup cooked long-grain brown rice
- 1 cup mild salsa
- 1¼ teaspoons chili powder
- 1 teaspoon salt
- ½ teaspoon ground cumin
- ½ teaspoon freshly ground black pepper
- Olive oil spray
- Chopped fresh cilantro, for garnish
Directions:

1. Insert the Crisper Basket and close the hood. Select AIR CRISP, set the temperature to 360°F, and set the time to 15 minutes. Select START/STOP to begin preheating.

2. In a large skillet over medium-high heat, cook the turkey, breaking it up with a spoon, until browned, about 5 minutes. Drain off any excess fat.

3. Cut about ½ inch off the tops of the peppers and then cut in half lengthwise. Remove and discard the seeds and set the peppers aside.

4. In a large bowl, combine the browned turkey, black beans, Cheddar cheese, rice, salsa, chili powder, salt, cumin, and black pepper. Spoon the mixture into the bell peppers.

5. Lightly spray the Crisper Basket with olive oil spray.

6. Place the stuffed peppers in the Crisper Basket. Close the hood and AIR CRISP for 10 to 15 minutes until heated through.

7. Garnish with cilantro and serve.

Cilantro-lime Chicken Thighs

Servings: 4
Cooking Time: 15 Minutes
Ingredients:
- ½ cup extra-virgin olive oil
- 4 tablespoons light brown sugar, packed
- 4 tablespoons soy sauce
- Juice of 2 key limes
- Zest of 1 key lime
- 2 teaspoons sea salt
- ½ teaspoon freshly ground black pepper
- 2 tablespoons minced garlic
- ½ cup chopped fresh cilantro
- 3 pounds bone-in, skin-on chicken thighs
Directions:
1. In a large bowl, whisk together the olive oil, brown sugar, soy sauce, lime juice, lime zest, salt, pepper, minced garlic, and cilantro. Place the chicken thighs in the marinade and turn so the meat is fully coated. Cover the bowl and refrigerate for at least 1 hour or up to overnight.

2. Insert the Grill Grate and close the hood. Select GRILL, set the temperature to LO, and set the time to 15 minutes. Select START/STOP to begin preheating.

3. When the unit beeps to signify it has preheated, place the chicken thighs skin-side up on the Grill Grate. Brush some of the marinade on the chicken. Close the hood and grill for 8 minutes.

4. After 8 minutes, open the hood and flip the chicken. Close the hood and continue cooking for 7 minutes more.

Turkey Meatballs With Cranberry Sauce

Servings: 4
Cooking Time: 20 Minutes
Ingredients:
- 2 tablespoons onion powder
- 1 cup plain bread crumbs
- 2 large eggs
- 2 tablespoons light brown sugar, packed
- 1 tablespoon salt
- 2 pounds ground turkey
- 1 (14-ounce) can cranberry sauce
Directions:

1. In a large bowl, mix together the onion powder, bread crumbs, eggs, brown sugar, and salt. Place the ground turkey in the bowl. Using your hands, mix the ingredients together just until combined (overmixing can make the meat tough and chewy). Form the mixture into 1½- to 2-inch meatballs. This should make 20 to 22 meatballs.
2. Insert the Grill Grate and close the hood. Select GRILL, set the temperature to MED, and set the time to 20 minutes. Select START/STOP to begin preheating.
3. When the unit beeps to signify it has preheated, place the meatballs on the Grill Grate. Close the hood and cook for 10 minutes.
4. After 10 minutes, open the hood and flip the meatballs. Close the hood and cook for 10 minutes more.
5. When cooking is complete, remove the meatballs from the grill. Place the cranberry sauce in a small bowl and use a whisk to stir it into more of a thick jelly sauce. Serve the meatballs with the sauce on the side.

Buttermilk Ranch Chicken Tenders

Servings: 4
Cooking Time: 10 Minutes
Ingredients:
- 2 cups buttermilk
- 1 (0.4-ounce) packet ranch seasoning mix
- 1½ pounds boneless, skinless chicken breasts (about 3 breasts), cut into 1-inch strips
- 2 cups all-purpose flour
- ¼ teaspoon paprika
- ¼ teaspoon garlic powder
- ¼ teaspoon baking powder
- 2 teaspoons salt
- 2 large eggs
- ¼ cup avocado oil, divided

Directions:
1. In a large bowl, whisk together the buttermilk and ranch seasoning. Place the chicken strips in the bowl. Cover and let marinate in the refrigerator for 30 minutes.
2. Create an assembly line with 2 large bowls. Combine the flour, paprika, garlic powder, baking powder, and salt in one bowl. In the other bowl, whisk together the eggs. One at a time, remove the chicken strips from the marinade, shaking off any excess liquid. Dredge the chicken strip in the seasoned flour, coating both sides, then dip it in the beaten egg. Finally, dip it back into the seasoned flour bowl again. Shake any excess flour off. Repeat the process with all the chicken strips, setting them aside on a flat tray or plate once coated.
3. Insert the Grill Grate and close the hood. Select GRILL, set the temperature to MED, and set the time to 10 minutes. Select START/STOP to begin preheating.
4. While the unit is preheating, use a basting brush to generously coat one side of the chicken strips with half of the avocado oil.
5. When the unit beeps to signify it has preheated, place the chicken strips on the grill, oiled-side down. Brush the top of the chicken strips with the rest of the avocado oil. Close the hood and grill for 5 minutes.
6. After 5 minutes, open the hood and flip the chicken strips. Close the hood and continue cooking for 5 minutes more.

7. When cooking is complete, the chicken strips will be golden brown and crispy. Remove them from the grill and serve.

Pecan-crusted Turkey Cutlets

Servings: 4
Cooking Time: 10 To 12 Minutes
Ingredients:
- ¾ cup panko bread crumbs
- ¼ teaspoon salt
- ¼ teaspoon pepper
- ¼ teaspoon dry mustard
- ¼ teaspoon poultry seasoning
- ½ cup pecans
- ¼ cup cornstarch
- 1 egg, beaten
- 1 pound turkey cutlets, ½-inch thick
- Salt and pepper, to taste
- Cooking spray

Directions:
1. Insert the Crisper Basket and close the hood. Select AIR CRISP, set the temperature to 360ºF, and set the time to 12 minutes. Select START/STOP to begin preheating.
2. Place the panko crumbs, salt, pepper, mustard, and poultry seasoning in a food processor. Process until crumbs are finely crushed. Add pecans and process just until nuts are finely chopped.
3. Place cornstarch in a shallow dish and beaten egg in another. Transfer coating mixture from food processor into a third shallow dish.
4. Sprinkle turkey cutlets with salt and pepper to taste.
5. Dip cutlets in cornstarch and shake off excess, then dip in beaten egg and finally roll in crumbs, pressing to coat well. Spray both sides with cooking spray.
6. Place 2 cutlets in Crisper Basket in a single layer. Close the hood and AIR CRISP for 10 to 12 minutes. Repeat with the remaining cutlets.
7. Serve warm.

Sriracha-honey Glazed Chicken Thighs

Servings: 4
Cooking Time: 17 Minutes
Ingredients:
- 1 cup sriracha
- Juice of 2 lemons
- ¼ cup honey
- 4 bone-in chicken thighs

Directions:
1. Place the sriracha, lemon juice, and honey in a large resealable plastic bag or container. Add the chicken thighs and toss to coat evenly. Refrigerate for 30 minutes.
2. Insert the Grill Grate and close the hood. Select GRILL, set the temperature to MEDIUM, and set the time to 14 minutes. Select START/STOP to begin preheating.
3. When the unit beeps to signify it has preheated, place the chicken thighs onto the Grill Grate, gently pressing them down to maximize grill marks. Close the hood and GRILL for 7 minutes.
4. After 7 minutes, flip the chicken thighs using tongs. Close the hood and GRILL for 7 minutes more.
5. Cooking is complete when the internal temperature of the meat reaches at least 165ºF on a food thermometer. If

necessary, close the hood and continue grilling for 2 to 3 minutes more.

6. When cooking is complete, remove the chicken from the grill, and let it rest for 5 minutes before serving.

Crispy Dill Pickle Chicken Wings

Servings: 4
Cooking Time: 26 Minutes
Ingredients:
- 2 pounds bone-in chicken wings (drumettes and flats)
- 1½ cups dill pickle juice
- 1½ tablespoons vegetable oil
- ½ tablespoon dried dill
- ¾ teaspoon garlic powder
- Sea salt, to taste
- Freshly ground black pepper, to taste

Directions:
1. Place the chicken wings in a large shallow bowl. Pour the pickle juice over the top, ensuring all of the wings are coated and as submerged as possible. Cover and refrigerate for 2 hours.
2. Insert the Crisper Basket and close the hood. Select AIR CRISP, set the temperature to 390ºF, and set the time to 26 minutes. Select START/STOP to begin preheating.
3. While the unit is preheating, rinse the brined chicken wings under cool water, then pat them dry with a paper towel. Place in a large bowl.
4. In a small bowl, whisk together the oil, dill, garlic powder, salt, and pepper. Drizzle over the wings and toss to fully coat them.
5. When the unit beeps to signify it has preheated, place the wings in the basket, spreading them out evenly. Close the hood and AIR CRISP for 11 minutes.
6. After 11 minutes, flip the wings with tongs. Close the hood and AIR CRISP for 11 minutes more.
7. Check the wings for doneness. Cooking is complete when the internal temperature of the chicken reaches at least 165ºF on a food thermometer. If needed, AIR CRISP for up to 4 more minutes.
8. Remove the wings from the basket and serve immediately.

Crispy Chicken Parmigiana

Servings: 4
Cooking Time: 15 Minutes
Ingredients:
- 2 large eggs
- 2 cups panko bread crumbs
- ½ cup shredded Parmesan cheese
- 1 tablespoon Italian seasoning
- 1 teaspoon garlic powder
- 1½ pounds boneless, skinless chicken breasts (about 3 breasts), halved lengthwise
- 3 cups marinara sauce, hot
- ½ cup grated Parmesan cheese

Directions:
1. Insert the Grill Grate and close the hood. Select GRILL, set the temperature to MED, and set the time to 15 minutes. Select START/STOP to begin preheating.
2. While the unit is preheating, create an assembly line with 2 large bowls. In one bowl, whisk the eggs. In the other bowl, combine the panko bread crumbs, shredded Parmesan

cheese, Italian seasoning, and garlic powder. Dip each chicken breast in the egg and then into the bread crumb mix until fully coated. Set the coated chicken on a plate or tray.
3. When the unit beeps to signify it has preheated, place the chicken on the Grill Grate. Close the hood and grill for minutes.
4. After 8 minutes, open the hood and flip the chicken. Close the hood and continue cooking for 7 minutes more.
5. When cooking is complete, remove the chicken from the grill and top with the marinara sauce and grated Parmesan cheese.

Potato Cheese Crusted Chicken

Servings: 4
Cooking Time: 22 To 25 Minutes
Ingredients:
- ¼ cup buttermilk
- 1 large egg, beaten
- 1 cup instant potato flakes
- ¼ cup grated Parmesan cheese
- 1 teaspoon salt
- ½ teaspoon freshly ground black pepper
- 2 whole boneless, skinless chicken breasts, halved
- Cooking spray

Directions:
1. Insert the Crisper Basket and close the hood. Select BAKE, set the temperature to 325ºF, and set the time to 2 minutes. Select START/STOP to begin preheating.
2. Line the Crisper Basket with parchment paper.
3. In a shallow bowl, whisk the buttermilk and egg until blended. In another shallow bowl, stir together the potato flakes, cheese, salt, and pepper.
4. One at a time, dip the chicken pieces in the buttermilk mixture and the potato flake mixture, coating thoroughly.
5. Place the coated chicken on the parchment and spritz with cooking spray.
6. Close the hood and BAKE for 15 minutes. Flip the chicken, spritz it with cooking spray, and bake for 7 to 1 minutes more until the outside is crispy and the inside is no longer pink. Serve immediately.

Dill Chicken Strips

Servings: 4
Cooking Time: 10 Minutes
Ingredients:
- 2 whole boneless, skinless chicken breasts, halved lengthwise
- 1 cup Italian dressing
- 3 cups finely crushed potato chips
- 1 tablespoon dried dill weed
- 1 tablespoon garlic powder
- 1 large egg, beaten
- Cooking spray

Directions:
1. In a large resealable bag, combine the chicken and Italian dressing. Seal the bag and refrigerate to marinate at least 1 hour.
2. In a shallow dish, stir together the potato chips, dill, and garlic powder. Place the beaten egg in a second shallow dish.
3. Remove the chicken from the marinade. Roll the chicken pieces in the egg and the potato chip mixture, coating thoroughly.

4. Select BAKE, set the temperature to 325ºF, and set the time to 10 minutes. Select START/STOP to begin preheating.
5. Place the coated chicken in a baking pan and spritz with cooking spray.
6. Place the pan directly in the pot. Close the hood and BAKE for 5 minutes. Flip the chicken, spritz it with cooking spray, and bake for 5 minutes more until the outsides are crispy and the insides are no longer pink. Serve immediately.

Simple Whole Chicken Bake

Servings: 2 To 4
Cooking Time: 1 Hour
Ingredients:
- ½ cup melted butter
- 3 tablespoons garlic, minced
- Salt, to taste
- 1 teaspoon ground black pepper
- 1 whole chicken

Directions:
1. Select BAKE, set the temperature to 350ºF, and set the time to 1 hour. Select START/STOP to begin preheating.
2. Combine the butter with garlic, salt, and ground black pepper in a small bowl.
3. Brush the butter mixture over the whole chicken, then place the chicken in a baking pan, skin side down.
4. Place the pan directly in the pot. Close the hood and BAKE for 1 hour, or until an instant-read thermometer inserted in the thickest part of the chicken registers at least 165ºF. Flip the chicken halfway through.
5. Remove the chicken from the grill and allow to cool for 15 minutes before serving.

Turkey And Cauliflower Meatloaf

Servings: 6
Cooking Time: 50 Minutes
Ingredients:
- 2 pounds lean ground turkey
- 1⅓ cups riced cauliflower
- 2 large eggs, lightly beaten
- ¼ cup almond flour
- ⅔ cup chopped yellow or white onion
- 1 teaspoon ground dried turmeric
- 1 teaspoon ground cumin
- 1 teaspoon ground coriander
- 1 tablespoon minced garlic
- 1 teaspoon salt
- 1 teaspoon ground black pepper
- Cooking spray

Directions:
1. Select BAKE, set the temperature to 350ºF, and set the time to 25 minutes. Select START/STOP to begin preheating.
2. Spritz a loaf pan with cooking spray.
3. Combine all the ingredients in a large bowl. Stir to mix well. Pour half of the mixture in the prepared loaf pan and press with a spatula to coat the bottom evenly. Spritz the mixture with cooking spray.
4. Place the pan directly in the pot. Close the hood and BAKE for 25 minutes, or until the meat is well browned and the internal temperature reaches at least 165ºF. Repeat with remaining mixture.
5. Remove the loaf pan from the grill and serve immediately

Seafood

Chili-lime Shrimp Skewers

Servings: 4
Cooking Time: 10 Minutes
Ingredients:
- 2 pounds jumbo shrimp, peeled
- 1 tablespoon chili powder
- ¼ teaspoon ground cumin
- ¼ teaspoon dried oregano
- ¼ teaspoon garlic powder
- 2 tablespoons honey
- Juice of 2 limes, divided
- Instant rice, prepared as directed

Directions:
1. Insert the Grill Grate and close the hood. Select GRILL, set the temperature to HI, and set the time to 5 minutes. Select START/STOP to begin preheating.
2. While the unit is preheating, thread 4 or 5 shrimp onto each of 8 skewers, leaving about an inch of space at the bottom. Place the skewers on a large plate.

3. In a small bowl, combine the chili powder, cumin, oregano, and garlic powder. Lightly coat the shrimp with the dry rub. In the same bowl, add the honey and the juice of ½ lime to any remaining seasoning. Mix together.
4. When the unit beeps to signify it has preheated, place 4 shrimp skewers on the Grill Grate. Brush the shrimp with some of the honey mixture. Close the hood and grill for 2 minutes, 30 seconds.
5. After 2 minutes, 30 seconds, open the hood and squeeze the juice of another ½ lime over the skewers and flip. Brush on more honey mixture. Close the hood and cook for 2 minutes, 30 seconds.
6. When cooking is complete, the shrimp should be opaque and pink. Remove the skewers from the grill. Select GRILL, set the temperature to HI, and set the time to 5 minutes. Select START/STOP to begin and press PREHEAT to skip preheating. Repeat steps 4 and 5 for the remaining 4 skewers. When all of the skewers are cooked, serve with the rice.

Grilled Mahi-mahi Tacos With Spicy Coleslaw

Servings: 4
Cooking Time: 10 Minutes
Ingredients:

- 1 teaspoon garlic powder
- 1 teaspoon onion powder
- 1 tablespoon paprika
- ¼ teaspoon salt
- 4 (8-ounce) mahi-mahi fillets
- Avocado oil
- Juice of 2 limes, divided
- 1 cup mayonnaise
- 1 tablespoon sriracha
- ⅛ teaspoon cayenne pepper
- ½ head red cabbage, shredded
- 8 (6-inch) corn tortillas

Directions:

1. Insert the Grill Grate and close the hood. Select GRILL, set the temperature to MED, and set the time to 10 minutes. Select START/STOP to begin preheating.
2. While the unit is preheating, in a small bowl, combine the garlic powder, onion powder, paprika, and salt. Place the mahi-mahi fillets on a large plate and rub avocado oil on both sides. Then squeeze the juice of 1 lime on top and generously coat the fillets with the seasoning mix.
3. When the unit beeps to signify it has preheated, place the fillets on the Grill Grate. Close the hood and grill for 8 minutes.
4. While the mahi-mahi is cooking, in a large bowl, combine the mayonnaise, sriracha, cayenne pepper, and the juice of the remaining lime. Add the shredded cabbage to the bowl and stir until combined.
5. After 8 minutes, open the hood and remove the fillets from the grill. Place the tortillas on the Grill Grate. Close the hood to warm them for 2 minutes. Feel free to flip after 1 minute, if desired.
6. Cut the mahi-mahi into ½-inch to 1-inch strips. To assemble the tacos, place the mahi-mahi pieces on the tortillas and dress with the spicy coleslaw mix. Serve.

Buttered Lobster Tails

Servings: 6
Cooking Time: 7 Minutes
Ingredients:

- 6 (4-ounce) lobster tails
- Paprika
- Salt
- Freshly ground black pepper
- 4 tablespoons (½ stick) unsalted butter, melted
- 3 garlic cloves, minced

Directions:

1. Place the lobster tails shell-side up on a cutting board. Using kitchen shears, cut each shell down the center, stopping at the base of the tail. Carefully crack open the shell by sliding your thumbs between the shell and meat and delicately pulling apart. Wiggle, pull, and lift the meat out of the shell. Remove the vein and digestive tract, if present. Rest the meat on top of the shell for a beautiful display.
2. Insert the Grill Grate and close the hood. Select GRILL, set the temperature to HI, and set the time to 7 minutes. Select START/STOP to begin preheating.
3. While the unit is preheating, season the lobster meat with paprika, salt, and pepper.
4. In a small bowl, combine the melted butter and garlic.
5. When the unit beeps to signify it has preheated, place the lobster tails on their shells on the Grill Grate. Close the hood and grill for 4 minutes.
6. After 4 minutes, open the hood and brush the garlic butter on the lobster meat. Close the hood and cook for 3 minutes more.
7. When cooking is complete, the lobster meat will be opaque and the shell will be orangey red. Serve with more melted butter or a sauce of your choice.

Shrimp Boil

Servings: 6
Cooking Time: 10 Minutes
Ingredients:

- 2 tablespoons lemon-pepper seasoning
- 2 tablespoons light brown sugar, packed
- 2 tablespoons minced garlic
- 2 tablespoons Old Bay seasoning
- ¼ teaspoon Cajun seasoning
- ¼ teaspoon paprika
- ¼ teaspoon cayenne pepper
- 1 teaspoon garlic powder
- 1½ cups (3 sticks) unsalted butter, cut into quarters
- 2 pounds shrimp

Directions:

1. Insert the Cooking Pot and close the hood. Select GRILL, set the temperature to MED, and set the time to 10 minutes. Select START/STOP to begin preheating.
2. While the unit is preheating, in a small bowl, combine the lemon pepper, brown sugar, minced garlic, Old Bay seasoning, Cajun seasoning, paprika, cayenne pepper, and garlic powder.
3. When the unit beeps to signify it has preheated, place the butter and the lemon-pepper mixture in the Cooking Pot. Insert the Grill Grate and place the shrimp on it in a single layer. Close the hood and grill for 5 minutes.
4. After 5 minutes, open the hood and use grill mitts to remove the Grill Grate. Place the shrimp in the Cooking Pot. Stir to combine. Close the hood and cook for 5 minutes more.
5. When cooking is complete, open the hood and stir once more. Then close the hood and let the butter set with the shrimp for 5 minutes. Serve.

Tomato-stuffed Grilled Sole

Servings: 6
Cooking Time: 7 Minutes
Ingredients:

- 6 tablespoons mayonnaise
- 1 teaspoon garlic powder
- 1 (14-ounce) can diced tomatoes, drained
- 6 (4-ounce) sole fillets
- Cooking spray
- 6 tablespoons panko bread crumbs

Directions:

1. Insert the Grill Grate and close the hood. Select GRILL, set the temperature to HI, and set the time to 7 minutes. Select START/STOP to begin preheating.
2. While the unit is preheating, in a small bowl, combine the mayonnaise and garlic powder. Slowly fold in the tomatoes, making sure to be gentle so they don't turn to mush. Place the sole fillets on a large, flat surface and spread the mayonnaise across the top of each. Roll up the fillets, creating pinwheels. Spray the top of each roll with cooking spray, then press 1 tablespoon of panko bread crumbs on top of each.
3. When the unit beeps to signify it has preheated, place the fillets on the Grill Grate, seam-side down. Close the hood and grill for 7 minutes.
4. When cooking is complete, the panko bread crumbs will be crisp, and the fish will have turned opaque. Remove the fish from the grill and serve.

Honey-walnut Shrimp

Servings: 4
Cooking Time: 8 Minutes
Ingredients:
- 2 ounces walnuts
- 2 tablespoons honey
- 1 egg
- 1 cup panko bread crumbs
- 1 pound shrimp, peeled
- ½ cup mayonnaise
- 1 teaspoon powdered sugar
- 2 tablespoons heavy (whipping) cream
- Scallions, both white and green parts, sliced, for garnish

Directions:
1. Insert the Grill Grate. In a small heat-safe bowl, combine the walnuts and honey, then place the bowl on the Grill Grate and close the hood. Select GRILL, set temperature to HI, and set the time to 8 minutes. Select START/STOP to begin preheating. After 2 minutes of preheating (set a separate timer), remove the bowl. Close the hood to continue preheating.
2. While the unit is preheating, create an assembly line with 2 large bowls. In the first bowl, whisk the egg. Put the panko bread crumbs in the other bowl. One at a time, dip the shrimp in the egg and then into the panko bread crumbs until well coated. Place the breaded shrimp on a plate.
3. When the unit beeps to signify it has preheated, place the shrimp on the Grill Grate in a single layer. Close the hood and cook for 4 minutes.
4. After 4 minutes, open the hood and flip the shrimp. Close the hood and cook for 4 minutes more.
5. While the shrimp are cooking, in a large bowl, combine the mayonnaise, powdered sugar, and heavy cream and mix until the sugar has dissolved.
6. When cooking is complete, remove the shrimp from the grill. Add the cooked shrimp and honey walnuts to the mayonnaise mixture and gently fold them together. Garnish with scallions and serve.

Crab Cakes With Lemon-garlic Aioli

Servings:12
Cooking Time: 16 Minutes
Ingredients:
- For the crab cakes
- 1 large egg
- 1 tablespoon Old Bay seasoning
- 1 tablespoon dried parsley
- 1 tablespoon soy sauce
- 1 tablespoon minced garlic
- ¼ cup grated Parmesan cheese
- ½ cup mayonnaise
- ½ cup panko bread crumbs
- 1 pound lump crabmeat
- Avocado oil cooking spray
- For the lemon-garlic aioli
- ½ cup mayonnaise
- 1 teaspoon garlic powder
- Juice of 1 lemon
- ¼ teaspoon paprika

Directions:
1. In a large bowl, whisk the egg, then add the Old Bay seasoning, parsley, soy sauce, garlic, Parmesan cheese, mayonnaise, and panko bread crumbs and mix well. Add the crabmeat and fold it in gently so the crabmeat does not fall apart. Form the mixture into 12 equal-size patties. Place the patties on a large baking sheet and refrigerate for at least 30 minutes.
2. Insert the Grill Grate and close the hood. Select Grill, set the temperature to HI, and set the time to 8 minutes. Select START/STOP to begin preheating.
3. When the unit beeps to signify it has preheated, spray avocado oil on both sides of 6 crab cakes and place them on the Grill Grate. Close the hood and cook for 4 minutes.
4. After 4 minutes, open the hood and flip the crab cakes. Close the hood and cook for 4 minutes more.
5. When cooking is complete, remove the crab cakes from the grill. Select GRILL, set the temperature to HI, and set the time to 8 minutes. Select START/STOP to begin and press PREHEAT to skip preheating. Repeat steps 3 and 4 for the remaining 6 crab cakes.
6. While the crab cakes are cooking, in a small bowl, combine the mayonnaise, garlic powder, lemon juice, and paprika. Feel free to add more lemon or a few dashes of hot sauce to adjust the taste to your liking.
7. When all of the crab cakes are cooked, serve with the sauce.

Crusted Codfish

Servings: 4
Cooking Time: 8 Minutes
Ingredients:
- 1 cup panko bread crumbs
- 2 tablespoons grated Parmesan cheese
- ¼ cup chopped pistachios
- 4 (4-ounce) frozen cod fillets, thawed
- 4 tablespoons Dijon mustard
- Cooking spray

Directions:
1. Insert the Grill Grate and close the hood. Select GRILL, set the temperature to HI, and set the time to 8 minutes. Select START/STOP to begin preheating.
2. While the unit is preheating, on a large plate, mix together the panko bread crumbs, Parmesan cheese, and pistachios. Evenly coat both sides of the cod fillets with the mustard, then press the fillets on the panko mixture on both sides to create a crust.

3. When the unit beeps to signify it has preheated, spray the crusted fillets with cooking spray and place them on the Grill Grate. Close the hood and grill for 4 minutes.

4. After 4 minutes, open the hood and flip the fillets. Close the hood and cook for 4 minutes more.

5. When cooking is complete, remove the fillets from the grill and serve.

Lemon-garlic Butter Scallops

Servings: 6
Cooking Time: 4 Minutes
Ingredients:
- 2 pounds large sea scallops
- Salt
- Freshly ground black pepper
- 3 tablespoons avocado oil
- 3 garlic cloves, minced
- 8 tablespoons (1 stick) unsalted butter, sliced
- Juice of 1 lemon
- Chopped fresh parsley, for garnish

Directions:
1. Insert the Cooking Pot and close the hood. Select GRILL, set the temperature to HI, and set the time to 4 minutes. Select START/STOP to begin preheating.

2. While the unit is preheating, pat the scallops dry with a paper towel and season them with salt and pepper. After 5 minutes of preheating (set a separate timer), open the hood and add the avocado oil and garlic to the Cooking Pot, then close the hood to continue preheating.

3. When the unit beeps to signify it has preheated, use a spatula to spread the oil and garlic around the bottom of the Cooking Pot. Place the scallops in the pot in a single layer. Close the hood and cook for 2 minutes.

4. After 2 minutes, open the hood and flip the scallops. Add the butter to the pot and drizzle some lemon juice over each scallop. Close the hood and cook for 2 minutes more.

5. When cooking is complete, open the hood and flip the scallops again. Spoon melted garlic butter on top of each. The scallops should be slightly firm and opaque. Remove the scallops from the grill and serve, garnished with the parsley.

Garlic Butter Shrimp Kebabs

Servings: 4
Cooking Time: 10 Minutes
Ingredients:
- 2 tablespoons unsalted butter, at room temperature
- 4 garlic cloves, minced
- 2 pounds jumbo shrimp, peeled
- 1 tablespoon garlic salt
- 1 teaspoon dried parsley

Directions:
1. Insert the Grill Grate. Place the butter and minced garlic in a heat-safe bowl, place the bowl on the Grill Grate, and close the hood. Select GRILL, set the temperature to HI, and set the time to 5 minutes. Select START/STOP to begin preheating. After 1 minute of preheating (set a separate timer), remove the bowl with the butter. Close the hood to continue preheating.

2. While the unit is preheating, place 4 or 5 shrimp on each of 8 skewers, with at least 1 inch left at the bottom. Place the skewers on a large plate. Lightly coat them with the garlic salt and parsley.

3. When the unit beeps to signify it has preheated, place 4 skewers on the Grill Grate. Brush some of the melted garlic butter on the shrimp. Close the hood and grill for 2 minutes, 30 seconds.

4. After 2 minutes, 30 seconds, open the hood and brush the shrimp with garlic butter again, then flip the skewers. Brush on more garlic butter. Close the hood and cook for 2 minutes, 30 seconds more.

5. When cooking is complete, the shrimp will be opaque and pink. Remove the skewers from the grill. Select GRILL, set the temperature to HI, and set the time to 5 minutes. Select START/STOP to begin and press PREHEAT to skip preheating. Repeat steps 3 and 4 for the remaining skewers. When all the skewers are cooked, serve.

Lobster Rolls

Servings: 4
Cooking Time: 7 Minutes
Ingredients:
- ¼ cup mayonnaise
- Juice of ½ lemon
- ¼ teaspoon sea salt
- ⅛ teaspoon freshly ground black pepper
- 1 teaspoon dried parsley
- Dash paprika
- 1 pound frozen lobster meat, thawed, cut into 1-inch pieces
- Unsalted butter, at room temperature
- 4 sandwich rolls, such as French rolls, hoagie rolls, or large hot dog buns
- 1 lemon, cut into wedges

Directions:
1. Insert the Grill Grate and close the hood. Select GRILL, set the temperature to MED, and set the time to 7 minutes. Select START/STOP to begin preheating.

2. While the unit is preheating, in a large bowl, combine the mayonnaise, lemon juice, salt, pepper, parsley, and paprika.

3. When the unit beeps to signify it has preheated, place the lobster meat on the Grill Grate. Close the hood and grill for 4 minutes.

4. While the lobster is cooking, spread the butter on the sandwich rolls.

5. After 4 minutes, open the hood and remove the lobster meat. Set aside on a plate. Place the sandwich rolls on the grill, buttered-side down. Close the hood and grill for 2 minutes.

6. After 2 minutes, open the hood and flip the rolls. Close the hood and cook for 1 minute more.

7. When the bread is toasted and golden brown, remove it from the grill. Add the lobster meat to the mayonnaise mixture and gently fold in until well combined. Spoon the lobster meat into the sandwich rolls. Serve with the lemon wedges.

Halibut With Lemon And Capers

Servings: 4
Cooking Time: 8 Minutes
Ingredients:
- 4 halibut steaks (at least 1 inch thick)
- Extra-virgin olive oil
- 1 lemon
- 1 cup white wine
- 3 garlic cloves, minced
- 4 tablespoons capers
- 4 tablespoons (½ stick) unsalted butter, sliced

Directions:
1. Insert the Cooking Pot and close the hood. Select GRILL, set the temperature to HI, and set the time to 8 minutes. Select START/STOP to begin preheating.
2. While the unit is preheating, drizzle the fish fillets with olive oil. Cut half the lemon into thin slices and place them on top of the fillets.
3. When the unit beeps to signify it has preheated, place the fillets in the Cooking Pot. Close the hood and cook for 4 minutes.
4. After 4 minutes, open the hood and add the white wine. Close the hood and cook for 2 minutes. After 2 minutes, open the hood and add the garlic, capers, and butter. Squeeze the juice of the remaining ½ lemon over the fish. Close the hood and cook for 2 minutes more.
5. When cooking is complete, open the hood and spoon the sauce over the fish. If the capers have not popped, give about half of them a tap with the spoon to pop them. Stir the sauce and serve with the fillets.

Coconut Shrimp With Orange Chili Sauce

Servings:44
Cooking Time: 16 Minutes
Ingredients:
- For the coconut shrimp
- 2 large eggs
- 1 cup sweetened coconut flakes
- 1 cup panko bread crumbs
- ½ teaspoon salt
- ¼ teaspoon freshly ground black pepper
- 2 pounds jumbo shrimp, peeled
- For the orange chili sauce
- ½ cup orange marmalade
- 1 teaspoon sriracha or ¼ teaspoon red pepper flakes

Directions:
1. Insert the Grill Grate and close the hood. Select GRILL, set the temperature to HI, and set the time to 16 minutes. Select START/STOP to begin preheating.
2. While the unit is preheating, create an assembly line with 2 large bowls. In one bowl, whisk the eggs. In the other bowl, combine the coconut flakes, panko bread crumbs, salt, and pepper. One at a time, dip the shrimp in the egg and then into the coconut flakes until fully coated.
3. When the unit beeps to signify it has preheated, place half the shrimp on the Grill Grate in a single layer. Close the hood and cook for 4 minutes.
4. After 4 minutes, open the hood and flip the shrimp. Close the hood and cook for 4 minutes more. After 4 minutes, open the hood and remove the shrimp from the grill.

5. Repeat steps 3 and 4 for the remaining shrimp.
6. To make the orange chili sauce
7. In a small bowl, combine the orange marmalade and sriracha. Serve as a dipping sauce alongside the coconut shrimp.

Crab Rangoons

Servings:40
Cooking Time: 10 Minutes
Ingredients:
- 8 ounces cream cheese, at room temperature
- 1 (8-ounce) package imitation crabmeat, diced
- 2 tablespoons chopped scallions, both white and green parts
- 1 teaspoon garlic powder
- 1 teaspoon soy sauce
- 1 teaspoon Worcestershire sauce
- 1 package wonton wrappers (40 to 50 wrappers)
- ¼ cup water
- 4 tablespoons avocado oil

Directions:
1. In a large bowl, combine the cream cheese, imitation crabmeat, scallions, garlic powder, soy sauce, and Worcestershire sauce.
2. Insert the Grill Grate and close the hood. Select GRILL, set the temperature to LO, and set the time to 5 minutes. Select START/STOP to begin preheating.
3. While the unit is preheating, place a wonton wrapper on a flat surface. Moisten the edges with water and place a heaping teaspoon of the crab mixture in the center. Bring the 4 sides together and then pinch the top, forming a cross. Make sure all the edges are sealed. Repeat with the remaining wrappers and crab mixture.
4. When the unit beeps to signify it has preheated, brush half the rangoons with avocado oil and place them on the Grill Grate. Close the hood and cook for 5 minutes.
5. When cooking is complete, the rangoons will be crispy and golden brown. Remove the rangoons from the grill. Select GRILL, set the temperature to HI, and set the time to 5 minutes. Select START/STOP to begin and press PREHEAT to skip preheating. Repeat step 4 for the remaining rangoons.
6. Serve the rangoons with sweet chili sauce or Orange Chili Sauce (here).

Seared Tuna With Citrus Ponzu Sauce

Servings: 4
Cooking Time: 6 Minutes
Ingredients:
- Extra-virgin olive oil
- 4 (4- to 5-ounce) ahi tuna steaks (at least 1 inch thick)
- Salt
- Freshly ground black pepper
- ¼ cup soy sauce
- ⅓ cup rice wine (mirin)
- 1 teaspoon granulated sugar
- Juice of 2 limes
- Juice of 2 lemons
- 1 tablespoon sesame seeds, for garnish (optional)
- Scallions, both white and green parts, sliced, for garnish

Directions:

1. Insert the Grill Grate and close the hood. Select GRILL, set the temperature to MAX, and set the time to 6 minutes. Select START/STOP to begin preheating.
2. While the unit is preheating, drizzle the olive oil over the tuna steaks and rub it in for a nice coat. Season both sides with salt and pepper.
3. When the unit beeps to signify it has preheated, place the tuna steaks on the Grill Grate. Close the hood and cook for 3 minutes.
4. After 3 minutes, open the hood and flip the steak. Close the hood and cook for 3 minutes more.
5. While the tuna steaks are cooking, in a small bowl, whisk together the soy sauce, rice wine, sugar, lime juice, and lemon juice until the sugar is dissolved.
6. When cooking is complete, open the hood and remove the tuna steaks from the grill. Garnish with sesame seeds (if using) and scallions. Serve with the citrus ponzu sauce for dipping.

Tilapia With Cilantro And Ginger
Servings: 4
Cooking Time: 8 Minutes
Ingredients:
- Extra-virgin olive oil
- 4 (8-ounce) tilapia fillets
- 2 tablespoons soy sauce
- 1 teaspoon sesame oil
- 1 tablespoon honey
- 1 tablespoon peeled minced fresh ginger
- ½ cup chopped fresh cilantro

Directions:
1. Insert the Cooking Pot and close the hood. Select GRILL, set the temperature to HI, and set the time to 8 minutes. Select START/STOP to begin preheating.
2. While the unit is preheating, drizzle the fish fillets with olive oil.
3. When the unit beeps to signify it has preheated, place the fillets in the Cooking Pot in a single layer. Close the hood and cook for 6 minutes.
4. While the fish is cooking, in a small bowl, whisk together the soy sauce, sesame oil, honey, ginger, and cilantro.
5. After 6 minutes, open the hood and pour the sauce over the fillets. Close the hood and cook for 2 minutes more.
6. When cooking is complete, remove the fillets from the grill and serve.

Orange-ginger Soy Salmon
Servings: 4
Cooking Time: 12 Minutes
Ingredients:
- ½ cup low-sodium soy sauce
- ¼ cup orange marmalade
- 3 tablespoons light brown sugar, packed
- 1 tablespoon peeled minced fresh ginger
- 1 garlic clove, minced
- 4 (8-ounce) skin-on salmon fillets

Directions:
1. In a large bowl, whisk together the soy sauce, orange marmalade, brown sugar, ginger, and garlic until the sugar is dissolved. Set aside one-quarter of the marinade in a small bowl. Place the salmon fillets skin-side down in the marinade in the large bowl.
2. Insert the Grill Grate and close the hood. Select GRILL, set the temperature to MED, and set the time to 12 minutes. Select START/STOP to begin preheating.
3. When the unit beeps to signify it has preheated, place the salmon fillets on the Grill Grate, skin-side down. Spoon the remaining marinade in the large bowl over the fillets. Close the hood and cook for 10 minutes.
4. After 10 minutes, open the hood and brush the reserved marinade in the small bowl over the fillets. Close the hood and cook for 2 minutes more.
5. When cooking is complete, the salmon will be opaque and should flake easily with a fork. (If you want, you can also use the Smart Thermometer at the end of cooking to check that the internal temperature of the salmon has reached 145°F.) Remove the fillets from the grill and serve.

Mom's Lemon-pepper Salmon
Servings: 4
Cooking Time: 8 Minutes
Ingredients:
- ¼ cup mayonnaise
- 4 (4- to 5-ounce) skin-on salmon fillets
- 1 tablespoon lemon-pepper seasoning

Directions:
1. Insert the Grill Grate and close the hood. Select GRILL, set the temperature to MED, and set the time to 8 minutes. Select START/STOP to begin preheating.
2. While the unit is preheating, spread the mayonnaise evenly on the flesh of each salmon fillet. Season with the lemon pepper.
3. When the unit beeps to signify it has preheated, place the fillets on the Grill Grate, skin-side down. Close the hood and cook for 8 minutes.
4. When cooking is complete, the salmon will be opaque and should flake easily with a fork. (If you want, you can also use the Smart Thermometer at the end of cooking to check that the internal temperature of the salmon has reached 145°F.) Remove the salmon from the grill and serve.

Striped Bass With Sesame-ginger Scallions

Servings: 4
Cooking Time: 8 Minutes
Ingredients:

- 4 (8-ounce) striped bass fillets
- Extra-virgin olive oil
- 2 (1-inch) pieces fresh ginger, peeled and thinly sliced
- ½ cup soy sauce
- ½ cup rice wine (mirin)
- 2 tablespoons sesame oil
- ¼ cup light brown sugar, packed
- ¼ cup water
- ¼ cup sliced scallions, both white and green parts, for garnish

Directions:

1. Insert the Cooking Pot and close the hood. Select GRILL, set the temperature to HI, and set the time to 8 minutes. Select START/STOP to begin preheating.
2. While the unit is preheating, drizzle the fish fillets with olive oil.
3. When the unit beeps to signify it has preheated, place the fillets in the Cooking Pot in a single layer. Place the ginger slices on top of the fillets. Close the hood and cook for 6 minutes.
4. While the fish is cooking, in a small bowl, whisk together the soy sauce, rice wine, sesame oil, brown sugar, and water until the sugar dissolves.
5. After 6 minutes, open the hood and pour the soy sauce mixture over the fish. Close the hood and cook for 2 minutes more.
6. When cooking is complete, open the hood and remove the fillets from the grill. Garnish with the scallions and serve

Sauces, Dips, And Dressings

Fresh Mixed Berry Vinaigrette

Servings:1
Cooking Time: 0 Minutes
Ingredients:

- 1 cup mixed berries, thawed if frozen
- ½ cup balsamic vinegar
- ⅓ cup extra-virgin olive oil
- 2 tablespoons freshly squeezed lemon or lime juice
- 1 tablespoon lemon or lime zest
- 1 tablespoon Dijon mustard
- 1 tablespoon raw honey or maple syrup
- 1 teaspoon salt
- ½ teaspoon freshly ground black pepper

Directions:

1. Place all the ingredients in a blender and purée until thoroughly mixed and smooth.
2. You can serve it over a bed of greens, grilled meat, or fresh fruit salad.

Garlic Lime Tahini Dressing

Servings:1
Cooking Time: 0 Minutes
Ingredients:

- ⅓ cup tahini
- 3 tablespoons filtered water
- 2 tablespoons freshly squeezed lime juice
- 1 tablespoon apple cider vinegar
- 1 teaspoon lime zest
- 1½ teaspoons raw honey
- ¼ teaspoon garlic powder
- ¼ teaspoon salt

Directions:

1. Whisk together the tahini, water, vinegar, lime juice, lime zest, honey, salt, and garlic powder in a small bowl until well emulsified.
2. Serve immediately, or refrigerate in an airtight container for to 1 week.

Ginger Sweet Sauce

Servings:1
Cooking Time: 5 Minutes
Ingredients:

- 3 tablespoons ketchup
- 2 tablespoons water
- 2 tablespoons maple syrup
- 1 tablespoon rice vinegar
- 2 teaspoons peeled minced fresh ginger root
- 2 teaspoons soy sauce (or tamari, which is a gluten-free option)
- 1 teaspoon cornstarch

Directions:

1. In a small saucepan over medium heat, combine all the ingredients and stir continuously for 5 minutes, or until slightly thickened.
2. Enjoy warm or cold.

Chimichurri

Servings:2
Cooking Time: 0 Minutes
Ingredients:
- 1 cup minced fresh parsley
- ½ cup minced fresh cilantro
- ¼ cup minced fresh mint leaves
- ¼ cup minced garlic
- 2 tablespoons minced fresh oregano leaves
- 1 teaspoon fine Himalayan salt
- 1 cup olive oil or avocado oil
- ½ cup red wine vinegar
- Juice of 1 lemon

Directions:
1. Thoroughly mix the parsley, cilantro, mint leaves, garlic, oregano leaves, and salt in a medium bowl. Add the olive oil, vinegar, and lemon juice and whisk to combine.
2. Store in an airtight container in the refrigerator and shake before using.
3. You can serve the chimichurri over vegetables, poultry, meats, and fish. It also can be used as a marinade, dipping sauce, or condiment.

Peanut-lime Dressing

Servings: 8
Cooking Time: 0 Minutes
Ingredients:
- 1 cup lite coconut milk
- ¼ cup freshly squeezed lime juice
- ¼ cup creamy peanut butter
- 2 tablespoons low-sodium soy sauce or tamari
- 3 garlic cloves, minced
- 1 tablespoon grated fresh ginger

Directions:
1. Place all the ingredients in a food processor or blender and process until completely mixed and smooth.
2. It's delicious served over grilled chicken or tossed with noodles and green onions.

Lemon Dijon Vinaigrette

Servings:6
Cooking Time: 0 Minutes
Ingredients:
- ¼ cup extra-virgin olive oil
- 1 garlic clove, minced
- 2 tablespoons freshly squeezed lemon juice
- 1 teaspoon Dijon mustard
- ½ teaspoon raw honey
- ¼ teaspoon salt
- ¼ teaspoon dried basil

Directions:
1. Place all the ingredients in a mason jar. Cover and shake vigorously until thoroughly mixed and well emulsified.
2. Serve chilled.

Pico De Gallo

Servings: 2
Cooking Time: 0 Minutes
Ingredients:
- 3 large tomatoes, chopped
- ½ small red onion, diced
- ⅛ cup chopped fresh cilantro
- 3 garlic cloves, chopped
- 2 tablespoons chopped pickled jalapeño pepper
- 1 tablespoon lime juice
- ¼ teaspoon pink Himalayan salt (optional)

Directions:
1. In a medium bowl, combine all the ingredients and mix with a wooden spoon.

Creamy Coconut Lime Dressing

Servings:1
Cooking Time: 0 Minutes
Ingredients:
- 8 ounces plain coconut yogurt
- 2 tablespoons chopped fresh parsley
- 2 tablespoons freshly squeezed lemon juice
- 1 tablespoon snipped fresh chives
- ½ teaspoon salt
- Pinch freshly ground black pepper

Directions:
1. Stir together the coconut yogurt, parsley, lemon juice, chives, salt, and pepper in a medium bowl until completely mixed.
2. Transfer to an airtight container and refrigerate until ready to use.
3. This dressing perfectly pairs with spring mix greens, grilled chicken, or even your favorite salad.

Cashew Vodka Sauce

Servings:3
Cooking Time: 5 Minutes
Ingredients:
- ¾ cup raw cashews
- ¼ cup boiling water
- 1 tablespoon olive oil
- 4 garlic cloves, minced
- 1½ cups unsweetened almond milk
- 1 tablespoon arrowroot powder
- 1 teaspoon salt
- 1 tablespoon nutritional yeast
- 1¼ cups marinara sauce

Directions:
1. Put the cashews in a heatproof bowl and add boiling water to cover. Let soak for 10 minutes. Drain the cashews and place them in a blender. Add ¼ cup boiling water and blend for 1 to 2 minutes or until creamy. Set aside.
2. In a small saucepan, heat the olive oil over medium heat. Add the garlic and sauté for 2 minutes until golden. Whisk in the almond milk, arrowroot powder, and salt. Bring to a simmer. Continue to simmer, whisking frequently, for about 5 minutes or until the sauce thickens.
3. Carefully transfer the hot almond milk mixture to the blender with the cashews. Blend for 30 seconds to combine, then add the nutritional yeast and marinara sauce. Blend for 1 minute or until creamy.

Creamy Ranch Dressing

Servings: 8
Cooking Time: 0 Minutes
Ingredients:

1 cup plain Greek yogurt
¼ cup chopped fresh dill
2 tablespoons chopped fresh chives
Zest of 1 lemon
1 garlic clove, minced
½ teaspoon sea salt
⅛ teaspoon freshly cracked black pepper

Directions:
1. Mix together the yogurt, dill, chives, lemon zest, garlic, sea salt, and pepper in a small bowl and whisk to combine.
2. Serve chilled.

Balsamic Dressing

Servings:1
Cooking Time: 0 Minutes
Ingredients:

2 tablespoons Dijon mustard
¼ cup balsamic vinegar
¾ cup olive oil

Directions:
1. Put all ingredients in a jar with a tight-fitting lid. Put on the lid and shake vigorously until thoroughly combined. Refrigerate until ready to use and shake well before serving.

Kale And Almond Pesto

Servings:1
Cooking Time: 0 Minutes
Ingredients:

2 cups chopped kale leaves, rinsed well and stemmed
½ cup toasted almonds
2 garlic cloves
3 tablespoons extra-virgin olive oil
3 tablespoons freshly squeezed lemon juice
2 teaspoons lemon zest
1 teaspoon salt
½ teaspoon freshly ground black pepper
¼ teaspoon red pepper flakes

Directions:
1. Place all the ingredients in a food processor and pulse until smoothly puréed.
2. It tastes great with the eggs, salads, soup, pasta, cracker, and sandwiches.

Hummus

Servings: 2

Cooking Time: 0 Minutes
Ingredients:
- 1 can chickpeas, drained and rinsed
- ¼ cup tahini
- 3 tablespoons cold water
- 2 tablespoons freshly squeezed lemon juice
- 1 garlic clove
- ½ teaspoon turmeric powder
- ⅛ teaspoon black pepper
- Pinch of pink Himalayan salt

Directions:
1. Combine all the ingredients in a food processor and blend until smooth.

Cashew Pesto

Servings:1
Cooking Time: 0 Minutes
Ingredients:
- ¼ cup raw cashews
- Juice of 1 lemon
- 2 garlic cloves
- ⅓ red onion
- 1 tablespoon olive oil
- 4 cups basil leaves, packed
- 1 cup wheatgrass
- ¼ cup water
- ¼ teaspoon salt

Directions:
1. Put the cashews in a heatproof bowl and add boiling water to cover. Soak for 5 minutes and then drain.
2. Put all ingredients in a blender and blend for 2 to 3 minutes or until fully combined.

Cashew Ranch Dressing

Servings: 12
Cooking Time: 0 Minutes
Ingredients:
- 1 cup cashews, soaked in warm water for at least 1 hour
- ½ cup water
- 2 tablespoons freshly squeezed lemon juice
- 1 tablespoon vinegar
- 1 teaspoon garlic powder
- 1 teaspoon onion powder
- 2 teaspoons dried dill

Directions:
1. In a food processor, combine the cashews, water, lemon juice, vinegar, garlic powder, and onion powder. Blend until creamy and smooth. Add the dill and pulse a few times until combined

Desserts

Coffee Chocolate Cake

Servings: 8
Cooking Time: 30 Minutes
Ingredients:
- Dry Ingredients:
- 1½ cups almond flour
- ½ cup coconut meal
- ⅔ cup Swerve
- 1 teaspoon baking powder
- ¼ teaspoon salt
- Wet Ingredients:
- 1 egg
- 1 stick butter, melted
- ½ cup hot strongly brewed coffee
- Topping:
- ½ cup confectioner's Swerve
- ¼ cup coconut flour
- 3 tablespoons coconut oil
- 1 teaspoon ground cinnamon
- ½ teaspoon ground cardamom

Directions:
1. Select BAKE, set the temperature to 330ºF, and set the time to 30 minutes. Select START/STOP to begin preheating.
2. In a medium bowl, combine the almond flour, coconut meal, Swerve, baking powder, and salt.
3. In a large bowl, whisk the egg, melted butter, and coffee until smooth.
4. Add the dry mixture to the wet and stir until well incorporated. Transfer the batter to a greased baking pan.
5. Stir together all the ingredients for the topping in a small bowl. Spread the topping over the batter and smooth the top with a spatula.
6. Place the pan directly in the pot. Close the hood and BAKE for 30 minutes, or until the cake springs back when gently pressed with your fingers.
7. Rest for 10 minutes before serving.

Ultimate Skillet Brownies

Servings: 6
Cooking Time: 40 Minutes
Ingredients:
- ½ cup all-purpose flour
- ¼ cup unsweetened cocoa powder
- ¾ teaspoon sea salt
- 2 large eggs
- 1 tablespoon water
- ½ cup granulated sugar
- ½ cup dark brown sugar
- 1 tablespoon vanilla extract
- 8 ounces semisweet chocolate chips, melted
- ¾ cup unsalted butter, melted
- Nonstick cooking spray

Directions:
1. In a medium bowl, whisk together the flour, cocoa powder, and salt.

2. In a large bowl, whisk together the eggs, water, sugar, brown sugar, and vanilla until smooth.
3. In a microwave-safe bowl, melt the chocolate in the microwave. In a separate microwave-safe bowl, melt the butter.
4. In a separate medium bowl, stir together the chocolate and butter until evenly combined. Whisk into the egg mixture. Then slowly add the dry ingredients, stirring just until incorporated.
5. Remove the Grill Grate from the unit. Select BAKE, set the temperature to 350ºF, and set the time to 40 minutes. Select START/STOP to begin preheating.
6. Meanwhile, lightly grease the baking pan with cooking spray. Pour the batter into the pan, spreading evenly.
7. When the unit beeps to signify it has preheated, place the pan directly in the pot. Close the hood and BAKE for 40 minutes.
8. After 40 minutes, check that baking is complete. A wooden toothpick inserted into the center of the brownies should come out clean.

Chocolate Coconut Brownies

Servings: 8
Cooking Time: 15 Minutes
Ingredients:
- ½ cup coconut oil
- 2 ounces dark chocolate
- 1 cup sugar
- 2½ tablespoons water
- 4 whisked eggs
- ¼ teaspoon ground cinnamon
- ½ teaspoons ground anise star
- ¼ teaspoon coconut extract
- ½ teaspoons vanilla extract
- 1 tablespoon honey
- ½ cup flour
- ½ cup desiccated coconut
- Sugar, for dusting

Directions:
1. Select BAKE, set the temperature to 355ºF, and set the time to 15 minutes. Select START/STOP to begin preheating.
2. Melt the coconut oil and dark chocolate in the microwave.
3. Combine with the sugar, water, eggs, cinnamon, anise, coconut extract, vanilla, and honey in a large bowl.
4. Stir in the flour and desiccated coconut. Incorporate everything well.
5. Lightly grease a baking pan with butter. Transfer the mixture to the pan.
6. Place the pan directly in the pot. Close the hood and BAKE for 15 minutes.
7. Remove from the grill and allow to cool slightly.
8. Take care when taking it out of the baking pan. Slice it into squares.
9. Dust with sugar before serving.

Everyday Cheesecake

Servings: 4
Cooking Time: 35 Minutes
Ingredients:
- 1 large egg
- 8 ounces cream cheese, at room temperature
- ¼ cup heavy (whipping) cream
- ¼ cup sour cream
- ¼ cup powdered sugar
- 1 teaspoon vanilla extract
- 5 ounces cookies, such as chocolate, vanilla, cinnamon, or your favorite
- 4 tablespoons (½ stick) unsalted butter, melted

Directions:
1. In a large bowl, whisk the egg. Then add the cream cheese, heavy cream, and sour cream and whisk until smooth. Slowly add the powdered sugar and vanilla, whisking until fully mixed.
2. Insert the Cooking Pot and close the hood. Select BAKE, set the temperature to 350°F, and set the time to 35 minutes. Select START/STOP to begin preheating.
3. While the unit is preheating, crush the cookies into fine crumbs. Place them in a 6-inch springform pan and drizzle evenly with the melted butter. Using your fingers, press down on the crumbs to form a crust on the bottom of the pan. Pour the cream cheese mixture on top of the crust. Cover the pan with aluminum foil, making sure the foil fully covers the sides of the pan and tucks under the bottom so it does not lift up and block the Splatter Shield as the air flows while baking.
4. When the unit beeps to signify it has preheated, place the springform pan in the Cooking Pot. Close the hood and cook for 25 minutes.
5. After 25 minutes, open the hood and remove the foil. Close the hood and cook for 10 minutes more.
6. When cooking is complete, remove the pan from the Cooking Pot and let the cheesecake cool for 1 hour, then place the cheesecake in the refrigerator for at least 3 hours. Slice and serve.

Banana And Walnut Cake

Servings: 6
Cooking Time: 25 Minutes
Ingredients:
- 1 pound bananas, mashed
- 8 ounces flour
- 6 ounces sugar
- 3.5 ounces walnuts, chopped
- 2.5 ounces butter, melted
- 2 eggs, lightly beaten
- ¼ teaspoon baking soda

Directions:
1. Select BAKE, set the temperature to 355°F, and set the time to 10 minutes. Select START/STOP to begin preheating.
2. In a bowl, combine the sugar, butter, egg, flour, and baking soda with a whisk. Stir in the bananas and walnuts.
3. Transfer the mixture to a greased baking pan. Place the pan directly in the pot. Close the hood and BAKE for 10 minutes.
4. Reduce the temperature to 330°F and bake for another 15 minutes. Serve hot.

Orange And Anise Cake

Servings: 6
Cooking Time: 20 Minutes
Ingredients:
- 1 stick butter, at room temperature
- 5 tablespoons liquid monk fruit
- 2 eggs plus 1 egg yolk, beaten
- ⅓ cup hazelnuts, roughly chopped
- 3 tablespoons sugar-free orange marmalade
- 6 ounces unbleached almond flour
- 1 teaspoon baking soda
- ½ teaspoon baking powder
- ½ teaspoon ground cinnamon
- ½ teaspoon ground allspice
- ½ ground anise seed
- Cooking spray

Directions:
1. Select BAKE, set the temperature to 310°F, and set the time to 20 minutes. Select START/STOP to begin preheating.
2. Lightly spritz a baking pan with cooking spray.
3. In a mixing bowl, whisk the butter and liquid monk fruit until the mixture is pale and smooth. Mix in the beaten eggs, hazelnuts, and marmalade and whisk again until well incorporated.
4. Add the almond flour, baking soda, baking powder, cinnamon, allspice, anise seed and stir to mix well.
5. Scrape the batter into the prepared baking pan. Place the pan directly in the pot. Close the hood and BAKE for 20 minutes, or until the top of the cake springs back when gently pressed with your fingers.
6. Transfer to a wire rack and let the cake cool to room temperature. Serve immediately.

Candied Pecans

Servings: 4
Cooking Time: 20 Minutes
Ingredients:
- 1 large egg white
- 1 teaspoon vanilla extract
- 1 tablespoon water
- ¼ cup granulated sugar
- ¼ cup light brown sugar, packed
- 1 teaspoon ground cinnamon
- 1 teaspoon salt
- 1 pound pecan halves

Directions:
1. Insert the Cooking Pot and close the hood. Select GRILL, set the temperature to MED, and set the time to 20 minutes. Select START/STOP to begin preheating.
2. While the unit is preheating, in a large bowl, whisk together the egg white, vanilla, and water until it becomes frothy.
3. In a small bowl, combine the granulated sugar, brown sugar, cinnamon, and salt. Add the pecans to the egg mixture, coating them well. Then add the sugar mixture and stir to coat the pecans evenly.
4. When the unit beeps to signify it has preheated, evenly spread the pecans in the Cooking Pot. Close the hood and grill for 5 minutes.

5. After 5 minutes, open the hood and stir the pecans. Close the hood and cook for 5 minutes. Repeat until the pecans have cooked for 20 minutes total.

6. When cooking is complete, remove the pecans from the Cooking Pot and spread them on a baking sheet to cool to room temperature. Store in a resealable bag or airtight container.

Cinnamon-sugar Dessert Chips

Servings: 4
Cooking Time: 10 Minutes
Ingredients:
- 10 (6-inch) flour tortillas
- 8 tablespoons (1 stick) unsalted butter, melted
- 1 tablespoon cinnamon
- ¼ cup granulated sugar
- ½ cup chocolate syrup, for dipping

Directions:
1. Insert the Grill Grate and close the hood. Select GRILL, set the temperature to HI, and set the time to 10 minutes. Select START/STOP to begin preheating.

2. While the unit is preheating, cut the tortillas into 6 equal wedges. In a large resealable bag, combine the tortillas, butter, cinnamon, and sugar and shake vigorously to coat the tortillas.

3. When the unit beeps to signify it has preheated, add half the tortillas to the Grill Grate. Close the hood and cook for 2 minutes, 30 seconds.

4. After 2 minutes, 30 seconds, open the hood and use a spatula to quickly flip the chips or move them around. Close the hood and cook for 2 minutes, 30 seconds more.

5. After 2 minutes, 30 seconds, open the hood and remove the grilled chips and repeat the process with the remaining tortillas.

6. Serve with the chocolate syrup for dipping.

Grilled Strawberry Pound Cake

Servings: 8
Cooking Time: 8 Minutes
Ingredients:
- 1 loaf pound cake, cut into ¼-inch-thick slices (8 slices)
- 4 tablespoons (½ stick) unsalted butter, melted
- 2 cups strawberries, sliced
- 1 tablespoon granulated sugar
- Juice of ¼ lemon

Directions:
1. Insert the Grill Grate and close the hood. Select GRILL, set the temperature to HI, and set the time to 8 minutes. Select START/STOP to begin preheating.

2. While the unit is preheating, brush both sides of the pound cake slices with the melted butter. In a small bowl, combine the strawberries, sugar, and lemon juice.

3. When the unit beeps to signify it has preheated, place 4 slices of pound cake on the Grill Grate. Close the hood and grill for 2 minutes.

4. After 2 minutes, open the hood and flip the pound cake slices. Top each with ¼ cup of strawberries. Close the hood and cook for 2 minutes.

5. After 2 minutes, open the hood and carefully remove the grilled pound cake. Repeat steps 3 and 4 with the remaining pound cake and strawberries. Serve.

Pecan Pie

Servings: 4
Cooking Time: 20 Minutes
Ingredients:
- 6 ounces cream cheese, at room temperature
- 4 tablespoons (½ stick) unsalted butter
- 2 large eggs
- 1 teaspoon vanilla extract
- 1 cup light brown sugar, packed
- 1 cup all-purpose flour
- ½ cup pecan halves

Directions:
1. Place the cream cheese and butter in a 7-inch silicon cake pan. Insert the Cooking Pot, place the cake pan in the pot, and close the hood. Select BAKE, set the temperature to 350°F, and set the time to 20 minutes. (If using a metal or glass cake pan, you may need to add 5 to 10 minutes to the baking time.) Select START/STOP to begin preheating. After 5 minutes of preheating (set a separate timer), open the hood and remove the cake pan. (The cream cheese and butter will be melted but not combined.) Close the hood to continue preheating.

2. While the unit is preheating, in a medium bowl, whisk together the eggs, vanilla, brown sugar, and 1½ tablespoons of the melted butter from the cake pan.

3. Transfer the remaining butter and cream cheese from the cake pan to a large bowl and mix to combine. (It may look a little like cottage cheese.) Slowly sift the flour into the bowl. Begin kneading and mixing the dough together with your hands. It may be sticky at first, but continue mixing until it forms into a smooth dough. Place the dough in the cake pan and press it into the bottom and up the sides of the pan to form a piecrust.

4. Pour the filling into the piecrust and top with the pecans.

5. When the unit beeps to signify it has preheated, place the cake pan in the Cooking Pot. Close the hood and bake for 20 minutes.

6. When cooking is complete, the crust edges will be golden brown. Remove the cake pan and let cool to room temperature before slicing and serving.

Strawberry Pizza

Servings: 4
Cooking Time: 6 Minutes
Ingredients:
- 2 tablespoons all-purpose flour, plus more as needed
- ½ store-bought pizza dough
- 1 tablespoon canola oil
- 1 cup sliced fresh strawberries
- 1 tablespoon sugar
- ½ cup chocolate-hazelnut spread

Directions:
1. Insert the Grill Grate and close the hood. Select GRILL, set the temperature to MAX, and set the time to 6 minutes. Select START/STOP to begin preheating.

2. While the unit is preheating, dust a clean work surface with the flour. Place the dough on the floured surface, and roll it out to a 9-inch round of even thickness. Dust your rolling pin and work surface with additional flour, as needed to ensure the dough does not stick.

3. Brush the surface of the rolled-out dough evenly with half the oil. Flip the dough over, and brush with the

remaining oil. Poke the dough with a fork 5 or 6 times across its surface to prevent air pockets from forming during cooking.
4. When the unit beeps to signify it has preheated, place the dough on the Grill Grate. Close the hood and GRILL for 3 minutes.
5. After 3 minutes, flip the dough. Close the hood and continue grilling for the remaining 3 minutes.
6. Meanwhile, in a medium mixing bowl, combine the strawberries and sugar.
7. Transfer the pizza to a cutting board and let cool. Top with the chocolate-hazelnut spread and strawberries. Cut into pieces and serve.

Blackberry Chocolate Cake

Servings: 8
Cooking Time: 22 Minutes
Ingredients:
- ½ cup butter, at room temperature
- 2 ounces Swerve
- 4 eggs
- 1 cup almond flour
- 1 teaspoon baking soda
- ⅓ teaspoon baking powder
- ½ cup cocoa powder
- 1 teaspoon orange zest
- ⅓ cup fresh blackberries

Directions:
1. Select BAKE, set the temperature to 335ºF, and set the time to 22 minutes. Select START/STOP to begin preheating.
2. With an electric mixer or hand mixer, beat the butter and Swerve until creamy.
3. One at a time, mix in the eggs and beat again until fluffy.
4. Add the almond flour, baking soda, baking powder, cocoa powder, orange zest and mix well. Add the butter mixture to the almond flour mixture and stir until well blended. Fold in the blackberries.
5. Scrape the batter to a baking pan. Place the pan directly in the pot. Close the hood and BAKE for 22 minutes. Check the cake for doneness: If a toothpick inserted into the center of the cake comes out clean, it's done.
6. Allow the cake cool on a wire rack to room temperature. Serve immediately.

Oatmeal And Carrot Cookie Cups

Servings: 16
Cooking Time: 8 Minutes
Ingredients:
- 3 tablespoons unsalted butter, at room temperature
- ¼ cup packed brown sugar
- 1 tablespoon honey
- 1 egg white
- ½ teaspoon vanilla extract
- ⅓ cup finely grated carrot
- ½ cup quick-cooking oatmeal
- ⅓ cup whole-wheat pastry flour
- ½ teaspoon baking soda
- ¼ cup dried cherries

Directions:
1. Select BAKE, set the temperature to 350ºF, and set the time to 8 minutes. Select START/STOP to begin preheating.

2. In a medium bowl, beat the butter, brown sugar, and honey until well combined.
3. Add the egg white, vanilla, and carrot. Beat to combine.
4. Stir in the oatmeal, pastry flour, and baking soda.
5. Stir in the dried cherries.
6. Double up 32 mini muffin foil cups to make 16 cups. Fill each with about 4 teaspoons of dough. Place the cookie cups directly in the pot.
7. Close the hood and BAKE for 8 minutes, 8 at a time, or until light golden brown and just set. Serve warm.

Vanilla Scones

Servings: 18
Cooking Time: 15 Minutes
Ingredients:
- For the scones
- 2 cups almond flour
- ¼ cup granulated sugar
- ¼ teaspoon salt
- 1 tablespoon baking powder
- 2 large eggs
- 1 teaspoon vanilla extract
- 4 tablespoons (½ stick) unsalted butter, melted
- 2 tablespoons heavy (whipping) cream
- For the icing
- 1 cup powdered sugar
- 2 tablespoons heavy (whipping) cream
- 1 tablespoon vanilla extract

Directions:
1. In a large bowl, combine the almond flour, granulated sugar, salt, and baking powder. In another large bowl, whisk the eggs, then whisk in the vanilla, butter, and heavy cream. Add the dry ingredients to the wet and mix just until a dough forms.
2. Insert the Cooking Pot and close the hood. Select BAKE, set the temperature to 325°F, and set the time to 15 minutes. Select START/STOP to begin preheating.
3. While the unit is preheating, divide the dough into 3 equal pieces. Shape each piece into a disc about 1 inch thick and 5 inches in diameter. Cut each into 6 wedges, like slicing a pizza.
4. When the unit beeps to signify it has preheated, place the scones in the Cooking Pot, spacing them apart so they don't bake together. Close the hood and cook for 15 minutes.
5. While the scones are baking, in a small bowl, combine the powdered sugar, heavy cream, and vanilla. Stir until smooth.
6. After 15 minutes, open the hood and remove the scones. They are done baking when they have turned a light golden brown. Place on a wire rack to cool to room temperature. Drizzle the icing over the scones, or pour a tablespoonful on the top of each scone for an even glaze.

Easy Blackberry Cobbler

Servings: 6
Cooking Time: 25 To 30 Minutes
Ingredients:
- 3 cups fresh or frozen blackberries
- 1¾ cups sugar, divided
- 1 teaspoon vanilla extract
- 8 tablespoons butter, melted
- 1 cup self-rising flour
- Cooking spray

Directions:
1. Select BAKE, set the temperature to 350ºF, and set the time to 30 minutes. Select START/STOP to begin preheating.
2. Spritz a baking pan with cooking spray.
3. Mix the blackberries, 1 cup of sugar, and vanilla in a medium bowl and stir to combine.
4. Stir together the melted butter, remaining sugar, and flour in a separate medium bowl.
5. Spread the blackberry mixture evenly in the prepared pan and top with the butter mixture.
6. Place the pan directly in the pot. Close the hood and BAKE for 20 to 25 minutes. Check for doneness and bake for another 5 minutes, if needed.
7. Remove from the grill and place on a wire rack to cool to room temperature. Serve immediately.

Apple, Peach, And Cranberry Crisp

Servings: 8
Cooking Time: 12 Minutes
Ingredients:
- 1 apple, peeled and chopped
- 2 peaches, peeled and chopped
- ⅓ cup dried cranberries
- 2 tablespoons honey
- ⅓ cup brown sugar
- ¼ cup flour
- ½ cup oatmeal
- 3 tablespoons softened butter

Directions:
1. Select BAKE, set the temperature to 370ºF, and set the time to 12 minutes. Select START/STOP to begin preheating.
2. In a baking pan, combine the apple, peaches, cranberries, and honey, and mix well.
3. In a medium bowl, combine the brown sugar, flour, oatmeal, and butter, and mix until crumbly. Sprinkle this mixture over the fruit in the pan.
4. Place the pan directly in the pot. Close the hood and BAKE for 10 to 12 minutes or until the fruit is bubbly and the topping is golden brown. Serve warm.

Pineapple And Chocolate Cake

Servings: 4
Cooking Time: 35 To 40 Minutes
Ingredients:
- 2 cups flour
- 4 ounces butter, melted
- ¼ cup sugar
- ½ pound pineapple, chopped
- ½ cup pineapple juice
- 1 ounce dark chocolate, grated
- 1 large egg
- 2 tablespoons skimmed milk

Directions:
1. Select BAKE, set the temperature to 370ºF, and set the time to 40 minutes. Select START/STOP to begin preheating.
2. Grease a cake tin with a little oil or butter.
3. In a bowl, combine the butter and flour to create a crumbly consistency.
4. Add the sugar, chopped pineapple, juice, and grated dark chocolate and mix well.
5. In a separate bowl, combine the egg and milk. Add this mixture to the flour mixture and stir well until a soft dough forms.
6. Pour the mixture into the cake tin and transfer to the grill.
7. Close the hood and BAKE for 35 to 40 minutes.
8. Serve immediately.

Churros With Chocolate-yogurt Sauce

Servings: 8
Cooking Time: 30 Minutes
Ingredients:
- 1 cup water
- 1 stick unsalted butter, cut into 8 pieces
- ½ cup sugar, plus 1 tablespoon
- 1 cup all-purpose flour
- 1 teaspoon vanilla extract
- 3 large eggs
- 2 teaspoons ground cinnamon
- Nonstick cooking spray
- 4 ounces dark chocolate, chopped
- ¼ cup Greek yogurt

Directions:
1. In a medium saucepan over medium-high heat, combine the water, butter, and the 1 tablespoon of sugar. Bring to a simmer. Add the flour, stirring it in quickly. Continue to cook, stirring constantly, until the mixture is thick, about 3 minutes. Transfer to a large bowl.
2. Using a spoon, beat the flour mixture for about 1 minute, until cooled slightly. Stir in the vanilla, then the eggs, one at a time.
3. Transfer the dough to a plastic bag or a piping bag. Let the dough rest for 1 hour at room temperature.
4. Insert the Crisper Basket and close the hood. Select AIR CRISP, set the temperature to 375ºF, and set the time to 30 minutes. Select START/STOP to begin preheating.
5. Meanwhile, in a medium shallow bowl, combine the cinnamon and remaining ½ cup of sugar.
6. When the unit beeps to signify it has preheated, spray the basket with the nonstick cooking spray. Take the plastic bag with your dough and cut off one corner. Pipe the batter directly into the Crisper Basket, making 6 churros, placed at least ½ inch apart. Close the hood and AIR CRISP for 10 minutes.
7. Meanwhile, in a small microwave-safe mixing bowl, melt the chocolate in the microwave, stirring it after every 30 seconds, until completely melted and smooth. Add the yogurt and whisk until smooth.

8. After 10 minutes, carefully transfer the churros to the sugar mixture and toss to coat evenly. Repeat piping and air crisping with the remaining batter, adding time as needed.
9. Serve the churros with the warm chocolate dipping sauce.

Chocolate S'mores

Servings: 12
Cooking Time: 3 Minutes
Ingredients:
- 12 whole cinnamon graham crackers
- 2 chocolate bars, broken into 12 pieces
- 12 marshmallows

Directions:
1. Insert the Crisper Basket and close the hood. Select BAKE, set the temperature to 350ºF, and set the time to 3 minutes. Select START/STOP to begin preheating.
2. Halve each graham cracker into 2 squares.
3. Put 6 graham cracker squares in the basket. Do not stack. Put a piece of chocolate into each. Close the hood and BAKE for 2 minutes.
4. Open the grill and add a marshmallow onto each piece of melted chocolate. Bake for 1 additional minute.
5. Remove the cooked s'mores from the grill, then repeat steps 2 and 3 for the remaining 6 s'mores.
6. Top with the remaining graham cracker squares and serve.

Curry Peaches, Pears, And Plums

Servings: 6 To 8
Cooking Time: 5 Minutes
Ingredients:
- 2 peaches
- 2 firm pears
- 2 plums
- 2 tablespoons melted butter
- 1 tablespoon honey
- 2 to 3 teaspoons curry powder

Directions:
1. Insert the Crisper Basket and close the hood. Select BAKE, set the temperature to 325ºF, and set the time to 8 minutes. Select START/STOP to begin preheating.
2. Cut the peaches in half, remove the pits, and cut each half in half again. Cut the pears in half, core them, and remove the stem. Cut each half in half again. Do the same with the plums.
3. Spread a large sheet of heavy-duty foil on the work surface. Arrange the fruit on the foil and drizzle with the butter and honey. Sprinkle with the curry powder.
4. Wrap the fruit in the foil, making sure to leave some air space in the packet.
5. Put the foil package in the basket. Close the hood and BAKE for 5 to 8 minutes, shaking the basket once during the cooking time, until the fruit is soft.
6. Serve immediately.

Chocolate Pecan Pie

Servings: 8
Cooking Time: 25 Minutes
Ingredients:
- 1 unbaked pie crust
- Filling:

- 2 large eggs
- ⅓ cup butter, melted
- 1 cup sugar
- ½ cup all-purpose flour
- 1 cup milk chocolate chips
- 1½ cups coarsely chopped pecans
- 2 tablespoons bourbon

Directions:
1. Select BAKE, set the temperature to 350ºF, and set the time to 25 minutes. Select START/STOP to begin preheating.
2. Whisk the eggs and melted butter in a large bowl until creamy.
3. Add the sugar and flour and stir to incorporate. Mix in the milk chocolate chips, pecans, and bourbon and stir until well combined.
4. Use a fork to prick holes in the bottom and sides of the pie crust. Pour the prepared filling into the pie crust. Place the pie crust in the pot.
5. Close the hood and BAKE for 25 minutes until a toothpick inserted in the center comes out clean.
6. Allow the pie cool for 10 minutes in the basket before serving.

Pumpkin Pudding

Servings: 4
Cooking Time: 15 Minutes
Ingredients:
- 3 cups pumpkin purée
- 3 tablespoons honey
- 1 tablespoon ginger
- 1 tablespoon cinnamon
- 1 teaspoon clove
- 1 teaspoon nutmeg
- 1 cup full-fat cream
- 2 eggs
- 1 cup sugar

Directions:
1. Select BAKE, set the temperature to 390ºF, and set the time to 15 minutes. Select START/STOP to begin preheating.
2. In a bowl, stir all the ingredients together to combine.
3. Scrape the mixture into a greased baking pan. Place the pan directly in the pot. Close the hood and BAKE for 15 minutes.
4. Serve warm.

Chocolate And Peanut Butter Lava Cupcakes

Servings: 8
Cooking Time: 10 To 13 Minutes
Ingredients:
- Nonstick baking spray with flour
- 1⅓ cups chocolate cake mix
- 1 egg
- 1 egg yolk
- ¼ cup safflower oil
- ¼ cup hot water
- ⅓ cup sour cream
- 3 tablespoons peanut butter
- 1 tablespoon powdered sugar

Directions:
1. Select BAKE, set the temperature to 350°F, and set the time to 13 minutes. Select START/STOP to begin preheating.
2. Double up 16 foil muffin cups to make 8 cups. Spray each lightly with nonstick spray; set aside.
3. In a medium bowl, combine the cake mix, egg, egg yolk, safflower oil, water, and sour cream, and beat until combined.
4. In a small bowl, combine the peanut butter and powdered sugar and mix well. Form this mixture into 8 balls.
5. Spoon about ¼ cup of the chocolate batter into each muffin cup and top with a peanut butter ball. Spoon remaining batter on top of the peanut butter balls to cover them.
6. Arrange the cups in the pot, leaving some space between each. Place the pan directly in the pot. Close the hood and BAKE for 10 to 13 minutes or until the tops look dry and set.
7. Let the cupcakes cool for about 10 minutes, then serve warm.

Rum Grilled Pineapple Sundaes

Servings: 6
Cooking Time: 8 Minutes
Ingredients:
- ½ cup dark rum
- ½ cup packed brown sugar
- 1 teaspoon ground cinnamon, plus more for garnish
- 1 pineapple, cored and sliced
- Vanilla ice cream, for serving

Directions:
1. In a large shallow bowl or storage container, combine the rum, sugar, and cinnamon. Add the pineapple slices and arrange them in a single layer. Coat with the mixture, then let soak for at least 5 minutes per side.
2. Insert the Grill Grate and close the hood. Select GRILL, set the temperature to MAX, and set the time to 8 minutes. Select START/STOP to begin preheating.
3. While the unit is preheating, strain the extra rum sauce from the pineapple.
4. When the unit beeps to signify it has preheated, place the fruit on the Grill Grate in a single layer (you may need to do this in multiple batches). Gently press the fruit down to maximize grill marks. Close the hood and GRILL for about 6 to 8 minutes without flipping. If working in batches, remove the pineapple, and repeat this step for the remaining pineapple slices.
5. When cooking is complete, remove, and top each pineapple ring with a scoop of ice cream. Sprinkle with cinnamon and serve immediately.

Classic Pound Cake

Servings: 8
Cooking Time: 30 Minutes
Ingredients:
- 1 stick butter, at room temperature
- 1 cup Swerve
- 4 eggs
- 1½ cups coconut flour
- ½ cup buttermilk
- ½ teaspoon baking soda

- ½ teaspoon baking powder
- ¼ teaspoon salt
- 1 teaspoon vanilla essence
- A pinch of ground star anise
- A pinch of freshly grated nutmeg
- Cooking spray

Directions:
1. Select BAKE, set the temperature to 320°F, and set the time to 30 minutes. Select START/STOP to begin preheating.
2. Spray a baking pan with cooking spray.
3. With an electric mixer or hand mixer, beat the butter and Swerve until creamy. One at a time, mix in the eggs and whisk until fluffy. Add the remaining ingredients and stir to combine.
4. Transfer the batter to the prepared baking pan. Place the pan directly in the pot. Close the hood and BAKE for 30 minutes until the center of the cake is springy. Rotate the pan halfway through the cooking time.
5. Allow the cake to cool in the pan for 10 minutes before removing and serving.

Peanut Butter-chocolate Bread Pudding

Servings: 8
Cooking Time: 10 To 12 Minutes
Ingredients:
- 1 egg
- 1 egg yolk
- ¾ cup chocolate milk
- 3 tablespoons brown sugar
- 3 tablespoons peanut butter
- 2 tablespoons cocoa powder
- 1 teaspoon vanilla
- 5 slices firm white bread, cubed
- Nonstick cooking spray

Directions:
1. Select BAKE, set the temperature to 330°F, and set the time to 12 minutes. Select START/STOP to begin preheating.
2. Spritz a baking pan with nonstick cooking spray.
3. Whisk together the egg, egg yolk, chocolate milk, brown sugar, peanut butter, cocoa powder, and vanilla until well combined.
4. Fold in the bread cubes and stir to mix well. Allow the bread soak for 10 minutes.
5. When ready, transfer the egg mixture to the prepared baking pan.
6. Place the pan directly in the pot. Close the hood and BAKE for 10 to 12 minutes, or until the pudding is just firm to the touch.
7. Serve at room temperature.

Sugar-glazed Biscuit Bites

Servings: 8
Cooking Time: 12 Minutes
Ingredients:
- ⅔ cup all-purpose flour, plus additional for dusting
- ⅔ cup whole-wheat flour
- 2 tablespoons granulated sugar
- 1 teaspoon baking powder
- ¼ teaspoon ground cinnamon
- ¼ teaspoon sea salt
- 4 tablespoons salted butter, cold and cut into small pieces
- ⅓ cup whole milk
- Nonstick cooking spray
- 2 cups powdered sugar
- 3 tablespoons water

Directions:
1. In a large bowl, combine the all-purpose flour, whole-wheat flour, sugar, baking powder, cinnamon, and salt. Add the cold butter pieces, and cut them into the flour mixture using a pastry cutter or a fork, until well-combined and the mixture resembles a course meal. Add the milk to the mixture, and stir together until the dough comes together into a ball.
2. Insert the Crisper Basket and close the hood. Select AIR CRISP, set the temperature to 350ºF, and set the time to 12 minutes. Select START/STOP to begin preheating.
3. While the unit is preheating, dust a clean work surface with the all-purpose flour. Place the dough on the floured surface, and knead until the dough is smooth and forms a cohesive ball, about 30 seconds. Cut the dough into 16 equal pieces. Gently roll each piece into a smooth ball.
4. When the unit beeps to signify it has preheated, coat the basket well with cooking spray. Place 8 biscuit bites in the basket, leaving room between each, and spray each with cooking spray. Close the hood and AIR CRISP for 10 to 12 minutes, until golden brown.
5. Meanwhile, in a medium mixing bowl, whisk together the powdered sugar and water until it forms a smooth glaze.
6. Gently remove the bites from the basket, and place them on a wire rack covered with aluminum foil. Repeat step 4 with the remaining biscuit bites.
7. Spoon half the glaze over the bites and let cool 5 minutes, then spoon over the remaining glaze.

Orange Cake

Servings: 8
Cooking Time: 23 Minutes
Ingredients:
- Nonstick baking spray with flour
- 1¼ cups all-purpose flour
- ⅓ cup yellow cornmeal
- ¾ cup white sugar
- 1 teaspoon baking soda
- ¼ cup safflower oil
- 1¼ cups orange juice, divided
- 1 teaspoon vanilla
- ¼ cup powdered sugar

Directions:
1. Select BAKE, set the temperature to 350ºF, and set the time to 23 minutes. Select START/STOP to begin preheating.
2. Spray a baking pan with nonstick spray and set aside.
3. In a medium bowl, combine the flour, cornmeal, sugar, baking soda, safflower oil, 1 cup of the orange juice, and vanilla, and mix well.
4. Pour the batter into the baking pan. Place the pan directly in the pot. Close the hood and BAKE for 23 minutes or until a toothpick inserted in the center of the cake comes out clean.
5. Remove the cake from the grill and place on a cooling rack. Using a toothpick, make about 20 holes in the cake.
6. In a small bowl, combine remaining ¼ cup of orange juice and the powdered sugar and stir well. Drizzle this mixture over the hot cake slowly so the cake absorbs it.
7. Cool completely, then cut into wedges to serve.

Lemon Squares

Servings: 4
Cooking Time: 35 Minutes
Ingredients:
- 1 cup all-purpose flour
- 8 tablespoons (1 stick) unsalted butter, at room temperature
- ⅓ cup powdered sugar, plus additional for dusting
- 2 large eggs
- ⅔ cup granulated sugar
- ½ teaspoon baking powder
- ¼ teaspoon salt
- Juice of 1 lemon

Directions:
1. Insert the Cooking Pot and close the hood. Select BAKE, set the temperature to 325°F, and set the time to 35 minutes. Select START/STOP to begin preheating.
2. While the unit is preheating, in a large bowl, combine the flour, butter, and powdered sugar. Use your hands to smash and mix until the mixture has a crumbly texture. Transfer the mixture to a 6-inch square pan, using your fingers to press the dough into the bottom of the pan to form a crust.
3. When the unit beeps to signify it has preheated, place the pan in the Cooking Pot. Close the hood and cook for 5 minutes.
4. While the crust is baking, in a small bowl, beat the eggs, then add the sugar, baking powder, salt, and lemon juice and mix until well combined.
5. After 5 minutes, open the hood and pour the lemon filling over the crust. Cover the pan with aluminum foil (use grill mitts), making sure the foil tucks under the bottom of the pan so it does not lift up and block the Splatter Shield as the air flows while baking. Close the hood and cook for 20 minutes.
6. After 20 minutes, open the hood and remove the foil. Close the hood and bake uncovered for 10 minutes more.
7. When cooking is complete, remove the pan and let cool for at least 1 to 2 hours. Dust with additional powdered sugar and serve.

Chocolate And Coconut Cake

Servings: 6
Cooking Time: 15 Minutes
Ingredients:
- ½ cup unsweetened chocolate, chopped
- ½ stick butter, at room temperature
- 1 tablespoon liquid stevia
- 1½ cups coconut flour
- 2 eggs, whisked
- ½ teaspoon vanilla extract
- A pinch of fine sea salt
- Cooking spray

Directions:
1. Place the chocolate, butter, and stevia in a microwave-safe bowl. Microwave for about 30 seconds until melted.
2. Let the chocolate mixture cool for 5 to 10 minutes.
3. Add the remaining ingredients to the bowl of chocolate mixture and whisk to incorporate.
4. Select BAKE, set the temperature to 330ºF, and set the time to 15 minutes. Select START/STOP to begin preheating.
5. Lightly spray a baking pan with cooking spray.
6. Scrape the chocolate mixture into the prepared baking pan.
7. Place the pan directly in the pot. Close the hood and BAKE for 15 minutes, or until the top springs back lightly when gently pressed with your fingers.
8. Let the cake cool for 5 minutes and serve.

Chia Pudding

Servings: 2
Cooking Time: 4 Minutes
Ingredients:
- 1 cup chia seeds
- 1 cup unsweetened coconut milk
- 1 teaspoon liquid stevia
- 1 tablespoon coconut oil
- 1 teaspoon butter, melted

Directions:
1. Select BAKE, set the temperature to 360ºF, and set the time to 4 minutes. Select START/STOP to begin preheating.
2. Mix together the chia seeds, coconut milk, and stevia in a large bowl. Add the coconut oil and melted butter and stir until well blended.
3. Divide the mixture evenly between the ramekins, filling only about ⅔ of the way. Transfer to the pot.
4. Close the hood and BAKE for 4 minutes.
5. Allow to cool for 5 minutes and serve warm.

Grilled Apple Fries With Caramel Cream Cheese Dip

Servings: 4
Cooking Time: 5 Minutes
Ingredients:
- 4 apples, such as Honeycrisp, Gala, Pink Lady, or Granny Smith, peeled, cored, and sliced
- ¼ cup heavy (whipping) cream
- 1 tablespoon granulated sugar
- ¼ teaspoon cinnamon
- ¼ cup all-purpose flour
- 4 ounces cream cheese, at room temperature
- 1 tablespoon caramel sauce
- 1 tablespoon light brown sugar, packed

Directions:
1. Insert the Grill Grate and close the hood. Select GRILL, set the temperature to MAX, and set the time to 5 minutes. Select START/STOP to begin preheating.
2. In a large bowl, toss the apple slices with the heavy cream, granulated sugar, and cinnamon to coat. Slowly shake in the flour and continue mixing to coat.
3. In a small bowl, mix together the cream cheese, caramel sauce, and brown sugar until smooth. Set aside.
4. When the unit beeps to signify it has preheated, place the apples on the Grill Grate in a single layer. Close the hood and grill for 2 minutes, 30 seconds.
5. After 2 minutes, 30 seconds, open the hood and flip and toss the apples around. Close the hood and cook for 2 minutes, 30 seconds more.
6. When cooking is complete, open the hood and remove the apple chips from the grill. Serve with the sauce.

Pound Cake With Mixed Berries

Servings: 6
Cooking Time: 8 Minutes
Ingredients:
- 3 tablespoons unsalted butter, at room temperature
- 6 slices pound cake, sliced about 1-inch thick
- 1 cup fresh raspberries
- 1 cup fresh blueberries
- 3 tablespoons sugar
- ½ tablespoon fresh mint, minced

Directions:
1. Insert the Grill Grate and close the hood. Select GRILL, set the temperature to MAX, and set the time to 8 minutes. Select START/STOP to begin preheating.
2. While the unit is preheating, evenly spread the butter on both sides of each slice of pound cake.
3. When the unit beeps to signify it has preheated, place the pound cake on the Grill Grate. Close the hood and GRILL for 2 minutes.
4. After 2 minutes, flip the pound cake and GRILL for 2 minutes more, until golden brown. Repeat steps 3 and 4 for all of the pound cake slices.
5. While the pound cake grills, in a medium mixing bowl, combine the raspberries, blueberries, sugar, and mint.
6. When cooking is complete, plate the cake slices and serve topped with the berry mixture.

Lemon Ricotta Cake

Servings: 6
Cooking Time: 25 Minutes
Ingredients:
- 17.5 ounces ricotta cheese
- 5.4 ounces sugar
- 3 eggs, beaten
- 3 tablespoons flour
- 1 lemon, juiced and zested
- 2 teaspoons vanilla extract

Directions:
1. Select BAKE, set the temperature to 320ºF, and set the time to 25 minutes. Select START/STOP to begin preheating.

2. In a large mixing bowl, stir together all the ingredients until the mixture reaches a creamy consistency.
3. Pour the mixture into a baking pan. Place the pan directly in the pot.
4. Close the hood and BAKE for 25 minutes until a toothpick inserted in the center comes out clean.
5. Allow to cool for 10 minutes on a wire rack before serving.

Grilled Peaches With Bourbon Butter Sauce

Servings: 4
Cooking Time: 12 Minutes
Ingredients:
- 4 tablespoons salted butter
- ¼ cup bourbon
- ½ cup brown sugar
- 4 ripe peaches, halved and pitted
- ¼ cup candied pecans

Directions:
1. Insert the Grill Grate and close the hood. Select GRILL, set the temperature to MAX, and set the time to 12 minutes. Select START/STOP to begin preheating.
2. While the unit is preheating, in a saucepan over medium heat, melt the butter for about 5 minutes. Once the butter is browned, remove the pan from the heat and carefully add the bourbon.
3. Return the saucepan to medium-high heat and add the brown sugar. Bring to a boil and let the sugar dissolve for 5 minutes, stirring occasionally.
4. Pour the bourbon butter sauce into a medium shallow bowl and arrange the peaches cut-side down to coat in the sauce.
5. When the unit beeps to signify it has preheated, place the fruit on the Grill Grate in a single layer (you may need to do this in multiple batches). Gently press the fruit down to maximize grill marks. Close the hood and GRILL for 10 to 12 minutes without flipping. If working in batches, repeat this step for all the peaches.
6. When cooking is complete, remove the peaches and top each with the pecans. Drizzle with the remaining bourbon butter sauce and serve immediately.

Ultimate Coconut Chocolate Cake

Servings: 10
Cooking Time: 15 Minutes
Ingredients:
- 1¼ cups unsweetened bakers' chocolate
- 1 stick butter
- 1 teaspoon liquid stevia
- ⅓ cup shredded coconut
- 2 tablespoons coconut milk
- 2 eggs, beaten
- Cooking spray

Directions:
1. Select BAKE, set the temperature to 330ºF, and set the time to 15 minutes. Select START/STOP to begin preheating.
2. Lightly spritz a baking pan with cooking spray.
3. Place the chocolate, butter, and stevia in a microwave-safe bowl. Microwave for about 30 seconds until melted. Let the chocolate mixture cool to room temperature.

4. Add the remaining ingredients to the chocolate mixture and stir until well incorporated. Pour the batter into the prepared baking pan.
5. Place the pan directly in the pot. Close the hood and BAKE for 15 minutes, or until a toothpick inserted in the center comes out clean.
6. Remove from the pan and allow to cool for about 10 minutes before serving.

Black Forest Pies

Servings: 6
Cooking Time: 15 Minutes
Ingredients:
- 3 tablespoons milk or dark chocolate chips
- 2 tablespoons thick, hot fudge sauce
- 2 tablespoons chopped dried cherries
- 1 sheet frozen puff pastry, thawed
- 1 egg white, beaten
- 2 tablespoons sugar
- ½ teaspoon cinnamon

Directions:
1. Insert the Crisper Basket and close the hood. Select BAKE, set the temperature to 350ºF, and set the time to 15 minutes. Select START/STOP to begin preheating.
2. In a small bowl, combine the chocolate chips, fudge sauce, and dried cherries.
3. Roll out the puff pastry on a floured surface. Cut into 6 squares with a sharp knife.
4. Divide the chocolate chip mixture into the center of each puff pastry square. Fold the squares in half to make triangles. Firmly press the edges with the tines of a fork to seal.
5. Brush the triangles on all sides sparingly with the beaten egg white. Sprinkle the tops with sugar and cinnamon.
6. Put in the Crisper Basket. Close the hood and BAKE for 15 minutes or until the triangles are golden brown. The filling will be hot, so cool for at least 20 minutes before serving.

Pear And Apple Crisp

Servings: 6
Cooking Time: 20 Minutes
Ingredients:
- ½ pound apples, cored and chopped
- ½ pound pears, cored and chopped
- 1 cup flour
- 1 cup sugar
- 1 tablespoon butter
- 1 teaspoon ground cinnamon
- ¼ teaspoon ground cloves
- 1 teaspoon vanilla extract
- ¼ cup chopped walnuts
- Whipped cream, for serving

Directions:
1. Select BAKE, set the temperature to 340ºF, and set the time to 20 minutes. Select START/STOP to begin preheating.
2. Lightly grease a baking pan and place the apples and pears inside.
3. Combine the rest of the ingredients, minus the walnuts and the whipped cream, until a coarse, crumbly texture is achieved.

4. Pour the mixture over the fruits and spread it evenly. Top with the chopped walnuts.
5. Place the pan directly in the pot. Close the hood and BAKE for 20 minutes or until the top turns golden brown.
6. Serve at room temperature with whipped cream.

Biscuit Raisin Bread

Servings: 6 To 8
Cooking Time: 20 Minutes
Ingredients:
- 1 (12-ounce) package refrigerated buttermilk biscuits (10 biscuits)
- 8 ounces cream cheese, cut into 40 cubes
- ¼ cup light brown sugar, packed
- 4 tablespoons (½ stick) unsalted butter, melted
- ½ cup raisins

Directions:
1. Insert the Cooking Pot and close the hood. Select GRILL, set the temperature to LO, and set the time to 20 minutes. Select START/STOP to begin preheating.
2. While the unit is preheating, separate the biscuits and cut each into quarters. Flatten each quarter biscuit with your palm and place 1 cream cheese cube on the center. Wrap the dough around the cream cheese and press to seal, forming a ball. Place the biscuit balls in a 9-by-5-inch bread loaf pan. They will be layered over each other.
3. In a small bowl, combine the brown sugar and melted butter. Pour this over the biscuit balls evenly.
4. When the unit beeps to signify it has preheated, place the loaf pan in the Cooking Pot. Close the hood and grill for 10 minutes.
5. After 10 minutes, open the hood and evenly scatter the raisins on the top layer. Close the hood and cook for 10 minutes more.
6. When cooking is complete, remove the loaf pan from the pot. Remove the bread from the pan, slice, and serve.

Grilled Banana S'mores

Servings: 4
Cooking Time: 6 Minutes
Ingredients:
- 4 large bananas
- 1 cup milk chocolate chips
- 1 cup mini marshmallows
- 4 graham crackers, crushed

Directions:
1. Insert the Cooking Pot and close the hood. Select GRILL, set the temperature to HI, and set the time to 6 minutes. Select START/STOP to begin preheating.
2. While the unit is preheating, prepare the banana boats. Starting at the bottom of a banana, slice the peel lengthwise up one side and then the opposite side. Pull the top half of the peel back, revealing the fruit underneath, but keeping the bottom of the banana peel intact. With a spoon, carefully scoop out some of the banana. (Eat it or set it aside.) Repeat with each banana. Equally divide the chocolate chips and marshmallows between the banana boats.
3. When the unit beeps to signify it has preheated, place the bananas in the Cooking Pot. Close the hood and cook for 6 minutes.
4. When cooking is complete, remove the bananas from the grill and sprinkle the crushed graham crackers on top. Serve.

Marshmallow Banana Boat

Servings: 4
Cooking Time: 6 Minutes
Ingredients:
- 4 ripe bananas
- 1 cup mini marshmallows
- ½ cup chocolate chips
- ½ cup peanut butter chips

Directions:
1. Insert the Grill Grate and close the hood. Select GRILL, set the temperature to MEDIUM, and set the time to 6 minutes. Select START/STOP to begin preheating.
2. While the unit is preheating, slice each banana lengthwise while still in its peel, making sure not to cut all the way through. Using both hands, pull the banana peel open like you would a book, revealing the banana inside. Divide the marshmallows, chocolate chips, and peanut butter chips among the bananas, stuffing them inside the skin.
3. When the unit beeps to signify it has preheated, place the stuffed banana on the Grill Grate. Close the hood and GRILL for 4 to 6 minutes, until the chocolate is melted and the marshmallows are toasted.

Rich Chocolate Cookie

Servings: 4
Cooking Time: 9 Minutes
Ingredients:
- Nonstick baking spray with flour
- 3 tablespoons softened butter
- ⅓ cup plus 1 tablespoon brown sugar
- 1 egg yolk
- ½ cup flour
- 2 tablespoons ground white chocolate
- ¼ teaspoon baking soda
- ½ teaspoon vanilla
- ¾ cup chocolate chips

Directions:
1. Select BAKE, set the temperature to 350ºF, and set the time to 9 minutes. Select START/STOP to begin preheating.
2. In a medium bowl, beat the butter and brown sugar together until fluffy. Stir in the egg yolk.
3. Add the flour, white chocolate, baking soda, and vanilla, and mix well. Stir in the chocolate chips.
4. Line a baking pan with parchment paper. Spray the parchment paper with nonstick baking spray with flour.
5. Spread the batter into the prepared pan, leaving a ½-inch border on all sides.
6. Place the pan directly in the pot. Close the hood and BAKE for 9 minutes or until the cookie is light brown and just barely set.
7. Remove the pan from the grill and let cool for 10 minutes. Remove the cookie from the pan, remove the parchment paper, and let cool on a wire rack.
8. Serve immediately.

Peaches-and-cake Skewers

Servings: 4
Cooking Time: 8 Minutes
Ingredients:

    1 loaf pound cake, cut into 1-inch cubes
    4 peaches, sliced
    ½ cup condensed milk

Directions:
1. Insert the Grill Grate and close the hood. Select GRILL, set the temperature to HI, and set the time to 8 minutes. Select START/STOP to begin preheating.
2. While the unit is preheating, alternate cake cubes and peach slices, 3 or 4 pieces of each, on each of 12 skewers. Using a basting brush, brush the condensed milk onto the cake and peaches and place the skewers on a plate or baking sheet.
3. When the unit beeps to signify it has preheated, place 6 skewers on the Grill Grate. Close the hood and cook for 2 minutes.
4. After 2 minutes, open the hood and flip the skewers. Close the hood to cook for 2 minutes more.
5. After 2 minutes, open the hood and remove the skewers. Repeat steps 3 and 4 with the remaining 6 skewers. Serve.

Black And White Brownies

Servings: 1
Cooking Time: 20 Minutes
Ingredients:

- 1 egg
- ¼ cup brown sugar
- 2 tablespoons white sugar
- 2 tablespoons safflower oil
- 1 teaspoon vanilla
- ⅓ cup all-purpose flour
- ¼ cup cocoa powder
- ¼ cup white chocolate chips
- Nonstick cooking spray

Directions:
1. Select BAKE, set the temperature to 340ºF, and set the time to 20 minutes. Select START/STOP to begin preheating.
2. Spritz a baking pan with nonstick cooking spray.
3. Whisk together the egg, brown sugar, and white sugar in a medium bowl. Mix in the safflower oil and vanilla and stir to combine.
4. Add the flour and cocoa powder and stir just until incorporated. Fold in the white chocolate chips.
5. Scrape the batter into the prepared baking pan.
6. Place the pan directly in the pot. Close the hood and BAKE for 20 minutes, or until the brownie springs back when touched lightly with your fingers.
7. Transfer to a wire rack and let cool for 30 minutes before slicing to serve.

Fudge Pie

Servings: 8
Cooking Time: 25 To 30 Minutes
Ingredients:

- 1½ cups sugar
- ½ cup self-rising flour
- ⅓ cup unsweetened cocoa powder
- 3 large eggs, beaten

- 12 tablespoons butter, melted
- 1½ teaspoons vanilla extract
- 1 unbaked pie crust
- ¼ cup confectioners' sugar (optional)

Directions:
1. Select BAKE, set the temperature to 350ºF, and set the time to 30 minutes. Select START/STOP to begin preheating.
2. Thoroughly combine the sugar, flour, and cocoa powder in a medium bowl. Add the beaten eggs and butter and whisk to combine. Stir in the vanilla.
3. Pour the prepared filling into the pie crust and transfer to the pot.
4. Close the hood and BAKE for 25 to 30 minutes until just set.
5. Allow the pie to cool for 5 minutes. Sprinkle with the confectioners' sugar, if desired. Serve warm.

Lemony Blackberry Crisp

Servings: 1
Cooking Time: 20 Minutes
Ingredients:

- 2 tablespoons lemon juice
- ⅓ cup powdered erythritol
- ¼ teaspoon xantham gum
- 2 cup blackberries
- 1 cup crunchy granola

Directions:
1. Select BAKE, set the temperature to 350ºF, and set the time to 15 minutes. Select START/STOP to begin preheating.
2. In a bowl, combine the lemon juice, erythritol, xantham gum, and blackberries. Transfer to a round baking pan and cover with aluminum foil.
3. Place the pan directly in the pot. Close the hood and BAKE for 12 minutes.
4. Take care when removing the pan from the grill. Give the blackberries a stir and top with the granola.
5. Return the pan to the grill and bake at 320ºF for an additional 3 minutes. Serve once the granola has turned brown and enjoy.

Simple Corn Biscuits

Servings: 6
Cooking Time: 15 Minutes
Ingredients:

- 1½ cups all-purpose flour, plus additional for dusting
- ½ cup yellow cornmeal
- 2½ teaspoons baking powder
- ½ teaspoon sea salt
- ⅓ cup vegetable shortening
- ⅔ cup buttermilk
- Nonstick cooking spray

Directions:
1. In a large bowl, combine the flour, cornmeal, baking powder, and salt.
2. Add the shortening, and cut it into the flour mixture, until well combined and the dough resembles a coarse meal. Add the buttermilk and stir together just until moistened.
3. Insert the Crisper Basket and close the hood. Select AIR CRISP, set the temperature to 350ºF, and set the time to 15 minutes. Select START/STOP to begin preheating.

4. While the unit is preheating, dust a clean work surface with flour. Knead the mixture on the floured surface until a cohesive dough forms. Roll out the dough to an even thickness, then cut into biscuits with a 2-inch biscuit cutter.

5. When the unit beeps to signify it has preheated, coat the basket with cooking spray. Place 6 to 8 biscuits in the basket, well spaced, and spray each with cooking spray. Close the hood and AIR CRISP for 12 to 15 minutes, until golden brown.

6. Gently remove the biscuits from the basket, and place them on a wire rack to cool. Repeat with the remaining dough.

Apple Pie Crumble

Servings: 4
Cooking Time: 20 Minutes
Ingredients:
- 3 small apples, such as Honeycrisp, Gala, Pink Lady, or Granny Smith, peeled, cored, and cut into ⅛-inch-thick slices
- ¼ cup granulated sugar
- ½ teaspoon cinnamon
- ½ cup quick-cooking oatmeal
- 4 tablespoons (½ stick) unsalted butter, at room temperature
- ½ cup all-purpose flour
- ½ cup light brown sugar, packed

Directions:
1. Insert the Cooking Pot and close the hood. Select GRILL, set the temperature to LO, and set the time to 20 minutes. Select START/STOP to begin preheating.
2. While the unit is preheating, put the apples in a large bowl and coat with the granulated sugar and cinnamon. In a medium bowl, combine the oatmeal, butter, flour, and brown sugar, stirring to make clumps for the top layer.
3. Place the apples in a 6-inch springform pan in an even layer. Spread the oatmeal topping over the apples.
4. When the unit beeps to signify it has preheated, place the pan in the Cooking Pot. Close the hood and cook for 20 minutes.
5. After 20 minutes, open the hood and remove the pan from the unit. The apples should be soft and the topping golden brown. Serve.

Mini Brownie Cakes

Servings:4
Cooking Time: 15 Minutes
Ingredients:
- 8 tablespoons (1 stick) unsalted butter
- 2 large eggs
- ¼ cup unsweetened cocoa powder
- ½ cup granulated sugar
- ½ teaspoon vanilla extract
- ⅛ teaspoon salt
- ½ cup all-purpose flour

Directions:
1. Cut the butter into quarters and divide them between 2 (6-ounce) ramekins. Insert the Cooking Pot, place the ramekins in the pot, and close the hood. Select GRILL, set the temperature to LO, and set the time to 15 minutes. Select START/STOP to begin preheating. After 3 minutes of preheating (set a separate timer), use grill mitts to remove the ramekins and set aside. Close the hood to continue preheating.

2. While the unit is preheating, in a large bowl, whisk the eggs together, then add the cocoa powder, sugar, vanilla, and salt. Sift or gradually shake the flour into the bowl as you continue mixing. Then stir in the melted butter to form a smooth batter. Divide the batter evenly among 4 (6-ounce) ramekins, filling them no more than three-quarters full.

3. When the unit beeps to signify it has preheated, place the ramekins in the Cooking Pot. Close the hood and cook for 15 minutes.

4. When cooking is complete, open the hood and remove the ramekins. The brownies are done when a toothpick inserted in the center comes out clean. (Cooking them for 15 minutes usually gives the brownies a crispy crust with a fudgy center. Add another 3 to 5 minutes if you wish to cook the center all the way through.)

Mixed Berry And Cream Cheese Puff Pastries

Servings: 4
Cooking Time: 8 Minutes
Ingredients:
- 1 sheet puff pastry (thawed if frozen)
- 4 tablespoons (½ stick) unsalted butter, melted
- 6 ounces cream cheese, at room temperature
- 1 cup mixed-berry jam

Directions:
1. Insert the Grill Grate and close the hood. Select GRILL, set the temperature to LO, and set the time to 8 minutes. Select START/STOP to begin preheating.
2. While the unit is preheating, unfold the pastry dough on a flat surface. Cut the dough into four equal-size pieces. Brush each piece with the butter. Fold in ¼ to ½ inch of each side of each piece of dough to create a pocket for the filling. Spread a layer of the cream cheese across each pastry pocket and then add ¼ cup of jam on top of each.
3. When the unit beeps to signify it has preheated, place the pastries on the Grill Grate. Close the hood and grill for 8 minutes.
4. When cooking is complete, the puff pastry will be golden brown and the cream cheese and jam may be infused and melted together. Remove the pastries from the grill and serve.

Chocolate Molten Cake

Servings: 4
Cooking Time: 10 Minutes
Ingredients:
- 3.5 ounces butter, melted
- 3½ tablespoons sugar
- 3.5 ounces chocolate, melted
- 1½ tablespoons flour
- 2 eggs

Directions:
1. Select BAKE, set the temperature to 375°F, and set the time to 10 minutes. Select START/STOP to begin preheating.
2. Grease four ramekins with a little butter.
3. Rigorously combine the eggs, butter, and sugar before stirring in the melted chocolate.
4. Slowly fold in the flour.

5. Spoon an equal amount of the mixture into each ramekin.
6. Put them in the pot. Close the hood and BAKE for 10 minutes.
7. Put the ramekins upside-down on plates and let the cakes fall out. Serve hot.

Sweet Potato Donuts

Servings:12
Cooking Time: 52 Minutes
Ingredients:
- 3 cups water
- 1 medium white sweet potato
- ⅔ cup all-purpose flour, plus more for dusting
- ½ cup granulated sugar
- Avocado oil

Directions:
1. Insert the Cooking Pot, pour in the water, and close the hood. Select BROIL, set the temperature to 500°F, and set the time to 20 minutes. Select START/STOP to begin preheating.
2. While the unit is preheating, peel the sweet potato and cut it into chunks.
3. When the unit beeps to signify it has preheated, add the sweet potato to the Cooking Pot, making sure the chunks are fully submerged in the water. Close the hood and cook for 20 minutes.
4. After 20 minutes, open the hood and pierce a potato chunk to check for doneness—it should be easy to slice into. Remove and drain the sweet potatoes.
5. In a large bowl, mash the sweet potato with a masher or fork. When it has cooled down, add ⅔ cup of flour and the sugar and mix until well combined. The dough will be sticky. Dust a clean work surface with some flour. Roll and knead the dough until it is no longer sticky and holds its form, using more flour as needed.
6. Divide the dough in half and then cut each half into 6 equal-size pieces. Roll each piece of dough into a cylinder about 4 inches long.
7. Insert the Cooking Pot and close the hood. Select GRILL, set the temperature to HI, and set the time to 16 minutes. Select START/STOP to begin preheating.
8. While the unit is preheating, brush avocado oil on a 6-ring donut pan and place 6 donuts in the molds. Brush more avocado oil on top.
9. When the unit beeps to signify it has preheated, place the donut pan in the Cooking Pot. Close the hood and grill for 8 minutes.
10. When cooking is complete, remove the pan and transfer the donuts to a rack to cool.
11. Repeat steps 8 through 10 with the remaining donuts. Serve.

Fresh Blueberry Cobbler

Servings: 6
Cooking Time: 30 Minutes
Ingredients:
- 4 cups fresh blueberries
- 1 teaspoon grated lemon zest
- 1 cup sugar, plus 2 tablespoons
- 1 cup all-purpose flour, plus 2 tablespoons
- Juice of 1 lemon
- 2 teaspoons baking powder
- ¼ teaspoon salt
- 6 tablespoons unsalted butter
- ¾ cup whole milk
- ⅛ teaspoon ground cinnamon

Directions:
1. In a medium bowl, combine the blueberries, lemon zest, 2 tablespoons of sugar, 2 tablespoons of flour, and lemon juice.
2. In a medium bowl, combine the remaining 1 cup of flour and 1 cup of sugar, baking powder, and salt. Cut the butter into the flour mixture until it forms an even crumb texture. Stir in the milk until a dough forms.
3. Select BAKE, set the temperature to 350°F, and set the time to 30 minutes. Select START/STOP to begin preheating.
4. Meanwhile, pour the blueberry mixture into the baking pan, spreading it evenly across the pan. Gently pour the batter over the blueberry mixture, then sprinkle the cinnamon over the top.
5. When the unit beeps to signify it has preheated, place the pan directly in the pot. Close the hood and BAKE for 30 minutes, until lightly golden.
6. When cooking is complete, serve warm.

Cinnamon Candied Apples

Servings: 4
Cooking Time: 12 Minutes
Ingredients:
- 1 cup packed light brown sugar
- 2 teaspoons ground cinnamon
- 2 medium Granny Smith apples, peeled and diced

Directions:
1. Select BAKE, set the temperature to 350°F, and set the time to 12 minutes. Select START/STOP to begin preheating.
2. Thoroughly combine the brown sugar and cinnamon in a medium bowl.
3. Add the apples to the bowl and stir until well coated. Transfer the apples to a baking pan.
4. Place the pan directly in the pot. Close the hood and BAKE for 9 minutes. Stir the apples once and bake for an additional 3 minutes until softened.
5. Serve warm.

Orange Coconut Cake

Servings: 6
Cooking Time: 17 Minutes
Ingredients:
- 1 stick butter, melted
- ¾ cup granulated Swerve
- 2 eggs, beaten
- ¾ cup coconut flour
- ¼ teaspoon salt
- ⅓ teaspoon grated nutmeg
- ⅓ cup coconut milk
- 1¼ cups almond flour
- ½ teaspoon baking powder
- 2 tablespoons unsweetened orange jam
- Cooking spray

Directions:

1. Select BAKE, set the temperature to 355ºF, and set the time to 17 minutes. Select START/STOP to begin preheating.
2. Coat a baking pan with cooking spray. Set aside.
3. In a large mixing bowl, whisk together the melted butter and granulated Swerve until fluffy.
4. Mix in the beaten eggs and whisk again until smooth. Stir in the coconut flour, salt, and nutmeg and gradually pour in the coconut milk. Add the remaining ingredients and stir until well incorporated.
5. Scrape the batter into the baking pan.
6. Place the pan directly in the pot. Close the hood and BAKE for 17 minutes until the top of the cake springs back when gently pressed with your fingers.
7. Remove from the grill to a wire rack to cool. Serve chilled.

Graham Cracker Cheesecake

Servings: 8
Cooking Time: 20 Minutes
Ingredients:
- 1 cup graham cracker crumbs
- 3 tablespoons softened butter
- 1½ packages cream cheese, softened
- ⅓ cup sugar
- 2 eggs
- 1 tablespoon flour
- 1 teaspoon vanilla
- ¼ cup chocolate syrup

Directions:
1. For the crust, combine the graham cracker crumbs and butter in a small bowl and mix well. Press into the bottom of a baking pan and put in the freezer to set.
2. For the filling, combine the cream cheese and sugar in a medium bowl and mix well. Beat in the eggs, one at a time. Add the flour and vanilla.
3. Select BAKE, set the temperature to 450ºF, and set the time to 20 minutes. Select START/STOP to begin preheating.
4. Remove ⅔ cup of the filling to a small bowl and stir in the chocolate syrup until combined.
5. Pour the vanilla filling into the pan with the crust. Drop the chocolate filling over the vanilla filling by the spoonful. With a clean butter knife, stir the fillings in a zigzag pattern to marbleize them.
6. Place the pan directly in the pot. Close the hood and BAKE for 20 minutes or until the cheesecake is just set.
7. Cool on a wire rack for 1 hour, then chill in the refrigerator until the cheesecake is firm.
8. Serve immediately

INDEX